MVFOL

Privacy and Surveillance
with New Technologies

MVFOL

Privacy and Surveillance with New Technologies

Peter P. Swire and Kenesa Ahmad, editors

International Debate Education Association

New York, London & Amsterdam

Published by
The International Debate Education Association

105 East 22nd Street
New York, NY 10010
Copyright © 2012 by International Debate Education Association

All rights reserved. No part of this publication may be reproduced or
transmitted in any form or by any means, electronic or mechanical,
including photocopy, or any information storage and retrieval system,
without permission from the publisher.

For permission to use in all or in part, please contact: idea@idebate.org

This book is published with the generous support of the Open Society
Foundations.

Library of Congress Cataloging-in-Publication Data

Privacy and surveillance with new technologies / Peter P. Swire and
Kenesa Ahmad, editors.
     pages cm
  ISBN 978-1-61770-058-3
  1. Electronic surveillance--Law and legislation--United States. 2. Pri-
vacy, Right of--United States. 3. Data mining in law enforcement--United
States. 4. Electronic surveillance--Government policy. I. Swire, Peter P.
II. Ahmad, Kenesa.
  KF5399.P75 2012
  342.7308'58--dc23
                                      2012029925

Design by Kathleen Hayes
Printed in the USA

 **IDEBATE Press**

Contents

Introduction

Imagine, if you will, that you are at home surfing the Net when you happen to turn around and notice that you are being watched. A man lurking in the shadows outside your window is watching every keystroke through powerful binoculars and recording every word you write and read.

The reality of this little scenario is creepier than fiction: the man with the binoculars lives in your computer. If that makes you uncomfortable, it should. Merchants, Internet sales sites, and business conglomerates all use cookies and tracking software to know what websites you visit in order to benefit from this information by trying to sell you their products. Pop-ups, proprietary ads, and directed advertising all derive from Internet surveillance on your computer. While this might be annoying, it rarely is harmful. However, what if the tracking software belonged to someone or something that wanted to harm you and was lurking in your email, copying and transmitting everything that you read and wrote? What if that insidious tracker was the government?

Computer intrusion is merely one aspect of surveillance with new technology. Consider the cameras at stoplights, in high-crime areas, at the mall, in banks, or behind the counter of your local convenience store. You are digitally captured for the police or other government agents to view nearly at every turn. Furthermore, the technology exists for cameras barely visible to the naked eye to peer through pinholes, unnoticed and undetectable. Looking back at all of the surveillance to which you have been subject, how many times have you been photographed without your knowledge? The answer in the tens of thousands, if not hundreds of thousands, of times.

By now, doubtless you are wondering in what ways your privacy rights are protected—and *not* protected? The answer is not particularly clear in a free society. As usual, law has not kept up with technology. That is a very big reason why you should be concerned. The legal, moral, and ethical questions about using new technology for surveillance are at the heart of this book. Perhaps you already have an opinion on the use of new technologies for surveillance. Perhaps after debating the issues herein, your opinion may change.

What Is Surveillance?

Surveillance has been part of the lexicon of espionage for about two centuries. It is rooted in the French *surveiller* (to watch over) and was first in regular usage about the time that Napoleon Bonaparte tried to conquer Europe at the beginning of the 19th century. In a military context, the word "surveillance" became nearly synonymous with "spying." Originally, the word suggested malignant intent toward the subject being watched; therefore, if one was the object of surveillance, it likely was by another who intended to do harm—for example, Napoleon's spies who watched the movements of Russian troops. The negative connotation generally remains today although it's not necessarily deserved. In fact, some surveillance is actually quite beneficial.

Cameras, satellites, sensors, and all manner of surveillance devices monitor everyday occurrences as mundane as, for example, the weather, helping us to plan our day, to fly our aircraft, to anticipate a drought, and so on. Understanding this should be a comfort because a host of professionals are evaluating and analyzing surveillance data to predict (i.e., forecast) the future. This analyzed information can help you decide whether to take an umbrella to work or school tomorrow or if you should expect weather delays in your cross-country flight. So, surveillance can help you.

On the other hand, military powers around the world constantly monitor satellite weather data to determine possible battlefield conditions or other aspects of warfare. Suddenly, mundane information gathered from weather surveillance has become malignant in the hands of those who may harm you. So, clearly it is the *intent* of the information collectors that determines malignancy, not necessarily the information itself. Thus, not all surveillance is necessarily bad, not all information collection is necessarily bad—but surely surveillance information can be used for harm against ordinary people, including you.

What Is Privacy?

The legal concept of privacy is relatively new and is still evolving. While such concepts as property rights are hundreds of years old, courts—and, indeed, the international community—recognized privacy as a right only in the 20th century. Why was the concept so late in appearing? Partly because the challenges to privacy emerged from modern technology. Before the advent of telephones, radios, and cameras, people could assume that what they did or said in private would remain private. Before the introduction of powerful computers, governments could not mine data and store and organize massive amounts of information on large numbers of people.[1]

Supreme Court Justice Louis Brandeis famously defined privacy as "the right to be left alone" and declared it "the most comprehensive of rights, and the right most valued by civilized men."[2] That right does not expressly appear in the U.S. Constitution or the Bill of Rights, yet the Framers were concerned about protecting certain aspects of privacy. The First Amendment guarantees freedom of association, the Fourth Amendment protects against unreasonable searches and seizures, and the Fifth Amendment grants immunity from self-incrimination, which protects the privacy of what you know. Over the years, courts have used these amendments to define the right to privacy as preventing government invasion of the private sphere. In the 21st century, courts and legislators face the task of reworking that definition to meet the challenges of a society in which not only government but also the private sector have the power of surveillance.

Technology, Surveillance, and the Law

Every generation has grappled with the challenges technological innovation present to privacy. By the 1840s, the electric telegraph had revolutionized long-distance communications, enabling Americans to send messages quickly over hundreds, even thousands, of miles. But telegraph operators had to transmit and transcribe the messages; accordingly, the messages were no longer private. Before the introduction of the dial phone in 1919, callers connected to each other through a human operator who could easily listen in on the call; and, until after World War II, most Americans received their telephone service over shared (party) lines that enabled neighbors to eavesdrop on conversations. While Americans may have found these intrusions annoying, they did not consider them significant. Concerns about abuses of new technology first centered on the police and federal government.

Soon after the invention of the telephone in the late 19th century, police began wiretapping conversations. During the 1920s, federal authorities used wiretaps to catch those violating the era's Prohibition laws. In this context, the issue of privacy came before the Supreme Court. Roy Olmstead, the head of a bootlegging ring, appealed his conviction of conspiracy to violate the National Prohibition Act on the grounds that evidence was obtained by federal wiretaps of private conversations. He argued that wiretaps were "searches" and thus required a search warrant under the provisions of the Fourth Amendment. In a 5–4 decision, the Court ruled in *Olmstead v. United States* that warrantless wiretaps were legal because they did not involve seizing tangible property—therefore, the bootlegger's Fourth and Fifth Amendment rights had not been not violated. The decision raised privacy concerns; six years later, Congress arrived at a compromise on wiretaps. The Federal Communications Act of 1934 permitted government agents to use them without a warrant but prohibited them from divulging the contents of the wiretap or using evidence from the wiretaps in court.

Under J. Edgar Hoover, the Federal Bureau of Investigation took full advantage of warrantless wiretapping, justifying their use not only in terms of criminal investigation but also national security. Hoover had long been convinced that radicals, particularly communists, represented a danger to the United States, and he utilized warrantless wiretaps to gather information on individuals and groups he deemed subversive. The information was not admissible in court, but it was passed on to Hoover's friends in government, including Sen. Joseph McCarthy, who used the information in his rabid attacks on the loyalties of many

Americans. Ultimately, the FBI created files on some 500,000 Americans, including Albert Einstein and Eleanor Roosevelt. By 1950, Hoover had compiled a list of 12,000 individuals whom he recommended that Pres. Harry Truman, using his powers as commander in chief, summarily imprison as "potentially dangerous" to national security.[3] Truman ignored Hoover.

In 1956, Hoover launched a full-fledged covert attack, COINTELPRO (Counter-Intelligence Program), against the already dying Communist Party in America. Emboldened by the program's success, he then targeted other individuals and groups. Justifying its actions on the grounds that it was protecting national security, preventing violence, and maintaining the existing social and political order, the FBI conducted illegal wiretaps and bugged individuals (including Martin Luther King, Jr.[4]) and organizations associated with radical groups and the civil rights and women's rights movements. The program was successfully kept secret until 1971, when exposure and a congressional investigation forced the FBI to discontinue it.

In 1967, the Supreme Court, in *Katz v. United States,* ruled that electronic eavesdropping required a search warrant because people have a reasonable expectation of privacy while speaking on a telephone,[5] a remarkable and long-overdue reversal of *Olmstead.* The Court limited the ruling to criminal cases, however, preserving for the future the decision on whether warrantless wiretapping on the authorization of the president or the attorney general might be permissible in national security cases. Five years later, the Court narrowed the *Katz* decision in what became known as the *Keith* case, ruling that the president's national security exception to warrantless electronic searches did not include domestic surveillance.[6]

Despite the Supreme Court rulings, privacy abuses from the executive branch continued during the Nixon administration, this time at the initiative of the president himself. For example, in 1969, Pres. Richard Nixon arranged for the FBI to tap the telephones of 17 government officials and news reporters to determine who had been leaking information to the press from the White House. The Justice Department cited national security as the motive behind the intercepts, although the more relevant purpose was to use federal assets to uncover Nixon's political enemies in government and elsewhere.[7]

In 1972, a burglary at the Democratic National Committee Headquarters in the Watergate Hotel in Washington, D.C., ignited a national scandal when investigations revealed illegal government wiretaps, bugging, and eavesdropping—along with dirty election campaign tricks, money laundering, burglary, and official cover-up of serious crimes—aimed at destroying Nixon's political opponents and ensuring his re-election. The evidence led directly to Richard Nixon as a primary player. The president resigned over the affair in August 1974.

Responding to the Watergate scandal, the Senate created a committee to investigate the involvement of the FBI and of other intelligence agencies in political repression. The Church Committee, named after its chairman, Sen. Frank Church of Idaho, found that the FBI had used electronic surveillance techniques to achieve "overly broad intelligence targeting and collection objectives" and warned that the very nature of these techniques made them a threat to personal privacy and constitutionally protected activities. That danger was compounded by an executive branch indifferent to constitutional restraints and lack of adequate standards limiting the use of such tactics and techniques.[8]

In response to the Church Committee's findings, Congress passed the Foreign Intelligence Surveillance Act of 1978 (FISA), which was designed to ensure that the president could never use the concept of "national security" to justify the electronic surveillance of political opponents and other citizens. The act attempted to balance the valid use of wiretaps against suspected enemy agents with protections of citizens' privacy. Under the law, the government was required to get a warrant to conduct national security surveillance. Authorities had to show a judge in a secret Foreign Intelligence Surveillance Court probable cause that the target was an agent of a foreign power. All other wiretaps were to be handled under Title III of The Omnibus Crime Control and Safe Streets Act of 1968, which set strict requirements for linking wiretaps to a specific criminal investigation.

Radio

The new radio industry of the early 20th century led to a sideline in surveillance: radio transmission tracking. It all began as a matter of counterespionage operations with direction-finding devices searching for radios operated by foreign agents contacting enemy governments in wartime. This evolved into domestic usage by law enforcement when portable radio transmitters were developed that could be clandestinely attached to cars suspected of being used by criminals. A perennial problem with early transmitters was that they often fell from the target car (early models were quite bulky); also their signal range was short. Although acquiring a warrant to affix a radio transmission device usually was not necessary in the 20th century, the technology was so unreliable that assessing the risk of losing the equipment was more often the determining factor in deciding to plant a device than the value of any information that might be acquired.

In time, these rudimentary devices were replaced by sophisticated GPS tracking systems that could give police a moment-by-moment record of the places an individual had been, again raising privacy issues. The issue of law enforcement's use of locational tracking devices came before the Supreme Court in 2011. In the course of an investigation into a suspected drug ring, police placed a clandestine GPS tracking device on Antoine Jones's car. The police acquired a warrant for the device but tracked the car far beyond the scope of the warrant and by so doing collected information about Jones's movements that led to his conviction on conspiracy to possess and sell drugs. Sentenced to life in prison, the defendant appealed on the grounds that the warrantless use of a tracking device on a motor vehicle constituted a "search" and therefore violated the Fourth Amendment. During oral arguments before the Supreme Court, Justice John Roberts asked the lawyer representing the government if placing clandestine tracking devices on the cars of all of the Supreme Court justices would be a "search" under the Fourth Amendment. The attorney said that in his opinion it would not. (The government argued that public information, in this case the movement of a car on a public road, is not protected by the Fourth Amendment.) Justice Stephen Breyer remarked that if this were the case then there would be nothing to stop the government from monitoring the movements of every American every day and added "[I]f you win, you suddenly produce what sounds like 1984. . . ."[9]

In *United States v. Jones* (2011), the Supreme Court ruled that the GPS evidence was inadmissible. Although the ruling was unanimous, the Court split on why the evidence should be thrown out. Five justices wrote that the physical attachment of the GPS device to the defendant's car constituted a search. The remaining four said that placing the device on the defendant's car was a violation of his reasonable expectation of privacy. In light of the government's responses to questions before the Court, it was not surprising that the ruling was unanimously in favor of the defendant; however, the split in the reasoning of the justices suggests that the Court views existing law as vague about what constitutes a search or seizure in an evolving technological environment.

Cameras, Schools, and Privacy

Communications was not the only area in which the use of new technologies raised privacy concerns. In the mid-1960s, surveillance cameras began to surface in business, industry, and government—initially to augment access controls at doors or gates. But, with the attachment of a videotape recorder and the introduction of smaller- and higher-resolution lenses, surveillance cameras expanded to other overseeing possibilities. Cameras began showing up behind retail counters and cash registers, ostensibly to record (or dissuade) robbers; however, they also recorded the actions of cashiers who might have their hand in the till. Cameras also monitored ATMS, recording customers utilizing the machines. Soon cameras became available for home installation to record those coming and going or activities inside the home. Cameras designed to capture burglars stealing the silverware instead captured kids sneaking in after curfew. In other words, expanding the world of camera surveillance offered new possibilities in the world of unintended consequences.

Police departments began installing surveillance cameras in high-crime areas and in high-traffic-density areas. No warrants were required for any of these cameras if they were installed in a public place. Some departments noted a significant reduction in crime in areas that had police cameras in plain view. Others noted waiting lists of neighborhoods hoping to have cameras installed on their streets to reduce or displace crime locally.

Nevertheless, civil liberties groups raised concerns about privacy rights since cameras record the actions of everyone, not just those engaged in inappropriate behavior. They point out that cameras in public send a message to the community that everyone is a suspect and everyone is being watched. As Steve Miller, president of the ACLU of Ohio Foundation said, "Freedom is dependent on whether the government does not treat every citizen as a suspect."[10]

Miniaturization and computerization have revolutionized surveillance but not necessarily always for the better. In 2009, a student in Pennsylvania noticed that a green webcam light was on while working on her school-issued laptop computer. Later, she learned that her school district had been using anti-theft webcam software to photograph her and her classmates remotely more than 56,000 times in two years. The federal lawsuit that followed charged the Lower Merion School District with invasion of privacy.[11] One plaintiff in the original complaint said that the school initiated an investigation into alleged drug use because he was photographed eating candy while at his computer. He was photographed (including while in bed) by the school every 15 minutes for 16 days as the school prepared its case against him. According to the complaint, cameras were remotely activated by the school to clandestinely view the student and photograph him in his home without his consent. In 2010, the suit was settled for $600,000.

Cameras in school buildings are no less controversial. Critics charge that oftentimes behavior that might be handled administratively by a school (e.g., a suspension following a fight) is now more often handled by the courts (e.g., prosecution for assault), merely because there is recorded evidence of the incident. Perilously little data on such in-school surveillance is available from either side of the issue, however. In the world of civil litigation, the term "reasonable" surfaces regularly. If, as a safety measure, a school can use camera surveillance of its property and the persons therein without intruding on privacy (no cameras in bathrooms, no cameras in locker rooms, no cameras in dressing rooms, etc.), what is a court's expectation of how a school should act reasonably? And, in a place such as a school, how much privacy can a student reasonably expect? Most important, if you were a student in a school considering routine camera surveillance, how would you feel? What if you were the principal?

9/11 and Surveillance

Following the attacks of September 11, the government began to use new technologies as a major weapon in the war on terror, often under the provisions of the PATRIOT Act. Passed in October 2001, this act significantly expanded the government's power to obtain personal records and conduct surveillance on and searches of suspected terrorists. The act also expanded the scope of surveillance permitted under the Foreign Intelligence Surveillance Act to encompass not only "foreign agents," but also "any U.S. person" in a terrorism-related investigation. It also permitted the government to expand its use of National Security Letters, which allow government agents to seize data about individuals from financial institutions, telephone companies, and Internet service providers, while requiring them to keep the seizure secret.

The PATRIOT Act had extremely strong bipartisan backing. Supporters argued that the FISA was woefully out-of-date and that the new law would give government the tools necessary to fight terrorism. Nevertheless, the measure drew criticism from civil liberties groups such as the ACLU, which maintained that the Bush administration was using the 9/11 attacks to expand government power and deprive Americans of their traditional liberties. In a 2011 review, the ACLU reported that the PATRIOT Act had led to many abuses of privacy, ranging from roving wire-taps of persons not suspected of crimes, surveillance of persons involved in lawful activities, and intrusion into public library records among others.[12] In 2004, a federal court ruled that the FBI's use of National Security Letters under the PATRIOT Act violated the First Amendment. Three years later, the FBI's own inspector general found that the agency had abused its power to issue National Security Letters.[13] Between 2003 and 2006, the FBI issued almost 200,000 NSLs, which led to only one convic-tion for terrorism.[14]

In one of his most controversial actions in the War on Ter-ror, Pres. George W. Bush initiated the Terrorist Surveillance Program (TSP). Claiming that his powers to "engage the enemy" as commander in chief trumped federal laws, he authorized the National Security Administration (NSA) to carry out warrantless electronic surveillance of international communications between persons in the United States and other countries where the gov-ernment suspected that at least one of the parties involved in the communication was a member of a terrorist organization. This surveillance was conducted outside the strictures of FISA and without the approval of any court. The program remained a secret, however, until the *New York Times* disclosed its existence in 2005. Bush ultimately ended the TSP in 2007 in response to public pressure. A 2009 internal report by the inspectors gen-eral of the CIA, NSA, and departments of Defense and Justice concluded that the program had resulted in "unprecedented" collection of data.[15]

Immediately after September 11, the NSA began another top-secret domestic spying program code named Stellar Wind, in which the agency turned programs developed for gathering foreign intelligence inward on the nation. Stellar Wind mined large communications databases, including e-mail communications, phone conversations, financial transactions, and Internet activity. It was extremely controversial even among administration officials and, in 2004, caused a near-mutiny among top leaders in the Justice Department who threatened to resign because it targeted large numbers of American citizens not suspected of involvement in terrorism. *USA Today* first revealed the data mining component of the program in 2006.

Surveillance in the New Century

Since the beginning of the 21st century, government agencies have used massive computers and powerful programs to conduct what the ACLU has called "dragnet surveillance." Agencies such as the FBI and NSA collect enormous amounts of private data to draw links and make predictions about people's behavior.[16] Supporters of the efforts maintain that innocent people have nothing to fear and that collection does not constitute use. Privacy advocates counter that data mining has fundamentally changed the nature of surveillance. To find illicit activity, government turns its forces to examining all digital behavior, even that of the innocent.[17] Agencies can use this massive amount of information to compile dossiers on vast numbers of innocent Americans.

We've spent a lot of time discussing federal government involvement in surveillance, but we have to remember that most modern surveillance comes from the private sector. Banks, insurance companies, and communications corporations, among others, collect massive amounts of information on Americans, which they use for a variety of purposes. For example, credit card companies use data mining to detect and stop fraud. And, as mentioned above, businesses use cookies to monitor Internet buying patterns to sell you products. More troubling for privacy advocates is that many businesses sell their data to improve their bottom line. Consumers are in the dark about who knows what about them. Regardless of the use, as John Markoff of the *New York Times* notes, "Millions of Americans have become enmeshed in a vast and growing data web that is constantly being examined by a legion of Internet-era software snoops."[18]

What Are the Challenges?

Since George Orwell's classic novel *1984* was released in 1949, the image of an Orwellian world has served as an instructive example of what government should not be. The oppressive government of *1984*'s Oceana controlled all information (including the revision of history) and was operated by an enigmatic leader called "Big Brother," the face of intrusive government. Intrusive surveillance by hidden cameras and government informants dominated the fictional landscape and no one could be trusted. Opposition to government was crushed and patriotism meant going with the flow no matter how inhuman the price.

Today, pundits often raise the specter of the Orwellian Big Brother as a moral and ethical warning that government's ability to conduct domestic surveillance has grown beyond reason or responsibility. They ask the rhetorical question, "If we have the technological capacity to conduct clandestine domestic surveillance, why should we expect the government to restrain itself from violating the privacy rights of its citizens?" Should

America's citizens expect that their government, which possesses the technological capacity to spy on them, will not?

In Orwell's cautionary tale, citizens of Oceana had no expectation that the government would restrain itself from anything; however, in the United States we have a judicial system that prides itself on protecting the civil liberties of its citizens as do most nations of the West. Accordingly, one might anticipate that the contemporary American justice system would offer protection through constitutional checks and balances if not immediately through the courts. Paraphrasing the law as it stands today: the government of the United States cannot interfere with the private lives of its citizens without a compelling reason.[19] Of course, what does and does not constitute "interference" and "compelling reason" is a matter that Congress and the courts must debate and decide.

Privacy is not an issue that involves government alone, however. Society must decide what privacy means in an electronically interconnected world. As Pres. Barack Obama wrote: "One thing should be clear, even though we live in a world in which we share personal information more freely than in the past, we must reject the conclusion that privacy is an outmoded value. It has been at the heart of our democracy from its inception, and we need it now more than ever."[20]

About the Book

Privacy and Surveillance with New Technologies presents the debate about the use of new technologies in surveillance focusing on the technologies students use every day—cameras, laptops, smartphones, location services, and social networks. The anthology begins with an overview of the issue, tracing the evolution of surveillance technology and introducing the broad question of whether the surveillance capabilities of new technologies are a threat to our rights. Part 2 explores how video surveillance by police and industry has changed America's expectations of privacy in public spaces, lowering the bar substantially. Proponents argue that video surveillance keeps us safe, opponents ask at what cost? Part 3 looks at an interesting exception to Fourth Amendment protections against warrantless searches and seizures. These protections do not apply at border crossings, and border agents now have the right, at their discretion, to access and download all of the files on a computer or smartphone. In 1994, Congress passed the Communications Assistance for Law Enforcement Act, which requires telephone systems to be made wiretap-ready, with built-in "backdoor" surveillance capability. Part 4 presents the debate over whether a software backdoor should be required for web-based communications as well. Part 5 examines the questions surrounding government use of locational tracking devices and mobile phone location data. Although these are useful tools for law enforcement, government could also use them to monitor the movements of innocent groups and individuals. Finally, Part 6 considers the issues surrounding online tracking, especially by private companies. This tracking reveals detailed information about individual preferences and behavior. Should this tracking be regulated?

Kenneth Ryan, PhD
Associate Professor
Department of Criminology
California State University, Fresno

NOTES

1. Ronald B. Standler, "Privacy Law in the United States," http://www.rbs2.com/privacy.htm

2. *Olmstead v. United States*, 1928.

3. Tim Weiner, "Hoover Planned Mass Jailings in 1950," *New York Times,* December 23, 2007, http://www.nytimes.com/2007/12/23/washington/23habeas.html?_r=1

4. David Robarge, "Chasing Spies: How the FBI Failed in Counterintelligence But Promoted the Politics of McCarthyism in the Cold War Years." CIA, April 2007, https://www.cia.gov/library/center-for-the-study-of-intelligence/csi-publications/csi-studies/studies/vol47no3/article07.html

5. *Katz v. United States*, 1967.

6. *United States v. United States District Court*, 1972.

7. "Washington Post Investigations: Top Secret America," *Washington Post*, http://voices.washingtonpost.com/washingtonpostinvestigations/2008/12/the_fbi_broke_into_civil.html

8. United States Senate, Select Committee to Study Governmental Operations with Respect to Intelligence Activities, *Final Report*, April, 1976, http://www.icdc.com/~paulwolf/cointelpro/churchfinalreportIIcc.htm

9. Peter Swire, "A Reasonableness Approach to Searches After the *Jones* GPS Tracking Case," SLR Online, February 2, 2012, http://www.stanfordlawreview.org/online/privacy-paradox/searches-after-jones

10. "Surveillance Cameras Threaten Privacy and Waste Taxpayer Money, Says ACLU," ACLU, February 28, 2012, http://www.aclu.org/technology-and-liberty/surveillance-cameras-threaten-privacy-and-waste-taxpayer-money-says-aclu

11. *Robbins v. Lower Merion School District*, 2010.

12. "Reform the Patriot Act: Myths and Realities," ACLU, May 26, 2011, http://www.aclu.org/free-speech-national-security-technology-and-liberty/reform-patriot-act-myths-realities#three

13. "FBI Audit Exposes Widespread Abuse of Patriot Act Powers," ACLU, March 13, 2008, http://www.aclu.org/national-security/fbi-audit-exposes-widespread-abuse-patriot-act-powers

14. Michael Kelley, "How Post-9/11 Surveillance Has Drastically Changed America," *Business Insider*, August 21, 2012, http://www.businessinsider.com/heres-how-surveillance-in-america-drastically-changed-after-911-2012-8#ixzz24UBX3L6b

15. *Dissent*, "Terrorist Surveillance Unplugged," July 10, 2009, http://www.pogowasright.org/?p=1731

16. "Surveillance and Privacy," ACLU, http://www.aclu.org/national-security/surveillance-privacy

17. John Markoff, "Taking Spying to Higher Level, Agencies Look for More Ways to Mine Data," *New York Times*, February 25, 2006. http://www.nytimes.com/2006/02/25/technology/25data.html?ei=5088&en=d231d2f98b31262a&ex=1298523600&pagewanted=prin

18. Ibid.

19. See, oddly enough, *Roe v. Wade*, 1973.

20. White House, "Consumer Data Privacy in a Networked World." February 23, 2012. http://www.whitehouse.gov/sites/default/files/privacy-final.pdf

PART 1:

Introduction to Surveillance

The terrorist attacks of September 11, 2001, changed the balance between government power and citizens' privacy. In the aftermath of the attacks, Congress passed the USA PATRIOT Act, which granted new and extensive surveillance powers to the government. Shortly thereafter, the federal government established the Department of Homeland Security, giving it the responsibility for the security of the nation and its borders. At that time of fear and uncertainty, the government implemented many new—and untested—forms of surveillance. Supporters of these measures argue that they are necessary to protect the nation against future attacks. Opponents claim that "terrorism" is used too frequently as a reason for imposing overbroad surveillance measures that infringe on privacy and constitutional rights. The balance between security and privacy is still hotly debated more than 10 years after the attacks.

This section begins with an article from *The Economist* that discusses the extent of modern surveillance capabilities and the collection and use of information by British, American, and other governments around the world. A series of four short essays follows; these pieces debate the purpose, extent, and use of surveillance today by the U.S. government. First, Glenn Greenwald argues that surveillance has expanded greatly since the September 11 terrorist attacks and continues to grow—with politicians invoking the specter of "terrorism" to justify increasing surveillance powers. Paul Rosenzweig counters that we do not have to be seriously concerned about extensive surveillance because "a strong and complex system of oversight and regulation of surveillance activity" has grown alongside increased surveillance. In another response essay, John Eastman contends that significant historical and legal precedent exists for surveillance during this time of "war." In a separate and final section essay, Greenwald concludes by explaining that Rosenzweig's and Eastman's claims are the sort of "fear-mongering" that has made us weak and too accepting of the current state of extensive government surveillance power.

While you read the articles, consider the following questions:

1. What are the benefits of government surveillance and what are the drawbacks?

2. Should the government be given expanded surveillance powers when we are at "war"? What limits, if any, should be imposed?

3. What personal information should be kept private from the government? What should not?

4. What factors should be considered in balancing privacy and surveillance?

Learning to Live with Big Brother

by The Economist*

It used to be easy to tell whether you were in a free country or a dictatorship. In an old-time police state, the goons are everywhere, both in person and through a web of informers that penetrates every workplace, community and family. They glean whatever they can about your political views, if you are careless enough to express them in public, and your personal foibles. What they fail to pick up in the café or canteen, they learn by reading your letters or tapping your phone. The knowledge thus amassed is then stored on millions of yellowing pieces of paper, typed or handwritten; from an old-time dictator's viewpoint, exclusive access to these files is at least as powerful an instrument of fear as any torture chamber. Only when a regime falls will the files either be destroyed, or thrown open so people can see which of their friends was an informer.

These days, data about people's whereabouts, purchases, behaviour and personal lives are gathered, stored and shared on a scale that no dictator of the old school ever thought possible. Most of the time, there is nothing obviously malign about this. Governments say they need to gather data to ward off terrorism or protect public health; corporations say they do it to deliver goods and services more efficiently. But the ubiquity of electronic data-gathering and processing—and above all, its acceptance by the public—is still astonishing, even compared with a decade ago. Nor is it confined to one region or political system.

In China, even as economic freedom burgeons, millions of city-dwellers are being issued with obligatory high-tech "residency" cards. These hold details of their ethnicity, religion, educational background, police record and even reproductive history—a refinement of the identity papers used by communist regimes.

Britain used to pride itself on respecting privacy more than most other democracies do. But there is not much objection among Britons as "talking" surveillance cameras, fitted with loudspeakers, are installed, enabling human monitors to shout rebukes at anyone spotted dropping litter, relieving themselves against a wall or engaging in other "anti-social" behaviour.

Even smarter technology than that—the sort that has been designed to fight 21st century wars—is being used in the fight against crime, both petty and serious. In Britain, Italy and America, police are experimenting with the use of miniature remote-controlled drone aircraft, fitted with video cameras and infra red night vision, to detect "suspicious" behaviour in crowds. Weighing no more than a bag of sugar and so quiet that it cannot be heard (or seen) when more than 50 metres (150 feet) from the ground, the battery-operated UAV (unmanned aerial vehicle) can be flown even when out of sight by virtue of the images beamed back to a field operator equipped with special goggles. MW Power, the firm that distributes the technology in Britain, has plans to add a "smart water" spray that would be squirted at suspects, infusing their skin and clothes with genetic tags, enabling police to identify them later.

Most of the time, the convenience of electronic technology, and the perceived need to fight the bad guys, seems to outweigh any worries about where it could lead. That is a recent development. On America's religious right, it was common in the late 1990s to hear dark warnings about the routine use of electronic barcodes in the retail trade: was this not reminiscent of the "mark of the beast" without which "no man might buy or sell", predicted in the final pages of the Bible? But today's technophobes, religious or otherwise, are having to get used to devices that they find even spookier.

Take radio-frequency identification (RFID) microchips, long used to track goods and identify family pets; increasingly they are being implanted in human beings. Such implants are used to help American carers keep track of old people; to give employees access to high-security areas (in Mexico and Ohio); and even to give willing night-club patrons the chance to jump entry queues and dispense with cash at the bar (in Spain and the Netherlands). Some people want everyone to be implanted with RFIDs, as the answer to identity theft.

Across the rich and not-so-rich world, electronic devices are already being used to keep tabs on ordinary citizens as never before. Closed-circuit television cameras (CCTV) with infra-red night vision peer down at citizens from street corners, and in banks, airports and shopping malls. Every time someone clicks on a web page, makes a phone call, uses a credit card, or checks in with a microchipped pass at work, that person leaves a data trail that can later be tracked. Every day, billions of bits of such personal data are stored, sifted, analysed, cross-referenced with other information and, in many cases, used to build up profiles to predict possible future behaviour.

Sometimes this information is collected by governments; mostly it is gathered by companies, though in many cases they are obliged to make it available to law-enforcement agencies and other state bodies when asked.

Follow the Data

The more data are collected and stored, the greater the potential for "data mining"—using mathematical formulas to sift through large sets of data to discover patterns and predict future behaviour. If the public had any strong concerns about the legitimacy of this process, many of them evaporated on September 11th 2001—when it became widely accepted that against a deadly and globally networked enemy, every stratagem was needed. Techniques for processing personal information, which might have raised eyebrows in the world before 2001, suddenly seemed indispensable.

Two days after the attacks on New York and Washington, Frank Asher, a drug dealer turned technology entrepreneur, decided to examine the data amassed on 450m people by his private data-service company, Seisint, to see if he could identify possible terrorists. After giving each person a risk score based on name, religion, travel history, reading preferences and so on, Mr Asher came up with a list of 1,200 "suspicious" individuals, which he handed to the FBI. Unknown to him, five of the terrorist hijackers were on his list.

The FBI was impressed. Rebranded the Multistate Anti-Terrorism Information Exchange, or Matrix, Mr Asher's programme, now taken over by the FBI, could soon access 20 billion pieces of information, all of them churned and sorted and analysed to predict who might one day turn into a terrorist. A new version, called the System to Assess Risk, or STAR, has just been launched using information drawn from both private and public databases. As most of the data have already been disclosed to third parties—airline tickets, job records, car rentals and the like—they are not covered by the American constitution's Fourth Amendment, so no court warrant is required.

In an age of global terror, when governments are desperately trying to pre-empt future attacks, such profiling has become a favourite tool. But although it can predict the behaviour of large groups, this technique is "incredibly inaccurate" when it comes to individuals, says Simon Wessely, a professor of psychiatry at King's College London. Bruce Schneier, an American security guru, agrees. Mining vast amounts of data for well-established behaviour patterns, such as credit-card fraud, works very well, he says. But it is "extraordinarily unreliable" when sniffing out terrorist plots, which are uncommon and rarely have a well-defined profile.

By way of example, Mr Schneier points to the Automated Targeting System, operated by the American Customs and Border Protection, which assigns a terrorist risk-assessment score to anyone entering or leaving the United States. In 2005 some 431m people were processed. Assuming an unrealistically accurate model able to identify terrorists (and innocent people) with 99.9% accuracy, that means some 431,000 false alarms annually, all of which presumably need checking. Given the unreliability of passenger data, the real number is likely to be far higher, he says.

Those caught up in terrorist-profiling systems are not allowed to know their scores or challenge the data. Yet their profiles, which may be shared with federal, state and even foreign governments, could damage their chances of getting a state job, a student grant, a public contract or a visa. It could even prevent them from ever being able to fly again. Such mistakes are rife, as the unmistakable Senator "Ted" Kennedy found to his cost. In the space of a single month in 2004, he was prevented five times from getting on a flight because the name "T Kennedy" had been used by a suspected terrorist on a secret "no-fly" list.

Watching Everybody

Another worry: whereas information on people used to be gathered selectively—following a suspect's car, for example—it is now gathered indiscriminately. The best example of such universal surveillance is the spread of CCTV cameras. With an estimated 5m CCTV cameras in public places, nearly one for every ten inhabitants, England and Wales are among the most closely scrutinised countries in the world—along with America which has an estimated 30m surveillance cameras, again one for every ten inhabitants. Every Briton can expect to be caught on camera on average some 300 times a day. Few seem to mind, despite research suggesting that CCTV does little to deter overall crime.

In any case, says Britain's "NO2ID" movement, a lobby group that is resisting government plans to introduce identity cards, cameras are a less important issue than the emergence of a "database state" in which the personal records of every citizen are encoded and too easily accessible.

Alongside fingerprints, DNA has also become an increasingly popular tool to help detect terrorists and solve crime. Here again Britain (minus Scotland) is a world leader, with the DNA samples of 4.1m individuals, representing 7% of the population, on its national database, set up in 1995. (Most other EU countries have no more than 100,000 profiles on their DNA databases.) The British database includes samples from one in three black males and nearly 900,000 juveniles between ten and 17—all tagged for life as possible criminals, since inclusion in the database indicates that someone has had a run-in with the law. This is because in Britain, DNA is taken from anyone arrested for a "recordable" offence—usually one carrying a custodial sentence, but including such peccadillos as begging or being drunk and disorderly. It is then stored for life, even if that person is never charged or is later acquitted. No other democracy does this.

In America, the federal DNA databank holds 4.6m profiles, representing 1.5% of the population. But nearly all are from convicted criminals. Since January 2006 the FBI has been permitted to take DNA samples on arrest, but these can be expunged, at the suspect's request, if no charges are brought or if he is later acquitted. Of some 40 states that have their own DNA databases, only California allows the permanent storage of samples of those charged, but later cleared. In Britain, where people cannot ask for samples to be removed from the database, it was recently proposed that the best way to prevent discrimination is therefore to include the whole population in the DNA database, plus all visitors to the country. Although this approach is commendably fair, it would be extremely expensive as well as an administrative nightmare.

In popular culture, the use of DNA has become rather glamorous. Tabloids and television dramas tell stories of DNA being used by police to find kidnappers or exonerate convicts on death row. According to a poll carried out for a BBC "Panorama" programme this week, two-thirds of Britons would favour a new law requiring that everyone's DNA be stored. But DNA is less reliable as a crime-detection tool than most people think. Although it almost never provides a false "negative" reading, it can produce false "positives". Professor Allan Jamieson, director of the Forensic Institute in Glasgow, believes too much faith is placed in it. As he points out, a person can transfer DNA to a place, or weapon, that he (or she) has never seen or touched.

Wiretapping Is Too Easy

More disturbing for most Americans are the greatly expanded powers the government has given itself over the past six years to spy on its citizens. Under the Patriot Act, rushed through after the 2001 attacks, the intelligence services and the FBI can now oblige third parties—internet providers, libraries, phone companies, political parties and the like—to hand over an individual's personal data, without a court warrant or that person's knowledge, if they claim that the information is needed for "an authorised investigation" in connection with international terrorism. (Earlier this month, a federal court in New York held this to be unconstitutional.)

Under the Patriot Act's "sneak and peek" provisions, a person's house or office can likewise now be searched without his knowledge or a prior court warrant. The act also expanded the administration's ability to intercept private e-mails and phone calls, though for this a court warrant was supposedly still needed. But in his capacity as wartime commander in chief, George Bush decided to ignore this requirement and set up his own secret "warrantless" eavesdropping programme.

The outcry when this was revealed was deafening, and the programme was dropped. But in August Mr Bush signed into law an amendment to the 1978 Foreign Intelligence Surveillance Act, allowing the warrantless intercept of phone calls and e-mails if at least one of the parties is "reasonably believed" to be outside America. So ordinary Americans will continue to be spied on without the need for warrants—but no one is protesting, because now it is legal.

Where's Your Warrant?

According to defenders of warrantless interception, requiring warrants for all government surveillance would dramatically limit the stream of foreign intelligence available. Privacy should not be elevated above all other concerns, they argue. But would it really impede law-enforcement that much if a judge was required to issue a warrant on each occasion? Technology makes wiretapping much easier than it used to be—too easy, perhaps—so requiring warrants would help to restore the balance, say privacy advocates.

Britain has long permitted the "warrantless" eavesdropping of its citizens (only the home secretary's authorisation is required), and few people appear to mind. What does seem to worry people is the sheer volume of information now being kept on them and the degree to which it is being made accessible to an ever wider group of individuals and agencies. The government is now developing the world's first national children's database for every child under 18. The National Health Service database, already the biggest of its kind in Europe, will eventually hold the medical records of all 53m people in England and Wales.

Even more controversial is Britain's National Identity Register, due to hold up to 49 different items on everyone living in the country. From 2009, everybody is to be issued with a "smart" biometric ID card, linked to the national register, which will be required for access to public services such as doctors' surgeries, unemployment offices, libraries and the like—leaving a new, readily traceable, electronic data-trail. America plans a similar system, with a string of personal data held on a new "smart" national driver's licence that would double up as an ID.

Companies are also amassing huge amounts of data about people. Most people do not think about what information they are handing over when they use their credit or shop "loyalty" card, buy something online or sign up for a loan. Nor do they usually have much idea of the use to which such data are subsequently put. Not only do companies "mine" them to target their advertising more effectively, for example, but also to give their more valued (ie, higher-spending) customers better service. They may also "share" their data with the police—without the individual's consent or knowledge.

Most democratic countries now have comprehensive data-protection and/or privacy laws, laying down strict rules for the collection, storage and use of personal data. There is also often a national information or privacy commissioner to police it all (though not in America). Intelligence agencies, and law-enforcement authorities often as well, are usually exempt from such data-protection laws whenever national security is involved. But such laws generally stipulate that the data be used only for a specific purpose, held no longer than necessary, kept accurate and up-to-date and protected from unauthorised prying

That all sounds great. But as a series of leaks in the past few years has shown, no data are ever really secure. Laptops containing sensitive data are stolen from cars, backup tapes go missing in transit and hackers can break into databases, even the Pentagon's. Then there are "insider attacks", in which people abuse the access they enjoy through their jobs. National Health Service workers in Britain were recently reported to have peeked at the intimate medical details of an unnamed celebrity. All of this can lead to invasions of privacy and identity theft. As the Surveillance Studies Network concludes in its recent report on the "surveillance society", drawn up for Britain's information commissioner, Richard Thomas, "The jury is out on whether privacy regulation...is not ineffective in the face of novel threats."

Boiling the Frog

If the erosion of individual privacy began long before 2001, it has accelerated enormously since. And by no means always to bad effect: suicide-bombers, by their very nature, may not be deterred by a CCTV camera (even a talking one), but security wonks say many terrorist plots have been foiled, and lives saved, through increased eavesdropping, computer profiling and "sneak and peek" searches. But at what cost to civil liberties?

Privacy is a modern "right". It is not even mentioned in the 18th-century revolutionaries' list of demands. Indeed, it was not explicitly enshrined in international human-rights laws and treaties until after the second world war. Few people outside the civil-liberties community seem to be really worried about its loss now.

That may be because electronic surveillance has not yet had a big impact on most people's lives, other than (usually) making it easier to deal with officialdom. But with the collection and centralisation of such vast amounts of data, the potential for abuse is huge and the safeguards paltry.

Ross Anderson, a professor at Cambridge University in Britain, has compared the present situation to a "boiled frog"—which fails to jump out of the saucepan as the water gradually heats. If liberty is eroded slowly, people will get used to it. He added a caveat: it was possible the invasion of privacy would reach a critical mass and prompt a revolt.

If there is not much sign of that in Western democracies, this may be because most people rightly or wrongly trust their own authorities to fight the good fight against terrorism, and avoid abusing the data they possess. The prospect is much scarier in countries like Russia and China, which have embraced capitalist technology and the information revolution without entirely exorcising the ethos of an authoritarian state where dissent, however peaceful, is closely monitored.

On the face of things, the information age renders impossible an old-fashioned, file-collecting dictatorship, based on a state monopoly of communications. But imagine what sort of state may emerge as the best brains of a secret police force—a force whose house culture treats all dissent as dangerous—perfect the art of gathering and using information on massive computer banks, not yellowing paper.

The Economist is a weekly news and international affairs publication based in the United Kingdom.

"Civil Liberties: Surveillance and Privacy: Learning to Live with Big Brother," *The Economist,* September 2007. http://www.economist.com/node/9867324.

© The Economist Newspaper Limited, London (September 2007).

Used by permission.

The Digital Surveillance State: Vast, Secret, and Dangerous

by Glenn Greenwald*

It is unsurprising that the 9/11 attack fostered a massive expansion of America's already sprawling Surveillance State. But what is surprising, or at least far less understandable, is that this growth shows no signs of abating even as we approach almost a full decade of emotional and temporal distance from that event. The spate of knee-jerk legislative expansions in the immediate aftermath of the 9/11 trauma—the USA-PATRIOT Act—has actually been exceeded by the expansions of the last several years—first secretly and lawlessly by the Bush administration, and then legislatively and out in the open once Democrats took over control of the Congress in 2006. Simply put, there is no surveillance power too intrusive or unaccountable for our political class provided the word "terrorism" is invoked to "justify" those powers.

The More-Surveillance-Is-Always-Better Mindset

Illustrating this More-Surveillance-is-Always-Better mindset is what happened after *The New York Times* revealed in December, 2005 that the Bush administration had ordered the National Security Agency to eavesdrop on American citizens without the warrants required by law and without any external oversight at all. Despite the fact that the 30-year-old FISA law made every such act of warrantless eavesdropping a felony[1], "punishable by a fine of not more than $10,000 or imprisonment for not more than five years, or both," and despite the fact that all three federal judges who ruled on the program's legality concluded that it was illegal[2], there was no accountability of any kind. The opposite is true: the telecom corporations which enabled and participated in this lawbreaking were immunized by a 2008 law supported by Barack Obama and enacted by the Democratic Congress. And that same Congress twice legalized the bulk of the warrantless eavesdropping powers which *The New York Times* had exposed: first with the 2007 Protect America Act, and then with the 2008 FISA Amendments Act, which, for good measure, even added new warrantless surveillance authorities.

Not even revelations of systematic abuse can retard the growth of the Surveillance State or even bring about some modest accountability. In 2007, the Justice Department's own Inspector General issued a report documenting continuous abuses by the FBI[3] of a variety of new surveillance powers vested by the Patriot Act, particularly the ability to obtain private, invasive records about Americans without the need for any judicial supervision (via so-called "National Security Letters" (NSLs))[4]. The following year, FBI Director Robert Mueller confirmed ongoing abuses subsequent to the time period covered by the initial IG report[5].

Again, the reaction of the political class in the face of these revelations was not only to resist any accountability but to further expand the very powers being abused. When then-candidate Obama infuriated many of his supporters in mid-2008 by announcing his support for the warrantless–surveillance expanding FISA Amendments Act, he assured everyone that he did so[6] "with the firm intention—once [he's] sworn in as President—to have [his] Attorney General conduct a comprehensive review of all our surveillance programs, and to make further recommendations on any steps needed to preserve civil liberties and to prevent executive branch abuse in the future."

Not only has nothing like that occurred, but Congress has twice brushed aside the privacy and abuse concerns about the Patriot Act highlighted by the DOJ's own report and long raised by Senator Russ Feingold[7]. They did so when voting overwhelmingly to extend the provisions of that law unchanged: first in 2006 by a vote of 89–10[8], and again this year—with the overt support of the Obama administration—when it once again extended the Patriot Act without even a single added oversight protection[9]. Even after *The New York Times* in 2009 twice revealed substantial and serious abuses[10] in the very warrantless eavesdropping powers which Obama voted to enact, the administration and the Congress show no interest whatsoever in imposing any added safeguards. The logic of the Surveillance State is that more is always better: not just more powers, but in increasingly unchecked form.

And this is to say nothing of the seemingly more mundane, though still invasive, surveillance powers which receive little attention. When Seung-Hui Cho went on a shooting rampage at Virginia Tech in 2007, this passage appeared buried in an ABC News report[11] on the incident: "Some news accounts have suggested that Cho had a history of antidepressant use, but senior federal officials tell ABC News that they can find no record of such medication in the government's files." Such "files" are maintained through a 2005 law[12] which, the Government claims, authorizes it to monitor and record all prescription drug use by all citizens[13] via so-called "Prescription Drug Monitoring Programs."[14] And there is a slew of other under-discussed surveillance programs whereby the U.S. government stores vast data on our private activities: everything from every domestic telephone call we make[15] to "risk assessment" records based on our travel activities[16]. A bipartisan group of Senators is currently promoting[17] mandated "biometric ID cards" for every American as a purported solution to illegal immigration.

Not only has Obama, in the wake of this massive expansion, blocked any reforms, he has taken multiple steps to further expand unaccountable and unchecked surveillance power. For the last year, the Obama Justice Department has been trying to convince federal courts[18] to extend its warrantless surveillance powers beyond even what the Patriot Act provides to encompass private email and Internet browsing records, a position which would allow the FBI and other federal agencies to acquire email and browsing records of American citizens—including those who are not suspected of any wrongdoing—without any warrants or judicial supervision of any kind. With defeat in the courts appearing likely, it was recently revealed by *The Washington Post*[19] that the administration is agitating for Congressional action to amend the Patriot Act to include such Internet and browsing data among the records obtainable by NSLs.

Blocking Even Modest Safeguards

Worse still, Obama has all but single-handedly prevented additional oversight mechanisms on the intelligence community by threatening to veto[20] even the modest oversight proposals favored by the House Democratic leadership. That veto threat just resulted in the removal of such mechanisms[21] by the

Senate Intelligence Committee from the latest rendition of the Intelligence Authorization Act. As *Time's* Massimo Calebresi recently reported[22], these reforms would merely have required the Executive Branch to notify the full House and Senate Intelligence Committees "when they launch any covert action or other controversial program," as well as vest those Committees with "the power to task the Government Accountability Office (GAO) with auditing any intelligence program" to ensure compliance with the law.

What makes Obama's vehement opposition even to these mild safeguards so striking is that this lack of oversight was one of the principal weapons used by the Bush administration to engage in illegal intelligence activities. The Bush administration, at best, would confine its briefings to extremely vague information disseminated only to the so-called "Gang of Eight"—comprised of 8 top-ranking members of the House and Senate—who were impeded by law and other constraints from taking any action even if they learned of blatantly criminal acts.

That's what makes the current oversight regime a sham process: it allows the administration to claim that it "briefed" selected Congressional leaders on illegal surveillance programs, but do so in a way that ensures there could be no meaningful action or oversight, because those individuals are barred from taking notes or even consulting their staff and, worse, because the full Intelligence Committees are kept in the dark and thus could do nothing even in the face of clear abuses. The process even allows the members who were briefed on illegal surveillance activities to claim they were powerless to stop illegal programs—which is exactly the excuse Democratic Senators who were briefed on the illegal NSA program[23] invoked to justify their inaction.

Here's how Richard Clarke explained the current "oversight" regime in July, 2009, on *The Rachel Maddow Show*:

MADDOW: Do you think that the current system, the gang of eight briefing system, allows the CIA to be good at spying and to be doing their work legally?

CLARKE: I think briefings of the gang of eight, those very sensitive briefings, as opposed to the broader briefings—the gang of eight briefings are usually often a farce. They catch them alone, one at the time usually. They run some briefing by them.

The congressman can't keep the briefing. They can't take notes. They can't consult their staff. They don't know what the briefings are about in advance. It's a box check so that the CIA can say it complied with the law. It's not oversight. It doesn't work.

And yet, the more surveillance abuse and even lawbreaking is revealed, the more emphatic is Executive Branch opposition to additional safeguards and oversights, let alone to scaling back some of those powers.

Thus, even when our National Security State gets caught red-handed breaking the law or blatantly abusing its powers, the reaction is to legalize their behavior and thus further increase their domestic spying authority. Apparently, eight years of the Bush assault on basic liberties was insufficient; there are still many remaining rights in need of severe abridgment in the name of terrorism. It never moves in the other direction: toward a reeling in of those post 9/11 surveillance authorities or at least the imposition of greater checks and transparency. The Surveillance State not only grows inexorably, but so does the secrecy and unaccountability behind which it functions.

The results of this mindset are as clear as they are disturbing. Last month's three-part *Washington Post* series, entitled

"Top Secret America," provided a detailed picture of what has long been clear: we live under a surveillance system so vast and secretive that nobody—not even those within the system—knows what it does or how it functions. Among the *Post's* more illustrative revelations: "Every day, collection systems at the National Security Agency intercept and store 1.7 billion e-mails, phone calls and other types of communications." To call that an out-of-control, privacy-destroying Surveillance State is to understate the case.

More Surveillance, Less Safety

What makes this leviathan particularly odious is that it does not even supply the security which is endlessly invoked to justify it. It actually does the opposite. As many surveillance experts have repeatedly argued, including House Intelligence Committee member Rush Holt[24], the more secret surveillance powers we vest in the government, the more unsafe we become. Cato's Julian Sanchez put it this way[25]: "We've gotten so used to the 'privacy/security tradeoff' that it's worth reminding ourselves, every now and again, that surrendering privacy does not automatically make us more secure—that systems of surveillance can themselves be a major source of insecurity."

That's because the Surveillance State already collects so much information about us, our activities and our communications—so indiscriminately and on such a vast scale—that it is increasingly difficult for it to detect any actual national security threats. NSA whistle blower Adrienne Kinne, when exposing NSA eavesdropping abuses[26], warned of what *ABC News* described as "the waste of time spent listening to innocent

Americans, instead of looking for the terrorist needle in the haystack." As Kinne explained:

> By casting the net so wide and continuing to collect on Americans and aid organizations, it's almost like they're making the haystack bigger and it's harder to find that piece of information that might actually be useful to somebody. You're actually hurting our ability to effectively protect our national security.

As the *Post* put it in its "Top Secret America" series:

> The NSA sorts a fraction of those [1.7 billion e-mails, phone calls and other types of daily collected communications] into 70 separate databases. The same problem bedevils every other intelligence agency, none of which have enough analysts and translators for all this work.

That article details how ample information regarding alleged Ft. Hood shooter Nidal Hassan and attempted Christmas Day bomber Umar Abdulmutallab was collected but simply went unrecognized. Similarly, *The Washington Post's* David Ignatius previously reported[27] that Abdulmutallab was not placed on a no-fly list despite ample evidence of his terrorism connections because information overload "clogged" the surveillance system and prevented its being processed. Identically, *Newsweek's* Mike Isikoff and Mark Hosenball documented[28] that U.S. intelligence agencies intercept, gather and store so many emails, recorded telephone calls, and other communications that it's simply impossible to sort through or understand what they have, quite possibly causing them to have missed crucial evidence in their possession about both the Fort Hood and Abdulmutallab plots:

> This deluge of Internet traffic—involving e-mailers whose true identity often is not apparent—is one indication of the volume of raw intelligence U.S. spy agencies have had to sort through . . . . The large volume of messages also may help to explain how

agencies can become so overwhelmed with data that sometimes it is difficult, if not impossible, to connect potentially important dots.

As a result, our vaunted Surveillance State failed to stop the former attack and it was only an alert airplane passenger who thwarted the latter. So it isn't that we keep sacrificing our privacy to an always-growing National Security State in exchange for greater security. The opposite is true: we keep sacrificing our privacy to the always-growing National Security State in exchange for less security.

The Privatization of the Surveillance State

Perhaps the most disturbing aspect of our mammoth Surveillance State is that the bulk of its actions are carried out not by shadowy government agencies, but by large private corporations which are beyond the reach of democratic accountability. At this point, perhaps it's more accurate to view the U.S. Government and these huge industry interests as one gigantic, amalgamated, inseparable entity—with a public division and a private one. In every way that matters, the separation between government and corporations is nonexistent, especially (though not only) when it comes to the Surveillance State. Indeed, so extreme is this overlap that when Michael McConnell was nominated to be Bush's Director of National Intelligence after serving for a decade as Vice President of Booz Allen (prior to which he was head of the NSA under Bush 41 and Clinton), he told *The New York Times* that[29] his ten years of working "outside the government," for Booz Allen, would not impede his ability to run the nation's intelligence functions. That's because his Booz Allen work was indistinguishable from working for the government, and therefore—as he put it—being at Booz Allen "has allowed me to stay focused on national security and intelligence communities as a strategist and as a consultant. Therefore, in many respects, I never left."

As the NSA scandal revealed, private telecom giants and other corporations now occupy the central role in carrying out the government's domestic surveillance and intelligence activities—almost always in the dark, beyond the reach of oversight or the law. As Tim Shorrock explained in his definitive 2007 *Salon* piece[30] on the relationship between McConnell, Booz Allen, and the intelligence community, in which (to no avail) he urged Senate Democrats to examine these relationships before confirming McConnell as Bush's DNI: "[Booz Allen's] website states that the Booz Allen team 'employs more than 10,000 TS/SCI cleared personnel.' TS/SCI stands for top secret-sensitive compartmentalized intelligence, the highest possible security ratings. This would make Booz Allen one of the largest employers of cleared personnel in the United States."

As the *Post* series documented, private contractors in America's Surveillance State are so numerous and unaccountably embedded in secret government functions that they are literally "countless":

> Making it more difficult to replace contractors with federal employees: The government doesn't know how many are on the federal payroll. Gates said he wants to reduce the number of defense contractors by about 13 percent, to pre-9/11 levels, but he's having a hard time even getting a basic head count.
>
> "This is a terrible confession," he said. "I can't get a number on how many contractors work for the Office of the Secretary of Defense," referring to the department's civilian leadership.

In sum, the picture that emerges from the *Post* series is that we have a Secret Government of 854,000 people, so vast and so secret that nobody knows what it does or what it is. That there is a virtually complete government/corporate merger when it comes to the National Security and Surveillance State is indisputable: "Private firms have become so thoroughly entwined with the government's most sensitive activities that without them important military and intelligence missions would have to cease or would be jeopardized."

As little oversight as Surveillance State officials have, corporate officials engaged in these activities have even less. Relying upon profit-driven industry for the intelligence community's "core mission" is to ensure that we have Endless War and an always-expanding Surveillance State. After all, the very people providing us with the "intelligence" that we use to make decisions are the ones who are duty-bound to keep this Endless War and Surveillance Machine alive and expanding because, as the Post put it, they are "obligated to shareholders rather than the public interest." The Surveillance State thus provides its own fuel and own rationale to ensure its endless expansion, all while resisting any efforts to impose transparency or accountability on it.

And as we acquiesce to more and more sacrifices of our privacy to the omnipotent Surveillance State, it builds the wall of secrecy behind which it operates higher and more impenetrable, which means it constantly knows more about the actions of citizens, while citizens constantly know less about it. We chirp endlessly about the Congress, the White House, the Supreme Court, the Democrats and Republicans, but this is the Real U.S. Government: a massive Surveillance State functioning in darkness, beyond elections and parties, so secret, vast and powerful

that it evades the control or knowledge of any one person or
even any organization.

URLS IN THIS POST

1. Made every such act of warrantless eavesdropping a felony: http://
   www.law.cornell.edu/uscode/50/usc_sec_50_00001809----000-.html

2. Concluded that it was illegal: http://www.salon.com/news/opinion/
   glenn_greenwald/2010/04/01/nsa

3. Documenting continuous abuses by the FBI: http://www.washingtonpost.
   com/wpdyn/content/article/2007/03/17/AR2007031701451.html

4. Via so-called "National Security Letters" (NSLs)): http://www.nytimes.
   com/2007/03/09/washington/09attorneys.html?hp

5. Confirmed ongoing abuses subsequent to the time period covered
   by the initial IG report: http://www.washingtonpost.com/wp-dyn/
   content/article/2008/03/05/AR2008030500463.html

6. He assured everyone that he did so: http://my.barackobama.com/
   page/community/post/rospars/gGxsZFf

7. Long raised by Senator Russ Feingold: http://tpmcafe.
   talkingpointsmemo.com/2005/12/13/update_on_the_patriot_act

8. First in 2006 by a vote of 89-10: http://edition.cnn.com/2006/
   POLITICS/03/07/patriot.act/

9. Once again extended the Patriot Act without even a single added
   oversight protection: http://www.eff.org/deeplinks/2010/02/epic-fail-
   congress-usa-patriot-act-renewed-without

10. Substantial and serious abuses: http://www.nytimes.com/2009/04/
    16/us/16nsa.html?_r=1&hp

11. An *ABC News* report: http://abcnews.go.com/US/story?id=3048108
    &page=2

12. A 2005 law: http://www.govtrack.us/congress/billtext.xpd?bill=
    h109-1132

13. Authorizes it to monitor and record all prescription drug use by all
    citizens: http://www.salon.com/news/opinion/glenn_greenwald/
    2007/04/18/surveillance/print.html

14. So-called "Prescription Drug Monitoring Programs.": http://www.ncsl.
    org/default.aspx?tabid=12726

15. Every domestic telephone call we make: http://www.usatoday.com/news/washington/2006-05-10nsa_ x.htm

16. "Risk assessment" records based on our travel activities: http://www.wired.com/threatlevel/2006/12/international_t/

17. Currently promoting: http://www.washingtonpost.com/wpdyn/ content/article/2010/03/17/AR2010031703115.html

18. Been trying to convince federal courts: http://www.salon.com/news/opinion/glenn_greenwald/2010/04/15/doj

19. Recently revealed by *The Washington Post*: http://www.washingtonpost.com/wpdyn/content/article/2010/07/28/AR2010072806141.html?hpid=topnews

20. Threatening to veto: http://www.salon.com/news/opinion/glenn_greenwald/2010/03/16/obama

21. Resulted in the removal of such mechanisms: http://pogoblog.typepad.com/pogo/2010/07/gao-inteloversight- provision-goes-missing-.html

22. *Time's* Massimo Calebresi recently reported: http://www.time.com/time/nation/article/0,8599,1999599,00.html

23. Excuse Democratic Senators who were briefed on the illegal NSA program: http://www.talkingpointsmemo.com/docs/rock-cheney1.html

24. House Intelligence Committee member Rush Holt: http://mobile.salon.com/opinion/greenwald/2008/10/09/eavesdropping/index.html

25. Put it this way: http://www.cato.org/pub_display.php?pub_id=11185

26. Exposing NSA eavesdropping abuses: http://abcnews.go.com/Blotter/Story?id=5987804&page=1

27. Previously reported: http://www.washingtonpost.com/wpdyn/ content/article/2010/01/05/AR2010010502986.html

28. Documented: http://blog.newsweek.com/blogs/declassified/archive/2010/01/05/intelligencesources- tens-of-thousands-of-e-mailers-corresponded-with-radical-cleric-linked-to-underpants-bomberand- ft-hood-shooter.aspx

29. He told *The New York Times* that: http://query.nytimes.com/gst/fullpage.html? res=9501EFDB1430F936A35752C0A9619C8B63&sec=&spon=&pagewanted=all

30. Explained in his definitive 2007 *Salon* piece: http://www.salon.com/news/feature/2007/01/08/mcconnell

***Glenn Greenwald** is a former constitutional and civil rights litigator and current contributing writer at Salon.com. He is the author of three *New York Times* best-selling books: *How Would a Patriot Act?*; *A Tragic Legacy*; and *With Liberty and Justice for Some*.

Greenwald, Glenn. "The Digital Surveillance State: Vast, Secret, and Dangerous," *Cato Unbound*, August 9, 2010. http://www.cato-unbound.org/2010/08/09/glenn-greenwald/the-digital-surveillance-statevast- secret-and-dangerous/.

Used by permission.

The Sky Isn't Falling

by Paul Rosenzweig*

Glenn Greenwald paints a grim image of America as a giant "Surveillance State."[1] But the image simply doesn't withstand scrutiny. Much as I admire Greenwald's writings, his pointillist picture of "abuses" and "excesses" is, from my perspective, an inaccurate picture. The idea that Los Angeles will soon be a hot-bed of Stasi-like surveillance is just not realistic.

Greenwald's essay, essentially, makes four interrelated assertions:

- The degree of surveillance in America is growing;

- More than is reasonably necessary to protect against terrorism;

- Without essential oversight; and

- In a manner that is ineffective even on its own terms.

The first of these assertions is manifestly true, and no sane person would deny it. The second is a value judgment at odds with the opinion of a vast majority of Americans and, in the end, impossible to prove or falsify, though perhaps in the discussion we can debate it. The third and fourth propositions are demonstrably wrong, and are the subject of this brief response.

Oversight Is Robust

Greenwald's principal complaint is that oversight of surveillance activity is inadequate. It must have been slightly embarrassing to have written that on the same day that the D.C. Circuit demonstrated the robustness of judicial oversight by limiting the use of GPS tracking surveillance systems.

Perhaps Greenwald sees court oversight as separate and apart from other institutions of control—but that would be a mistake. What we have seen, since September 11, is the growth of a robust and complex system of oversight and regulation of surveillance activity with many elements. It includes: courts that are willing to overturn executive branch action; investigative and legislative Congressional activity; the growth of investigative journalism in the blogosphere; the rise of the public interest groups (who are, in effect, the "canary in the mineshaft," serving as an early warning system of abuse); and a more empowered and aware public.

To cite an example, nobody can doubt the extensive Congressional engagement over the past nine years on issues of surveillance. The Patriot Act has been considered substantively on four separate occasions. Various systems like Total Information Awareness and Secure Flight have been subject to repeated Congressional scrutiny. And with the Intelligence Reform and Terrorism Prevention Act and the Implementing Recommendations of the 9/11 Commission Act, Congress has twice made major substantive revisions to the structures and rules governing surveillance.

Non-governmental oversight is equally robust. I'm not one who views Wikileaks as a beneficial development. But it would blink reality to deny its effectiveness as a check on governmental activity and to understand that the panoply of oversight ranges from the official to the informal.

Beyond these external mechanisms, Greenwald gives no weight to the truly significant structural changes we have made in internal institutional oversight of surveillance activity. The Department of Homeland Security was created with a statutorily required Privacy Officer (and another Officer for Civil Rights and Civil Liberties), the first of its kind in American history. Now Privacy Officers proliferate in virtually every Federal agency. More recently, Congress created a Civil Liberties Protection Officer within the intelligence community. Inspectors General in the various agencies have been active in their constructive review, with the IG at the Department of Justice being particularly effective. If the Administration were to staff the independent Privacy and Civil Liberties Oversight Board (a failure which I join Greenwald in decrying) it would be a significant further step. Surely Greenwald should at least be willing to acknowledge (if only grudgingly) the utility of these new structures.

Of even greater significance, the very same surveillance systems used to advance our counterterrorism interests are equally well suited to assure that government officials comply with the limitations imposed on them in respect of individual privacy. Indeed, there are already indications that these strong audit mechanisms work quite well. Recall the incident in the last Presidential campaign in which contractors hacked Barack Obama's passport file. There was no lawful reason to disclose the file; it was done solely for prurient, political reasons. As a result, candidate Obama suffered an adverse consequence of disclosure which had not met any legal trigger that would have permitted the disclosure. The same was true of the Toledo Police Department employees who released "Joe the Plumber's" tax returns.

A strong audit function quickly identified the wrongdoers and allowed punitive action to be taken.

Finally, it is not beneficial to the debate to mischaracterize the precise contours of the law. Greenwald, for example, characterizes the National Security Letters (NSLs) as "the ability to obtain private, invasive records about Americans without the need for any judicial supervision." But the truth is less scary: Under 18 USC §3511, an NSL recipient may file a petition for review of the NSL in District Court and the court may set aside the NSL request for records if compliance would be unreasonable, oppressive, or otherwise unlawful.

This not-so-small detail shows that Greenwald's real complaint is not that oversight is lacking. Rather, he considers the level of oversight insufficient. It seems he wants NSLs to be subject to some form of relevancy requirement, just as grand jury subpoenas are, or perhaps a notice requirement. Those are reasonable positions to take—though I wouldn't take them. But to leap from there to an overwrought condemnation of America as a "Surveillance State" simply leaps too far. While reasonable minds can disagree, Greenwald seems to think that any disagreement with his concerns is "dangerous" and unreasonable.

Effectiveness

Greenwald's other argument is that the system simply does not work. That would be a powerful indictment of our efforts, were it true. Thankfully, it is not.

To be sure, it is difficult to discern successes for surveillance techniques when those successes often occur in a classified domain. Rare is the case where a catalog of successes is declassified, as former DHS Secretary Chertoff did in May 2007.

But a careful observer can detect the outlines of other intelligence successes based on surveillance in recent events. When David Headley was arrested for allegedly seeking to commit terrorist acts in Denmark, news reports suggested that one of the key factors in his identification was his pattern of travel to the Middle East and his efforts to conceal those trips from the government. Review of his travel both provided the trigger to ask questions and the factual cross-check on the veracity of his answers. Likewise, when Najibullah al-Zasi was arrested, one factor that was publicly disclosed as a ground for suspicion was surveillance of his travel to Pakistan. And surveillance tapes from a shopping center in Bridgeport, Conn., played a modest role in the hunt for failed Times Square bomber Faisal Shahzad.

It is difficult to be certain how effective our surveillance efforts are, and Greenwald is right that the flood of data is increasing, not decreasing. But the evidence in the public record doesn't support a claim that the surveillance we undertake is ineffective.

To be sure, failures result when our surveillance techniques are used ineffectively. That was the case with the 2009 Christmas bomb plot. Not only was Umar Farouk Abdulmutallab's name provided by his father, but the gathered evidence suggests that other, less specific NSA intercepts existed that might have generated a suspicion of Nigerian travelers. Add in his reported purchase of a cash ticket and the alleged rejection of his visa application by the U.K., and the case seems to be the precise sort of concatenation of facts which, individually, amount to little but, collectively, paint a more cautionary picture. Greenwald is correct to portray this as a failure.

But even this complaint of ineffectiveness rings hollow. Opposition to data analytical techniques of the sort that would have made sense of the Abdulmutallab information has been a hallmark of privacy lobby. Programs like Secure Flight have languished because of opposition from privacy advocates who should not now be heard to condemn the ineffectiveness of the systems they have worked so hard to hobble. Though Greenwald would surely disagree, one answer to the ineffectiveness claim is more and better analytical techniques, not abandonment of the essential enterprise.

The Sky Is Not Falling

Finally, two other points are worth making to highlight matters of real concern.

First, Greenwald's critique would be far more persuasive if it were offered in a more even handed manner, with an internationalist perspective. Whatever one may say about the United States, our system is far more protective of civil liberties and privacy than, say, China or Russia or any of a dozen other readily-named nations. And yet, Greenwald seems to think that concern over Chinese activity is nothing more than an effort to distract Americans from what they should really be concerned about—American abuses. That kind of false moral equivalence drains his critique of much of its persuasive value.

But even more troubling, I fear that Greenwald's "the sky is falling" approach to surveillance will inevitably lead the public to disregard his complaints. As his essay makes clear, his concerns are held only by a minority of Americans. As efforts to portray America as a "Surveillance State" grow shriller, the disregard for those efforts will only grow deeper—and that would be a shame. Real abuses—like MKUltra, not the hypothetical ones that Greenwald posits—have happened in the past. I don't want Americans to simply ignore alarms about real abuses in the future because they've grown inured to the sound of the siren.

URLS IN THIS POST

1. "Surveillance State.": http://www.cato-unbound.org/2010/08/09/ glenn-greenwald/the-digitalsurveillance-state-vast-secret-and- dangerous/.

*Paul Rosenzweig is the founder of Red Branch Consulting PLLC, a home-land security consulting company, and is a senior advisor to The Chertoff Group. Mr. Rosenzweig formerly served as deputy assistant secretary for policy in the Department of Homeland Security.

Rosenzweig, Paul. "The Sky Isn't Falling," *Cato Unbound,* August 13, 2010. http://www.cato-unbound.org URL to article: http://www.cato-unbound. org/2010/08/13/paul-rosenzweig/the-sky-isnt-falling/.

Used by permission.

Surveillance of Our Enemies During Wartime? I'm Shocked!

by John Eastman*

Reading Glenn Greenwald's lead essay, "The Digital Surveillance State: Vast, Secret, and Dangerous," I could not help but recall a visit to my great aunt a quarter century ago. She showed me a shoe box of old World War I letters sent home from the front in France by my grandfather, who was then serving as an ambulance driver in the American Expeditionary Force. The letters—from a U.S. soldier home to his mother and sister—had been cut up by U.S. military censors like paper dolls, lest they inadvertently fall into enemy hands and unwittingly reveal some minor tactical detail about . . . the ambulance corps! I've not confirmed it yet, but I seriously doubt that the censors obtained a warrant before intercepting my grandfather's letters or taking the scissors to them.

Nor did they need to. Contrary to popular perception, fed by erroneous claims from the law professoriate and punditry, the Fourth Amendment does not require a warrant before any search or seizure can be undertaken. It simply requires that the search or seizure be "reasonable," and while warrants are the peacetime norm for "reasonableness" (and even then, there are exceptions), they are not the norm in wartime. This most basic fact of war seems entirely lost on Greenwald.

Not once in his article does Greenwald even acknowledge that we are at war with a global enemy bent on destroying us. He does refer to 9/11 as an "attack," but later describes it as a "trauma," as if it were some multi-car highway accident that overloaded the local emergency rooms. Most tellingly, he describes Congress's efforts to kick U.S. surveillance into high gear after the 9/11 attack as "knee-jerk," and bemoans the fact that our surveillance efforts have not abated "even as we approach almost a full decade of emotional and temporal distance from that event." Greenwald seems not to understand that the trigger date for a reduction in wartime surveillance efforts should be the conclusion of the war, not its onset! I will be more than happy to join Mr. Greenwald in expressing concern about our surveillance efforts if they are still in place ten years (or even one or two years) after the war ends, but I'd like to see us first defeat the enemy who would destroy us before unilaterally dismantling our efforts in the single most important front of this asymmetrical war.

Greenwald's extremely flawed (and dangerous) mindset discolors the rest of his analysis, and I want to focus on his legal claims. They are numerous, but they all tee off a single contention, that the Bush administration's surveillance efforts were "lawless," and that when they were disclosed, Congress "legalized" them rather than repudiating them. The evidence for the "lawless" charge? Two federal district court judges (Judge Anna Diggs Taylor and Judge Vaughn Walker—yes, the same Vaughn Walker that just held California's traditional marriage law unconstitutional) and an appellate court judge (Judge Ronald Gilman, writing in dissent!) have said so.

Judge Taylor's laughably simplistic and erroneous decision has already been reversed on appeal, and Judge Walker's is pending appeal, with the Obama administration vigorously challenging its holding. But even if that holding is upheld, it stands simply for the proposition that the surveillance program violated the Foreign Intelligence Surveillance Act ("FISA"). It does not resolve the following much more difficult questions: 1) whether the Authorization for the Use of Military Force ("AUMF"), Pub. L. No. 107-40, § 2(a), 115 Stat. 224, 224 (Sept. 18, 2001), passed by Congress one week after 9/11, gave authority to the President beyond that conveyed in FISA; and if it did not, 2) whether Congress's attempt with FISA to curtail the President's Commander-in-Chief powers, if applied in wartime, is constitutional.

On the former, the Supreme Court has already held that another federal statute—the Anti-Detention Act of 1971—was superseded by the AUMF because detention of enemy combatants is a well-established incident of military authority in time of war. See *Hamdi v. Rumsfeld*, 542 U.S. 507, 518 (2004). Surely surveillance of enemy communications, which is what the NSA Surveillance program targeted, equally qualifies as a well-established incident of military authority in time of war.

But even absent the authority granted by Congress to the President under the AUMF, the President has authority of his own directly from Article II of the Constitution, authority that cannot be restricted by an Act of Congress. The open question is whether the ability to conduct surveillance of enemy communications during time of war, even if one end of those communications is within the borders of the United States, is part of the President's constitutional authority. Existing Supreme Court precedent in analogous contexts strongly suggests that it is, and an intermediate appellate court decision dealing specifically with FISA expressly so states.

Here's the ruling by the highest court to have considered the issue, directly on point: "We take for granted that the President does have [inherent authority to conduct warrantless searches to obtain foreign intelligence information], and, assuming that is so, *FISA could not encroach on the President's constitutional power.*" *In re Sealed Case*, 310 F.3d 717 (U.S. Foreign Intell. Surveillance Ct. Rev. 2002) (emphasis added). As I elaborated upon in my 2006 testimony before the U.S. House of Representatives Permanent Select Committee on Intelligence, and again in my 2007 testimony before the U.S. Commission on Civil Rights, the point that the FISA Court of Review took for granted is well-grounded in Supreme Court precedent, in such cases as *United States v. Curtiss-Wright Export Corp.*, 299 U.S. 304, 319 (1936) ("[t]he President is the sole organ of the nation in its external relations," "and Congress itself is powerless to invade" the President's constitutional authority in that realm), *United States v. Reynolds*, 345 U.S. 1, 10 (1953) (upholding government's claim of privilege to prevent disclosure of classified information about military electronics equipment), and *United States v. Ramsey*, 431 U.S. 606 (1977) (upholding warrantless searches of mail at the border and even at a postal facility inside the border, as an exercise of inherent sovereign power).

Congress itself recognized in the AUMF that the President has inherent authority, when it noted that "the President has authority *under the Constitution* to take action to deter and prevent acts of international terrorism against the United States . . . ." AUMF, Preamble, PL 107-40, 115 Stat. 224 (Sept. 18, 2001) (emphasis added). The AUMF preamble also reflects the view of Congress prior to the adoption of FISA, when it expressly recognized the "*constitutional power* of the President to take such measures as he deems necessary to protect the Nation against actual or potential attack . . . , *[and] to obtain foreign intelligence information* deemed essential to the security of the United States. . . ." 82 Stat. 214, formerly codified at 18 U.S.C. § 2511(3) (emphasis added).

Every presidential administration since electronic surveillance technology was developed has taken the same view. Indeed, the notion that Congress cannot by mere statute truncate powers the President holds directly from the Constitution is a common feature of executive branch communications with the Congress. Two examples from a thorough and persuasive 2006 report from the Department of Justice entitled "Legal Authorities Supporting the Activities of the National Security Agency Described by the President" ("DOJ Report"), are particularly revealing. Griffin Bell, President Jimmy Carter's Attorney General, testified during debate in Congress over the adoption of FISA that, although FISA did not recognize any inherent power of the President, it "does not take away the power [of] the President under the Constitution." DOJ Report at 8 (citing Foreign Intelligence Electronic Surveillance Act of 1978: Hearings on H.R. 5764, H.R. 9745, H.R. 7308, and H.R. 5632 Before the Subcomm. on Legislation of the House Comm. on Intelligence, 95th Cong., 2d Sess. 15 (1978) (Statement of Attorney General Bell)). And President Clinton's Deputy Attorney General, Jamie Gorelick, made a similar point while testifying before Congress when amendments to FISA were being considered in 1994: "[T]he Department of Justice believes, and the case law supports, that the President has inherent authority to conduct warrantless physical searches for foreign intelligence purposes . . . ." DOJ Report at 8 (citing "Amending the Foreign Intelligence Surveillance Act: Hearings Before the House Permanent Select Comm. On Intelligence, 103d Cong. 2d Sess. 61 (1994) (statement of Deputy Attorney General Jamie S. Gorelick)). An equally compelling historical analysis, elaborating on the longstanding recognition of presidential power in wartime, was published by Cato's own Roger Pilon in the 2009 Chapman Law Review. I commend that work to Greenwald's attention as well.

In his dissenting opinion in *Terminiello v. Chicago,* 337 U.S. 1, 37 (1949), Justice Robert Jackson famously warned of the "danger that, if the court does not temper its doctrinaire logic with a little practical wisdom, it will convert the constitutional Bill of Rights into a suicide pact." Nowhere is that warning more appropriate than in wartime, and arguably at no time in our nation's history has it been more urgent than now.

*John C. Eastman** is the Henry Salvatori Professor of Law & Community Service at Chapman University School of Law in California. He is the founding director of the Center for Constitutional Jurisprudence, a public interest law firm affiliated with the Claremont Institute.

Eastman, John. "Surveillance of Our Enemies During Wartime? I'm Shocked!," Cato Unbound, August 11, 2010. http://www.cato-unbound.org/2010/08/11/john-eastman/surveillance-of-our-enemiesduring-wartime-i%e2%80%99m-shocked/.

Used by permission.

The Surveillance State Thrives on Fear

by Glenn Greenwald*

I'm particularly appreciative of the responses to my initial essay by John Eastman[1] and Paul Rosenzweig[2]. Those two replies—especially the former—perfectly illustrate the continuous stream of manipulative fear-mongering over the last decade which has reduced much of the American citizenry into a meek and submissive faction for whom no asserted government power is too extreme, provided the scary menace of "Terrorism" is uttered to justify it.

That more *surveillance-is-always-better* mentality is what allows Eastman and Rosenzweig to dismiss concerns over surveillance excesses a mere four weeks after the establishment-supporting *Washington Post* documented[3] that our Surveillance State is "so large, so unwieldy and so secretive" that not even top intelligence and defense officials know what it does. For those who are so fearful of Terrorism and/or so authoritarian in their desire to exploit and exaggerate that threat for greater government power, not even the construction of a "Top Secret America"—"an alternative geography of the United States" that operates in the dark and with virtually no oversight—is cause for concern.

Eastman's essay centers around one three-word slogan: *We're at war!* For almost a full decade, this has been the all-justifying cliché for everything the U.S. government does—from torture, renditions and due process-free imprisonments to wars of aggression, occupations, assassination programs aimed at U.S. citizens, and illegal domestic eavesdropping. Thus does Eastman thunder, with the melodrama and hysteria typical of this scare tactic: "Not once in his article does Greenwald even acknowledge that we are at war with a global enemy bent on destroying us." *A global enemy bent on destroying us! Scary: be very afraid.*

By invoking The War Justification for America's Surveillance State, Eastman wants to trigger images of America's past glorious wars. He's not particularly subtle about that, as he begins with a charming story of how his grandfather's letters were censored during World War I (how censorship of a soldier deployed in a foreign war justifies surveillance of American civilians on U.S. soil is anyone's guess). But, for several reasons, this war justification is as misleading as it is dangerous:

First, unlike for past wars (such as World War I), the current "war" has no possibility of any finite duration or definitive end. Even its most enthusiastic proponents—as well as the U.S. government—acknowledge that it is more akin to an ideological conflict (like the Cold War) than a traditional combat war. Islamic extremism is highly unlikely to end in the foreseeable future, to put it mildly. Thus, this "war" will drag on not for years but for decades, probably even generations. When President Obama unveiled his proposal for "preventive detention" [4] last June, he said that "unlike the Civil War or World War II, we can't count on a surrender ceremony to bring this journey to an end" and that we'll still be fighting this "war" "a year from now, five years from now, and—in all probability—10 years from now."

Thus, people like Eastman who want to radically expand government power in the name of this "war" are not defending temporary alterations to the American political system. Rather, they are urging its permanent transformation. We are, as the military historian Andrew Bacevich has repeatedly documented[5], a nation in a state of "perpetual war." War-justified powers will be vested in the government not—as people like Eastman imply—temporarily, but rather forever.

Second, Eastman's fear-inducing, glorifying description of a handful of Muslim extremists—"*a global enemy bent on destroying us*"—is so hyperbolic as to be laughable. Earlier this month, the State Department published its annual Report on Terrorism[6]. Among its findings, as highlighted by McClatchy's Warren Strobel[7], was this: "There were just 25 U.S. noncombatant fatalities from terrorism worldwide. (The U.S. government definition of terrorism excludes attacks on U.S. military personnel). While we don't have the figures at hand, undoubtedly more American citizens died overseas from traffic accidents or intestinal illnesses than from terrorism."

Eastman wants to drastically expand the power of the American government and subject U.S. citizens to sprawling, unaccountable surveillance, all because he's petrified of a handful of extremists hiding in caves who cause fewer deaths to Americans than stomach diseases (or, at least he wants Americans to be that petrified). That's how America has become a nation racked with fear. Compare that mentality to what the U.S. did in the face of an actually threatening "global enemy": the Soviet Union, which possessed a huge army and hundreds of nuclear-tipped intercontinental ballistic missiles aimed at U.S. cities.

Even at the height of the Cold War, the United States enacted the FISA statute, which criminalized government eavesdropping on American citizens without warrants. Every President until George W. Bush—including Ronald Reagan—was able to keep the country safe while adhering to that surveillance safeguard. But while even the most hawkish Americans in the 1980s—facing the Soviet threat—understood that domestic eavesdropping should be conducted only with judicial warrants, the war cheerleaders of the current decade insist that the far less formidable threat from Muslim extremists means we must vest the government with the power of warrantless surveillance—even on American citizens, on U.S. soil. That's how far we've descended into the pit of submission, thanks to the toxic mix of fear-mongers and the authoritarian cowards they exploit.

Third, there's no "war exception" in the Constitution. Even with real wars—i.e., those involving combat between opposing armies—the Constitution actually continues to constrain what government officials can do, most stringently as it concerns U.S. citizens. But strictly speaking, we're not really "at war." Congress has merely authorized the use of military force but has not formally or constitutionally declared war. Even the Bush administration conceded that this is a vital difference when it comes to legal rights. In 2006, the Bush DOJ insisted[8] that the wartime provision of FISA—allowing the Government to eavesdrop for up to 15 days without a warrant—didn't apply because Congress only enacted an AUMF, not a declaration of war:

> The contrary interpretation of section 111 also ignores the important differences between a formal declaration of war and a resolution such as the AUMF. As a historical matter, a formal declaration of war was no longer than a sentence, and thus Congress would not expect a declaration of war to outline the extent to which Congress authorized the President to engage in various incidents of waging war. Authorizations for the use of military force, by contrast, are typically more detailed and are made for the *specific purpose* of reciting the manner in which Congress has authorized the President to act.

The Bush DOJ went on to explain that declarations of war trigger a whole variety of legal effects (such as terminating diplomatic relations and abrogating or suspending treaty obligations) which AUMFs do not trigger (see p. 27). To authorize military force is not to declare war.

Indeed, the U.S. is fighting numerous undeclared wars, including ones involving military action—such as the "War on Drugs." Given that our "War on Drugs" continues to rage, should the U.S. government be able to eavesdrop on accused "drug kingpins" or associates without warrants? After all, terrorists blow up airplanes but drug kingpins kill our kids!!! The mindset that cheers for unlimited presidential powers in the name of "war" invariably leads to exactly these sorts of expansions.

From its founding, the United States has been grounded in the need to balance security with freedom; that means sometimes sacrificing the former for the latter (which is why, for instance, the Constitution limits the state's power to conduct searches or imprison people even though those limits will sometimes enable violent criminals to escape). People like Eastman evince no appreciation for that balance. Security is the only recognized value, and thus, like a frightened child calling out for a parent, they insist that the government must have unrestrained power to do what it wants to Keep Us Safe. A country wallowing in that level of blinding fear will not be great for very long.

Rosenzweig's reply is much more substantive and reasonable, and I'll leave it to readers to compare on their own our competing claims about the nature of the surveillance abuses and the lack of oversight and safeguards. I do, however, want to flag one component of his response as illustrative of the erosion of liberty which the United States continues to suffer and the way in which it has been normalized.

It was quite common during the "debate" over America's torture regime for Bush defenders to resort to the defense that even if we engaged in harsh or even illegal tactics, they paled in comparison to, say, the torture techniques employed by Saddam Hussein. *It's not like we have rape rooms and mass graves*, they'd argue (leave aside the fact that mass graves, at least figuratively, are exactly what we're leaving behind in Iraq[9], among other places). Our descent into brutality and lawlessness was epitomized by the fact that this became our new standard: *as long as we're not as bad as history's most despicable monsters, there's nothing to complain about.*

Rosenzweig's dismissals of America's Surveillance State abuses is redolent of that severe bar-lowering. He pronounces, as though it's comforting: "Whatever one may say about the United States, our system is far more protective of civil liberties and privacy than, say, China or Russia or any of a dozen other readily named nations." The United States once proclaimed itself "the Land of the Free" and our President "Leader of the Free World." We're now reduced to this sloganeering boast: Not as Tyrannical as Communist Regimes!

Is it really a comfort to anyone that the American Surveillance State is not as invasive or out-of-control as Russia's and "a dozen other nations"? Moreover, that premise is highly debatable. As I noted in my initial essay, quoting *The Washington Post*: "Every day, collection systems at the National Security Agency intercept and store 1.7 billion e-mails, phone calls and other types of communications." [. . .]

[. . .] For a society claiming to be devoted to principles of individual liberty and restrained government power, is that supposed to be some sort of comfort that we do not, in fact, now live under an out-of-control, increasingly entrenched and inherently abusive Surveillance State?

URLS IN THIS POST

1. John Eastman: http://www.cato-unbound.org/2010/08/11/john-eastman/surveillance-of-ourenemies-during-wartime-i%E2%80%99m-shocked/

2. Paul Rosenzweig: http://www.cato-unbound.org/2010/08/13/paul-rosenzweig/the-sky-isnt-falling/

3. Documented: http://projects.washingtonpost.com/top-secret-america/articles/a-hidden-world-growingbeyond- control/

4. Unveiled his proposal for "preventive detention": http://www.salon.com/news/opinion/glenn_greenwald/2009/05/22/preventive_detention

5. Repeatedly documented: http://cantate-domino.blogspot.com/2010/08/andrew-bacevich-on-perpetualwar.html

6. Annual Report on Terrorism: http://www.state.gov/s/ct/rls/crt/2009/index.htm

7. Highlighted by McClatchy's Warren Strobel: http://blogs.mcclatchydc.com/nationalsecurity/2010/08/terrorism-in-2009.html

8. The Bush DOJ insisted: http://epic.org/privacy/terrorism/fisa/doj11906wp.pdf

9. Exactly what we're leaving behind in Iraq: http://www.guardian.co.uk/world/2008/mar/19/iraq

*Glenn Greenwald is a former constitutional and civil rights litigator and current contributing writer at Salon.com. He is the author of three *New York Times* best-selling books: *How Would a Patriot Act?*, *A Tragic Legacy*, and *With Liberty and Justice for Some.*

Greenwald, Glenn. "The Surveillance State Thrives on Fear," Cato Unbound, August 26, 2010. http://www.cato-unbound.org/2010/08/26/glenn-greenwald/the-surveillance-statethrives- on-fear/.

Used by permission.

PART 2:

Video Surveillance

Video cameras are watching us. Where? Everywhere! During the last decade, video surveillance has become ubiquitous in public spaces. Earlier, property owners and banks used cameras to protect against break-ins and theft. Today, cameras are a common law enforcement surveillance tool, monitoring everything from traffic speed and pedestrian movements on public streets to libraries and schools. Surveys have shown that Americans accept this form of passive observation as a way to ensure public safety and to discourage unlawful behavior; however, the increasing use of the technology raises issues about how widespread surveillance should be and where to draw the line between acceptable use and unwarranted, unconstitutional invasion of privacy.

Proponents of widespread video surveillance argue that cameras play a critical role in identifying criminals and solving crimes. Video footage of crimes provides incontrovertible evidence in criminal investigations. "Smart" computer systems and cameras may be able to prevent crime by detecting suspicious activity before a crime has occurred. They contend that law enforcement is not the only beneficiary of widespread use of video cameras—the cameras that monitor civilians also monitor the police, serving as a check on their actions.

Opponents of video surveillance argue that cameras do little to deter or reduce crime. Instead, they maintain, routine surveillance erodes civil liberties. The same "smart" computer systems and cameras that help prevent crime are also capable of targeting minorities, foreigners, and political opponents. Advanced video technology capable of recording conversations on the street may have a chilling effect on speech and behavior. Further, video data collected for law enforcement purposes could be misused if they fall into the hands of unscrupulous parties. Opponents point to the fact that video surveillance has gone to extremes, even creeping into our homes. For example, a school district in Pennsylvania stirred controversy in 2010 when administrators used cameras installed in school-issued laptops to remotely monitor students without the knowledge of students or their families.

The presence of video surveillance has significantly affected our expectations of privacy in public spaces. As video surveillance becomes more sophisticated and accessible, how do we balance individual privacy rights with public safety interests? This section begins with a 1996 essay by David Brin. He maintains that the loss of privacy in public spaces is inevitable. However, he maintains that by embracing and sharing the power of observation among all citizens, rather than concentrating that power in the hands of a small number of authority figures, we can become a freer society. In the second article, David Rapp examines the various benefits and drawbacks of using cameras in schools. Journalist James Vlahos then explores the pervasive use of video cameras today and warns against unrestricted surveillance. The final article is an excerpt from a Police Executive Research Forum report; it discusses various real-life cases where cameras were integral to crime prevention and investigation.

As you read the materials in this section, consider the following questions:

1. What are the benefits of using cameras in public spaces? What are the drawbacks?

2. Should limits be imposed on the use of video surveillance in public spaces, and, if so, what should those limits be?

3. How does video surveillance affect our expectation of privacy today?

The Transparent Society

The cameras are coming. They're getting smaller and nothing will stop them. The only question is: who watches whom?

*by David Brin**

This is a tale of two cities. Cities of the near future, say, 20 years from now.

Barring something unforeseen, you are apt to live in one of these two places. Your only choice may be *which*.

At first sight, this pair of near-future municipalities look pretty much alike. Both contain dazzling technological marvels, especially in the realm of electronic media. Both suffer familiar urban quandaries of frustration and decay. If some progress is being made at solving human problems, it is happening gradually. Perhaps some kids seem better educated. The air may be marginally cleaner. People still worry about overpopulation, the environment, and the next international crisis.

None of these features is of interest to us right now, for we have noticed something about both 21st-century cities that *is* radically different. A trait that marks them distinctly apart from any metropolis of the late 1990s.

Street crime has nearly vanished from both towns. But that is only a symptom, a result.

The real change peers down from every lamppost, rooftop, and street sign.

Tiny *cameras*, panning left and right, surveying traffic and pedestrians, observing everything in open view.

Have we entered an Orwellian nightmare? Have the burghers of both towns banished muggings at the cost of creating a Stalinist dystopia?

Consider City Number One. In this place, the myriad cameras report their urban scenes straight to Police Central, where security officers use sophisticated image processors to scan for infractions against the public order—or perhaps against an established way of thought. Citizens walk the streets aware that any word or deed may be noted by agents of some mysterious bureau.

Now let's skip across space and time.

At first sight, things seem quite similar in City Number Two. Again, there are ubiquitous cameras, perched on every vantage point. Only here we soon find a crucial difference. The devices do *not* report to the secret police. Rather, each and every citizen of this metropolis can lift his or her wristwatch/TV and call up images from any camera in town.

Here, a late-evening stroller checks to make sure no one lurks beyond the corner she is about to turn.

Over there, a tardy young man dials to see if his dinner date still waits for him by the city hall fountain.

A block away, an anxious parent scans the area and finds which way her child has wandered off.

Over by the mall, a teenage shoplifter is taken into custody gingerly, with minute attention to ritual and rights, because the arresting officer knows the entire process is being scrutinized by untold numbers who watch intently, lest his neutral professionalism lapse.

In City Two, such microcameras are banned from many indoor places . . . except Police Headquarters! There, any citizen may tune in on bookings, arraignments, and especially the camera control room itself, making sure that the agents on duty look out for violent crime—and only crime.

Despite their similarities, these are very different cities. Disparate ways of life representing completely opposite relationships between citizens and their civic guardians. The reader may find both situations somewhat chilling. Both futures may seem undesirable. But can there be any doubt which city we'd rather live in, if these two make up our only choice?

Alas, they may be our only options. For the cameras *are* on their way, along with data networks that will send myriad images flashing back and forth, faster than thought.

In fact, the future has already arrived. Today, in Britain, several dozen cities and towns have already followed the example first set by King's Lynn, near Norwich, where 60 remote-controlled videocameras were installed to scan known "trouble spots," reporting directly to police headquarters. The resulting reduction in street crime exceeded all predictions, dropping to one-seventieth of the former amount in or near zones covered by surveillance. The savings in patrol costs alone paid for the equipment within a few months. Today, more than 250,000 cameras are in place throughout the United Kingdom, transmitting round-the-clock images to 100 constabularies, all of them reporting decreases in public misconduct. Polls report that the cameras are extremely popular with citizens, though British civil libertarian John Wadham and others bemoan this proliferation of snoop technology. "It could be used for any other purpose," he says. "And of course it could be abused."

The trend has been slower coming to North America, but it appears about to take off. After initial experiments garnered widespread public approval, the city of Baltimore plans to have police cameras scanning 106 downtown intersections by the end of 1996.

No one denies the obvious and dramatic short-term benefits of this early surveillance technology. But that is not the real issue. Over the long run, the sovereign folk of Baltimore and countless other communities will have to make the same choices as the inhabitants of mythical cities One and Two. *Who will ultimately control the cameras?*

Consider a few more examples:

Already, engineers can squeeze the electronics for a video pickup into a package smaller than a sugar cube. Inexpensive units half the size of a pack of cigarettes are offered for sale by the Spy Shop, a little store two blocks from the United Nations. Soon, cheap pickups will be so small that passersby won't be able to spot them.

Cameras aren't the only surveillance devices proliferating in our cities. Starting with Redwood City, California, south of San Francisco, several police departments have begun lacing neighborhoods with sound pickups that transmit directly back to headquarters. Using triangulation techniques, officials can now pinpoint bursts of gunfire and send patrol units swiftly to the scene, without having to wait for vague phone reports from neighbors. In 1995, the Defense Department awarded a US$1.7 million contract for Secures, a prototype system created by Alliant Techsystems, to test more advanced pickup networks in Washington, DC, and other cities. The department hopes to distinguish not only types of gunfire, but human voices crying for help. From there, further refinements are only logical.

Or take another piece of James Bond apparatus now available to anyone with ready cash. Today you can order from a catalog night-vision goggles that use state-of-the-art infrared optics equal to those used by the military. They cost about the same as a videocamera. Military and civilian enhanced-vision technologies now move in lockstep, as they have in the computer field for years.

What difference will this make in our lives?

It means that *darkness* no longer offers even a promise of privacy.

Nor does your garden wall. In late 1995, Admiral William A. Owens, vice chair of the Joint Chiefs of Staff, described a sensor system that he expected to be operational within about a year. It uses a pilotless drone, equipped with a TV camera and two-way video links, to provide airborne surveillance for soldiers in the field. Of course, camera drones in the $1 million range have been flying in the military for many years, allowing aerial reconnaissance without risk to human pilots. The difference this time is the new system's low cost and simplicity. Instead of requiring a crew of dozens, it is controlled by one semiskilled soldier. The price per drone will be minimal, since each unit fits in the palm of the hand. Minuscule and nearly silent, such remote-piloted vehicles, or RPVs, can flit between trees and over fences to survey the zone near a rifle platoon, seeking potential threats.

Owens expects them to be mass-produced in huge quantities, driving down unit prices.

Can civilian models be far behind? So much for the supposed privacy enjoyed by sunbathers in their own backyards.

Might we prevent this outcome by restricting such cameras to the military?

Of course not. No law will stop their proliferation. Oh, citizens will surely call for legislation. Official regulations may multiply, in response to public outrage. (Should we pass laws banning the private ownership of model airplanes?)

But no matter how many bills are passed, the arrival of such implements in our towns and cities will not be much delayed. The rich, the powerful, and figures of authority will have them, whether legally or surreptitiously. The contraptions are going to spread. And they will get smaller, faster, cheaper, and smarter with each passing year.

Moreover, surveillance cameras are the tip of the proverbial iceberg. Just another entrancing and invasive innovation of the information age. Other examples abound.

Will a paper envelope protect your correspondence, sent by old-fashioned surface mail, when new-style scanners can trace the patterns of ink inside without ever breaking the seal?

OK, let's say you correspond by email and use a computerized encryption program to ensure that your messages are read only by the intended recipient. What good will all the ciphers and codes do if some adversary can fly a gnat-sized camera into your room, station it above your desk, and watch every keystroke that you type?

The same issues arise when we contemplate the proliferation of vast databases containing information about our lives, habits, tastes, and personal histories. From the cash-register scanners in a million supermarkets, video stores, and pharmacies, there already pours a steady flow of statistical data about customers and their purchases, ready to be correlated, helping companies serve us more efficiently—or else giving them an unfair advantage, knowing vastly more about us than we do about them. Soon, computers will hold financial and educational records, legal documents, and medical analyses that parse you all the way down to your genes. Any of this might be accessed by strangers without your knowledge or even against your stated will.

As with our allegorical street lamp cameras, the choices we make regarding the future information networks—how they will be controlled and who can access the data—will affect our lives, those of our children, and their descendants.

In fact, it is already far too late to prevent the invasion of cameras and databases. The djinn cannot be crammed back into the bottle. No matter how many laws are passed, it will prove quite impossible to legislate away the new tools and techniques. They are here to stay. Light is going to shine into every aspect of our lives.

The real issue facing citizens of a new century will be how mature adults choose to live—how they might compete, cooperate, and thrive—in such a world. A transparent society.

Regarding those cameras for instance—the ones topping every lamppost in both City One and City Two—we can see that very different styles of urban life resulted from just one decision. From how people in each town answered the following questions: *Will average citizens share, along with the mighty, the right to these universal monitors? Will common folk have, and exercise, a sovereign power to watch the watchers?*

Back in City Number One, Jane and Joe Doe may walk through an average day never thinking about the microcameras overhead. They might even believe statements made by officials claiming that all the spy eyes were banished and dismantled a year or two ago. (When in fact they were only made smaller, harder to detect.) Jane and Joe stroll secure that their neighbors cannot spy on them. (Except, of course, for those casually peering down from windows on all sides—a burden people have lived with for centuries without much apparent harm.) In other words, Jane and Joe blissfully believe they have *privacy*.

The inhabitants of City Number Two know better. They realize that—out of doors at least—privacy has always been an illusion. They know that anyone in town can tune into that camera on the lamppost over there . . . and *they don't much care*. They perceive what really matters . . . that they live in a town where the police are efficient, respectful, and above all accountable. A place where homes are sacrosanct, but out on the street any citizen, from the richest to the poorest, can walk both safely and with the godlike power to zoom at will from vantage point to vantage point, viewing all the lively wonders of the vast but easily spanned village the metropolis has become—as if by some magic power it had turned into a city not of men and women but of birds.

Sometimes, citizens of City Number Two find it tempting to wax nostalgic about the old days, before there were so many cameras . . . or before TV invaded the home . . . or before the telephone and automobile. But for the most part, City Two's denizens know those times are gone, never to return. Above all, one thing makes life bearable—the surety that each person knows what is going on and has a say in what will happen next. A say equal to any billionaire or chief of police.

Of course, this little allegory—like all allegories—is a gross oversimplification. For instance, in our projected city of "open access," citizens will have 10,000 decisions to make.

Can a person order a routine search to pick another person's face out of a crowd?

Since one might conceivably use these devices to follow someone home, should convicted felons be forbidden access to the camera network? Or will that problem be solved by having the system tell you the identity of anyone who is watching you? (The mutual-transparency solution.)

When should merchants be allowed to bring these cameras indoors? True, it might hinder shoplifting, but whose business is it what aisle of the bookstore I go browsing in?

If cameras keep getting smaller and mobile (e.g., mosquito scale drones), what kind of defenses might protect us against Peeping Toms, or police spies, flying such devices through the open windows of our homes?

The list of possible quandaries goes on and on. Such an endless complexity of choices may cause some citizens of City Two to envy the simplicity of life in City One, where only big business, the State, and certain well-heeled criminals possess these powers.

That élite will, in turn, try to foster a widespread illusion among the populace that the cameras don't exist, that no one is actually watching. Some folk will prefer a fantasy of privacy over the ambiguity and arduous decisions faced by citizens of City Two.

There is nothing new in this, of course. All previous generations faced quandaries, the outcomes of which changed history. When Thomas Jefferson prescribed a revolution every few decades, he spoke not only politically but about the constant need to remain *flexible*, ready to adapt to changing circumstances—to innovate at need, while at the same time staying true to those values we hold unchanging and precious.

Our civilization is already a noisy one for precisely that reason—because we have chosen freedom and mass sovereignty, which means that the citizenry itself must constantly argue out all the details, instead of leaving them to some committee of sages.

What differs today is not only the pace of events, but also our toolkit for facing the future.

Above all, what marks our civilization as different has been its knack for applying one extremely hard-won lesson from the past:

In all of history, there has been only one cure for error discovered, one partial antidote against making grand, foolish mistakes. One remedy against self-deception.

That antidote is criticism.

Alas, criticism has always been what human beings—especially leaders—hate most to hear.

I call this contradiction the "Paradox of the Peacock." Its effects have been profound and tragic for centuries. Accounts from the past are filled with woeful events in which societies and peoples suffered largely because openness and free speech were suppressed, leaving the powerful at liberty to make devastating blunders without comment or dissent from below.

If Western Civilization has one new trick in its repertoire, a technique more responsible than any other for its success, that trick is *accountability*. Especially the knack—which no other culture ever mastered—of making accountability apply to the mighty. True, we still don't manage it perfectly. Gaffes, bungles, and inanities still get covered up.

And yet, one can look at any newspaper or television and see an eager press corps at work, supplemented by hordes of righteously indignant individuals (and their lawyers), all baying for waste or corruption to be exposed, secrets to be unveiled, and nefarious schemes to be nipped in the bud. *Disclosure* is a watchword of the age, and politicians grudgingly have responded by passing the Freedom of Information Act, a truth-in-lending law, open-meeting rules, then codes to enforce candor in housing, in dietary content of foodstuffs, in the expense accounts of lobbyists, and so on.

This morality pervades our popular culture, in which nearly every modern film or novel seems to preach the same message—suspicion of authority.

Nor is this phenomenon new to our generation. Schoolbooks teach that freedom is guarded by constitutional "checks and balances."

But those same provisions were copied, early in the 19th century, by nearly every new nation of Latin America, and *not one* of them remained consistently free. In North America, constitutional balances worked only because they were supplemented by a powerful mythic tradition, expounded in story, song—and now every Hollywood film: that any undue accumulation of power should be looked on with concern.

Above all, we are encouraged to distrust government.

In *The Open Society and Its Enemies*, philosopher Karl Popper pointed out the importance of this mythology during the dark days before and after the Second World War. Only by insisting on accountability can we constantly remind our public servants that they are servants. It is also how we maintain some confidence that merchants aren't cheating us, or that factories aren't poisoning the water. As inefficient and irascibly noisy as it seems at times, this habit of questioning authority ensures freedom far better than any of the older social systems that were based on reverence or trust.

And yet, another paradox rears up every time one interest group tries to hold another accountable in today's society:

Whenever a conflict appears between privacy and accountability, people demand the former for themselves and the latter for everybody else.

This rule seems to hold in almost every realm of modern life, from the NIMBY (not in my backyard) syndrome to demands that criminal records of sex offenders be made public, and in the battles over things like credit reporting and Caller ID. The penchant is especially profound in recent debates over how to organize new institutions of the information age—from the Internet to new cable and broadcast media.

Above all, floods of books, articles, and public pronouncements have appeared, proclaiming dire threats to our precious right of *privacy*.

In just the last year or so, there have erupted widespread calls to "empower" citizens and corporations with tools of encryption—the creation of ciphers and secret codes—so that the once open corridors of the Internet, and even our telephone lines, may soon fill with a blinding fog of static and concealed messages, of habitual masks and routine anonymity.

Some of society's best and brightest minds have taken recently to extolling a coming "golden age of privacy," when no one need fear snooping by the big, bad government anymore.

It is a risky thing to stand against such a near-universal outpouring of moral umbrage. John Perry Barlow, Mike Godwin, John Gilmore, and other members of the Electronic Frontier Foundation have been especially indignant, demanding that citizens be armed with unlimited power to conceal their words, actions, and identities. If not, claim the paladins of privacy, freedom itself will surely be forfeit.

In opposing this modern mania for personal secrecy, let me first emphasize that I happen to *like* privacy. Moreover, as a novelist and public figure, I need it, probably as much or more than the next guy. All my instincts run toward reticence, to protecting my family from invasions of our private space. Going back to the earlier example, I would find it hard to get used to living in *either* of the cities described in those early paragraphs.

I don't care to be peered at by hovering cameras.

But a few voices out there—Stewart Brand, Nick Arnett, and Bruce Sterling, for instance—have begun pointing out the obvious: that those cameras on every street corner are coming, as surely as the new millennium. Nothing will stop them.

Oh, we can try. We might agitate, demonstrate, legislate. But in rushing to pass so-called privacy laws, we will not succeed in preventing hidden eyes from peering into our lives. The devices will get tinier, more mobile, and more clever. In software form, they will cruise the data highways. The rich, the powerful, police agencies, and a technologically skilled élite will always be able to find out whatever they want to know about you and me.

In the end, as author Robert Heinlein prophesied years ago, the chief effect that "privacy" laws have is to "make the bugs smaller."

And, I might add, to prevent you and me from learning anything about the rich and powerful.

Given a choice between privacy and accountability, I must sadly conclude that there is no choice at all.

Privacy is a highly desirable *product* of liberty. If we remain free and sovereign, then we'll have a little privacy—in our bedrooms and sanctuaries. As citizens, we'll be able to demand some.

But *accountability* is no side benefit. It is the one fundamental ingredient on which liberty thrives. Without the accountability that derives from openness—enforceable upon even the mightiest individuals and institutions—freedom must surely die.

As this was true in the past, so it will be a thousandfold in the information age to come, when cameras and databases will sprout like crocuses—or weeds—whether we like it or not.

One of the basic decisions we all face in times ahead will be this:

Can we stand living our lives exposed to scrutiny . . . our secrets laid out in the open . . . if in return we get flashlights of our own, that we can shine on the arrogant and strong?

Or is privacy's illusion so precious that it is worth any price, including surrendering our own right to pierce the schemes of the powerful?

There are no easy answers, but asking questions can be a good first step.

***David Brin** is a scientist, technology speaker, and writer. His 15 novels, including *New York Times* best-sellers, have been translated into more than 20 languages. This article was later expanded into his nonfiction book—*The Transparent Society: Will Technology Make Us Choose Between Freedom and Privacy?*—which has won the Freedom of Speech Award of the American Library Association. http://www.davidbrin.com/

Brinn, David. "The Transparent Society," *Wired*, December 1996.

Used by permission.

Privacy vs. Security: Are You Prepared for the Thorny Issues Surrounding Student Surveillance?

by David Rapp*

A lot of school administrators are looking into installing security cameras in their districts. They want to keep their students safe. They want to keep tabs on people entering and leaving their schools. They want to cut down on vandalism and theft, and they want to do it now.

What's the urgency? Look at these numbers: During the 2005–06 school year, according to the most recent statistics available from the U.S. Department of Education, 86 percent of public schools nationwide reported that one or more serious violent incidents, thefts, or other crimes had occurred at their school, for a total of roughly 2.2 million crimes. That works out to about one crime reported for every 20 students. And that doesn't include vandalism and graffiti: Nearly 100,000 incidents of vandalism are reported in the United States public school system every year.

Cameras are expensive, with some high-end systems costing $500,000 or more, plus annual maintenance fees. But some

Rapp, David. "Privacy vs. Security: Are You Prepared for the Thorny Issues Surrounding Student Surveillance?" Scholastic.com, *Administr@tor Magazine*, 2009. http://www.scholastic.com/browse/article.jsp?id=3751958.

Used by permission.

administrators seem to think that installing security cameras will solve their problems. Even administrators in low-crime districts want the cameras, if only to deter potential crime. Anecdotally, cameras appear to be effective at detecting and deterring crime, though hard numbers are difficult to come by.

Installing cameras, however, can be controversial. There have been protests and legal action surrounding camera installation at schools nationwide, and there are a number of issues to consider before signing off on surveillance. What problems are you trying to solve with cameras? If you do install cameras, what kind of atmosphere will it create at your school? Most importantly, what do parents and students think?

When word got out that administrators at the Seaholm and Groves high schools in Oakland County, Michigan, were considering installing security cameras, it led students to organize the group Students Against Security Cameras (SASC). Its members have attended school board meetings to protest the plan, which they feel would be an unnecessary expense and would promote an atmosphere of distrust in the schools. SASC students even have a Facebook page spelling out their concerns, with more than 850 members so far. At press time, the school board had yet to make a decision about security cameras.

Terry Piper, the principal at Seaholm High School in Birmingham, Michigan, feels the time is right for security cameras at his school. After all, dozens of schools in their county have already done it, and with some success. "There are 30 high schools in Oakland County, and every single one of them has security cameras except Seaholm and Groves," Piper says. "They've seen thefts go down. They've been able to solve instances of vandalism on occasion, and there have been student altercations where they've been helpful. They also serve as a deterrent, so you never know how many things might have happened if you hadn't had them."

Some of the student group's arguments, Piper maintains, rest on incorrect assumptions—for example, that the cameras will be prohibitively expensive. "We haven't taken any bids yet," he says. "They don't know much about school funding, so they don't know that it's not going to take away from instructional programs. There's a separate budget for that kind of capital outlay."

Piper is convinced that security cameras are a valuable tool for combatting petty theft. Many such thefts take place in locker rooms; though cameras are barred from locker rooms and bathrooms, Piper plans to install cameras outside Seaholm's locker rooms, as well as in the main hallway, and outside at the main entrance. The question is: How do you determine whom you're going to question if you've got video of 50 kids walking out of a locker room following a theft? Do you interview them all?

Shelli Weisberg, the legislative director at the American Civil Liberties Union of Michigan, asked a Michigan principal that same question, and she found that it all boiled down to profiling. "He actually said, 'We know who the bad kids are,'" she says. This made her wonder: Well, then, why do you need the camera?

Weisberg, with the Michigan ACLU, has worked with students across the state to fight security cameras in schools, and she doubts the necessity of cameras in many schools. She points out that many of the schools that install the cameras tend to be in well-to-do districts, with some of the lowest crime rates. Ann Arbor Pioneer High School, which plans to install 53 cameras on its campus, is a prime example. "Ann Arbor does not have a high crime rate," Weisberg says. "They're a very affluent district, so there's a lot of eyes in the hall. [Administrators] did say, anecdotally, that they thought [cameras] made people feel safer. But students said it made them feel like they were being watched."

So the ACLU assisted the students in their fight, and provided them with academic studies in the US and UK that argued that surveillance cameras had little effect on crime. (You can read about these studies at the ACLU site.) "The students did a good job of using the research we gave them to develop their arguments—a lot of Big Brother–type arguments, asserting their due-process rights as students—because they are in schools to learn how to be adults," Weisberg says.

The students' "Big Brother" fears may not be completely off the mark. At a high school in Novi, Michigan, for example, administrators don't only monitor the cameras themselves—they also allow police access to the footage. And public schools in Demarest, New Jersey, have gone a step further: In 2007, they began allowing police to monitor live feeds from school security cameras. "It concerns me that schools would, without thinking about due process, simply turn over access to the police," Weisberg says. "I think it's a matter of schools looking very myopically at how they think their students are safe, and not really thinking about the consequences of it."

The danger, she says, is that with cameras recording every student infraction, more and more activities in schools will become criminalized. A scuffle between two kids in a hallway, which once would have been solved with detention or suspension, could now been seen as criminal activity—especially if the police are involved. "Kids are not only getting kicked out of school, but also sent to the police," Weisberg says. "There's this tendency, with all of this stuff on tape, to send more kids to jail."

Schools need to have a compelling reason for the cameras before installing them, Weisberg says, or they may be abused. "I think schools are worried—they have to keep their student body safe, and they have to keep parents assured that their children are safe," she says. "The general public seems to think that a camera means safety. It does bring in a slippery slope, because there is going to be a tendency to use the camera tapes to look at every little thing."

Seaholm's Piper points out that there have been cameras in his schools' parking lots for a decade, without protest or problems. "I've asked students, 'Do you know of anybody whose rights or privacy has been violated by those cameras watching you come in and out of the building?'" he says. "They said no. I said, 'So what makes you think that having cameras inside the doorways, when we already have them outside the doorways, is going to make us change the way we do business?' Their arguments were more emotional than logical."

Weisberg grants that security cameras can be useful tools, if used sensibly. "I think the ACLU and the students agree that there may be room at schools to have cameras at entrance doors," she says. "I think everyone's concerned about who has access to schools, especially elementary schools. But it's worth thinking about what you're trying to achieve."

When administrators consider installing security cameras, it's crucial to involve parents and students in the process.

Administrators who don't involve them can create huge problems for themselves down the road. A few examples:

During a 2003 girls' basketball game at Livingston Middle School in Overton County, Tennessee, visiting team members noticed a security camera in the girls' locker room. It turned out the camera had recorded images of the team members in their undergarments when they changed their clothes. Several other students had been similarly videotaped over the previous months. The scandal led to Brannum v. Overton County School Board, a lawsuit on behalf of 24 students. In a key legal decision last year, the U.S. Sixth Circuit Court of Appeals ruled that a school may not install security cameras inside locker rooms, where students have an expectation of privacy.

In late 2007, student newspaper reporters uncovered the fact that the principal at Newton South High School in Newton Centre, Massachusetts, had installed five security cameras outside a locker room without informing faculty, the school committee, or the rest of the community. It caused an uproar among committee members, teachers, students, and parents—a situation that any administrator would rather avoid.

Kenneth Trump, the president of National School Safety and Security Services, a Cleveland, Ohio–based consulting firm, stresses the need for open communication. "There has to be an education process by the administration, to explain the purpose of the technology to parents and students and staff, and how it fits into the overall school-safety program," he says. "The communication piece is one that can easily turn around and bite school administrators, if they haven't done a good job at informing people on the front end."

Trump tells administrators that an effective safety program is less about technology than it is about people. "Technology is an extra tool, and technology is only as good as the human element behind it," he says. "The first and best line of defense is always a well-trained, highly alert staff and student body who will recognize strangers on campus, or report rumors, or report a student having a weapon on campus, and so on." If you don't have the school community in your corner as part of a comprehensive safety and security policy, then even the most sophisticated security camera system won't be effective.

Administrators also need to address the idea that security cameras bring up a lot of hot-button emotional issues, such as child safety and privacy. "You tend to find people are on one extreme or the other on this issue," says Trump. "Either they're totally anti-equipment, or they believe totally that equipment is the solution and cure-all for everything. Neither is necessarily the right position."

In any case, parents should be kept well informed about every step of the process. In Trump's experience, he says, "a majority of parents tend to support it, and like the presence of those cameras, because it provides a clear indicator that there's some additional measures to protect their children."

Michigan ACLU's Weisberg agrees that parents tend to go along with a decision to install cameras, but she isn't sure that's a good thing. "You know, most people trust their schools, and they trust that they're doing the right things by their students—so there's great leeway given to an administrator's request," she says. "Parents don't like to fight that. So I'm particularly proud of the students who take on that fight—and, hopefully, it helps enlighten the school boards and administrators in terms of what they're doing and what they're spending their money on."

As you weigh whether to install security cameras, it pays to listen to students, parents, and faculty. If you engage people one-on-one and address their concerns about safety and privacy, you may be able to make everyone in the community a part of your security plan. You may find that you only need a few cameras—or none at all. In the end, it's all about keeping students safe. And that's something everyone can agree on.

A Question of Trust

Ronald D. Stephens is the executive director of the National School Safety Center, an independent nonprofit that focuses on school crime prevention and safe-school planning. As a former teacher and assistant superintendent, he shared his views on security cameras with Scholastic Administrator.

First and foremost, schools have to ask hard questions about what kind of climate they want to create, Stephens says. "When they put a four-way camera in the intersection I go through on my way to work every day, I wasn't pleased about that. It tends to say, 'Hey, we don't trust you.'" Many students, he adds, feel the same way about cameras in schools. "How do we create a climate that's conducive to education without making the place look like a juvenile detention facility?" Stephens says it has to be a decision that is well thought through and that involves students, parents, and the community.

Stephens also cautions against seeing cameras as a quick fix. Cameras don't stop all crimes, he warns, and he uses the example of Red Lake, Minnesota, where a 16-year-old high school student shot and killed five students, a teacher, and an unarmed security guard in 2005. "They had camera surveillance, they had a safe-school plan, they had metal [detectors]," he says. "They had two security officers at the front door. But the student still came in, overpowered them, and still committed those heinous acts." But he understands why cameras are so appealing, especially when high-profile school violence hits the news. "People want to do something after a crisis, and sometimes they pick the thing that is tangible, visible and easy to measure."

Cameras work best, notes Stephens, when they are deployed to take on a specific, here-and-now problem. "I was working with a school district in a midwestern state," he says. "These kids would come up to the school's double-entry doors with their Jeeps, run a chain through the door handles, hook it up to the back bumper, and pull the doors off. We told the district, 'Put in a surveillance camera. Do it until you find your culprit, and then you can pull it out.' What they found was that when they put the surveillance cameras in, vandalism at the school went down by 95 percent."

Students do not shed their rights at the schoolhouse doors, Stephens warns. "If the school does something that does not use common sense or good judgment, they will ultimately have to answer for that in the courts," he says. "Let's be thoughtful about what we do and how we do it."

*David Rapp is a contributing editor to Scholastic Administr@tor.

Surveillance Society: New High-Tech Cameras Are Watching You

In the era of computer-controlled surveillance, your every move could be captured by cameras, whether you're shopping in the grocery store or driving on the freeway. Proponents say it will keep us safe, but at what cost?

by James Vlahos*

The ferry arrived, the gangway went down and 7-year-old Emma Powell rushed toward the Statue of Liberty. She climbed onto the grass around the star-shaped foundation. She put on a green foam crown with seven protruding rays. Turning so that her body was oriented just like Lady Liberty's, Emma extended her right arm skyward with an imaginary torch. I snapped a picture. Then I took my niece's hand, and we went off to buy some pretzels.

Other people were taking pictures, too, and not just the other tourists—Liberty Island, name notwithstanding, is one of the most heavily surveilled places in America. Dozens of cameras record hundreds of hours of video daily, a volume that strains the monitoring capability of guards. The National Park Service has enlisted extra help, and as Emma and I strolled around, we weren't just being watched by people. We were being watched by machines.

Liberty Island's video cameras all feed into a computer system. The park doesn't disclose details, but fully equipped, the system is capable of running software that analyzes the imagery and automatically alerts human overseers to any suspicious events. The software can spot when somebody abandons a bag or backpack. It has the ability to discern between ferryboats, which are allowed to approach the island, and private vessels, which are not. And it can count bodies, detecting if somebody is trying to stay on the island after closing, or assessing when people are grouped too tightly together, which might indicate a fight or gang activity. "A camera with artificial intelligence can be there 24/7, doesn't need a bathroom break, doesn't need a lunch break and doesn't go on vacation," says Ian Ehrenberg, former vice president of Nice Systems, the program's developer.

Most Americans would probably welcome such technology at what clearly is a marquee terrorist target. An ABC News/ *Washington Post* poll in July 2007 found that 71 percent of Americans favor increased video surveillance. What people may not realize, however, is that advanced monitoring systems such as the one at the Statue of Liberty are proliferating around the country. High-profile national security efforts make the news—wiretapping phone conversations, Internet monitoring—but state-of-the-art surveillance is increasingly being used in more every-day settings. By local police and businesses. In banks, schools and stores. There are an estimated 30 million surveillance cameras now deployed in the United States shooting 4 billion hours of footage a week. Americans are being watched, all of us, almost everywhere.

We have arrived at a unique moment in the history of surveillance. The price of both megapixels and gigabytes has plummeted, making it possible to collect a previously unimaginable quantity and quality of data. Advances in processing power and software, meanwhile, are beginning to allow computers to surmount the greatest limitation of traditional surveillance—the ability of eyeballs to effectively observe the activity on dozens of video screens simultaneously. Computers can't do all the work by themselves, but they can expand the capabilities of humans exponentially.

Security expert Bruce Schneier says that it is naive to think that we can stop these technological advances, especially as they become more affordable and are hard-wired into everyday businesses. (I know of a local pizzeria that warns customers with a posted sign: "Stop stealing the spice shakers! We know who you are, we have 24-hour surveillance!") But it is also reckless to let the advances proceed without a discussion of safeguards against privacy abuses. "Society is fundamentally changing and we aren't having a conversation about it," Schneier says. "We are entering the era of wholesale surveillance."

Earlier this year, on a hot summer afternoon, I left my Brooklyn apartment to do some shoplifting.

I cruised the aisles of the neighborhood grocery store, a Pathmark, tossing items into my cart like a normal shopper would—Frosted Mini-Wheats, Pledge Wipes, a bag of carrots. Then I put them on the belt at checkout. My secret was on the lower level of the cart: a 12-pack of beer, concealed and undetectable. Or so I thought. Midway through checkout the cashier addressed me, no malice in her voice, but no doubt either. "Do you want to ring up that beer?"

My heist had been condoned by Pedro Ramos, Pathmark's vice president of loss prevention, though he didn't know precisely when or where I was going to attempt it. The beer was identified by an object-recognition scanner at ankle level—a LaneHawk, manufactured by Evolution Robotics—which prompted the cashier's question. Overhead, a camera recorded the incident and an alert was triggered in Ramos's office miles away on Staten Island. He immediately pulled up digital video and later relayed what he saw. "You concealed a 12-pack of Coronas on the bottom of the cart by strategically placing newspaper circulars so as to obstruct the view of the cashier."

Busted.

Pathmark uses StoreVision, a powerful video analytic and data-mining system. There are as many as 120 cameras in some stores, and employees with high-level security clearances can log on via the Web and see what any one of them is recording in real time. An executive on vacation in Brussels could spy on the frozen-food aisle in Brooklyn.

In 2006 theft and fraud cost American stores $41.6 billion, an all-time high. Employee theft accounted for nearly half of the total (shoplifting was only a third), so much of the surveillance aims to catch in-house crooks. If the cashier had given me the beer for free—employees often work with an outside accomplice—the system would know by automatically comparing what the video recorded with what the register logged. The technologies employed by Pathmark don't stop crime but they make a dent; weekly losses are reduced by an average of 15 percent.

Pathmark archives every transaction of every customer, and the grocery chain is hardly alone. Amazon knows what you read; Netflix, your taste in movies. Search engines such as Google and Yahoo retain your queries for months, and can identify searches by IP address—sometimes by individual computer. Many corporations log your every transaction with a stated goal of reducing fraud and improving marketing efforts. Until fairly recently it was impractical to retain all this data. But now the low cost of digital storage—you can get a terabyte hard drive for less than $350—makes nearly limitless archiving possible.

So what's the problem? "The concern is that information collected for one purpose is used for something entirely different down the road," says Ari Schwartz, deputy director of the Center for Democracy and Technology, a Washington, D.C., think tank.

This may sound like a privacy wonk's paranoia. But examples abound. Take E-ZPass. Drivers signed up for the system to speed up toll collection. But 11 states now supply E-ZPass records—when and where a toll was paid, and by whom—in response to court orders in criminal cases. Seven of those states provide information in civil cases such as divorce, proving, for instance, that a husband who claimed he was at a meeting in Pennsylvania was actually heading to his lover's house in New Jersey. (New York divorce lawyer Jacalyn Barnett has called E-ZPass the "easy way to show you took the offramp to adultery.")

On a case-by-case basis, the collection of surveillance footage and customer data is usually justifiable and benign. But the totality of information being amassed combined with the relatively fluid flow of that data can be troubling. Corporations often share what they know about customers with government agencies and vice versa. AT&T, for example, is being sued by the Electronic Frontier Foundation, a San Francisco-based civil liberties group, for allowing the National Security Agency almost unlimited access to monitor customers' e-mails, phone calls and Internet browsing activity.

"We are heading toward a total surveillance society in which your every move, your every transaction, is duly registered and recorded by some computer," says Jay Stanley, a privacy expert with the American Civil Liberties Union.

In the late 18th century, English philosopher Jeremy Bentham dreamed up a new type of prison: the panopticon. It would be built so that guards could see all of the prisoners at all times without their knowing they were being watched, creating "the sentiment of an invisible omniscience," Bentham wrote. America is starting to resemble a giant panopticon, according to surveillance critics like Bob Barr, a former Republican congressman from Georgia. "Were Bentham alive today, he probably would be the most sought-after consultant on the planet," he recently wrote in a Washington Times op-ed.

One of the most popular new technologies in law enforcement is the license-plate reader, or LPR. The leading manufacturer is Remington-Elsag, based in Madison, N.C. Its Mobile Plate Hunter 900 consists of cameras mounted on the outside of a squad car and connected to a computer database in the vehicle. The plate hunter employs optical-character-recognition technology originally developed for high-speed mail sorting. LPRs automate the process of "running a plate" to check if a vehicle is stolen or if the driver has any outstanding warrants. The sensors work whether the police car is parked or doing 75 mph. An officer working the old-fashioned way might check a couple dozen plates a shift. The LPR can check 10,000.

New York's Long Beach Police Department is one of more than 200 agencies around the country that use LPRs, and I rode in a squad car with Sgt. Bill Dodge to see the technology at work. A computer screen mounted in front of the glovebox flashed black-and-white images of every photographed plate; low alarms, like the sounds of your character dying in an '80s video game, droned for the problem cars. Over the course of a couple of hours we didn't net any car thieves or kidnappers, but Dodge's LPR identified dozens of cars with suspended or revoked registrations. He said that the system doesn't violate anyone's privacy—"there's no magic technology that lets it see inside a garage"—and praised its fairness. "It doesn't matter if you're black, white, old, young, a man or a woman, the system cannot discriminate. It looks at everyone and everything."

In July, New York City officials unveiled the Lower Manhattan Security Initiative, modeled after London's "Ring of Steel," which will include license-plate readers, automated roadblocks and 3000 new surveillance cameras—adding to the 250 already in place. Chicago, meanwhile, which has 560 anti-crime cameras deployed on city streets, revealed plans in September to add a sophisticated IBM video analytic system that would automatically detect abandoned bags, suspicious behaviors (such as a vehicle repeatedly circling the Sears Tower) and vehicles sought by the police. Expanded surveillance is perhaps to be expected for these high-profile cities, but they're hardly alone. Richmond, Calif.; Spokane, Wash.; and Greenville, N.C., are among the cities that have recently announced plans to add electronic spying eyes. According to iSuppli, a market research firm, the global surveillance-camera business is expected to grow from $4.9 billion in 2006 to $9 billion in 2011.

The ability of cameras to deter criminals is unproven, but their value in helping to solve crimes is not. Recall how videos led to several arrests in the July 7, 2005, London subway bombings. The problem with surveillance video is that there's simply too much of it. "It's impossible for mere mortals with eyeballs and brains to process all the information we're gathering," says

Stephen Russell, the chief executive of 3VR, a company that makes video analytic software.

An investigator looking for a particular piece of video is like a researcher working in a library with a jumbled card catalog—or in books with no tables of contents. The solution of 3VR and other similar companies is software that automatically analyzes and tags video contents, from the colors and locations of cars to the characteristics of individual faces that pass before the lens. The goal is to allow rapid digital search; instead of functioning like a shoddy library, 3VR hopes to be "the Google of surveillance video," Russell says. "It took 1000 [British agents] six weeks to review all the video after July 7. Had 3VRs been in place, it might have taken a dozen or so agents a weekend," he claims.

I recently spent a night at Chicago's Talbott Hotel, a luxurious small retreat where the staff addresses you by name and you have to clear a dozen pillows from the cushy king-size bed before lying down. The Talbott is surveilled by 70 cameras, which cover every public area of the hotel and feed into a 3VR system.

Troy Strand, general manager of the hotel, showed me a computer screen divided into 16 panes with different camera views. He looked up my check-in time and seconds later retrieved video of my arrival the previous day. There I was, towing my carry-on toward room 1504.

Strand found a few other shots showing me, then instructed the software to begin facial analysis. The system assessed the balance of light and dark areas of skin tone and hair and gauged the distance between my eyes, nose and mouth. Strand instructed the system to search for all recorded videos showing my face, and the computer retrieved several dozen faces, none of which was mine. There was a woman and a black man. But Strand went through a few pages of results, and I started to show up. When he clicked on any image, an associated video of me played—crossing the lobby to go to breakfast, chatting with the front-desk clerk.

So-called "facial profiling" has been surveillance's next big thing for nearly a decade, and it is only now showing tentative signs of feasibility. It's easy to see why people are seduced by the promise of this technology. Twelve bank companies employ 3VR systems at numerous locations, which build a facial template for every single person that enters any branch. If somebody cashes a check that is later determined to be stolen, the person's face can be flagged in the system, and the next time the con artist comes in, the system is supposed to alert the tellers.

For Strand, the security system's fancier features are just a bonus. The cameras are in plain sight, so he believes that would-be criminals and misbehaving employees are deterred. "You can't have security people on every floor monitoring every angle of the building," he says.

There's a man in Salt Lake City who knows what I did last summer. Specifically, he knows what I did on Aug. 24, 2007. He knows that I checked my EarthLink e-mail at 1:25 pm, and then blew a half an hour on ESPN's Web site. He also knows that my wife, Anne, wanted new shoes, from Hush Puppies or DSW, and that she synced her electronic planner—"she has quite a busy schedule," the man noted—and downloaded some podcasts. We both printed out passes for free weeklong trials at 24 Hour Fitness, but instead of working out, apparently spent the evening watching a pay-per-view movie. It was *Bridge to Terabithia* or *Zodiac*, he thinks.

The man's name is Joe Wilkinson, and he works for Raytheon Oakley Systems. The company specializes in "insider risk management," which means dealing with the problem of employees who, whether through innocent accident or nefarious plot, do things they really shouldn't be doing at work. Oakley's software, developed for the U.S. government and now used by ten Fortune 100 companies, monitors computer use remotely and invisibly. Wilkinson had agreed to run a surveillance trial with me as the subject, and after accessing my computer via the Web, he installed an "agent" that regularly reported my activities back to him.

The modern desktop machine is a multimedia distraction monster: friend, lover, shopping mall, stereo, television, movie theater and adult video store are mere mouse clicks away. Raytheon Oakley's software caught me wasting valuable work time checking personal e-mails and reading digital camera reviews online. Companies are also concerned about hostile work environments caused by employees openly surfing porn in the office—consequently, my 10:14 am visit to a risqué site was duly noted. Employees also leak trade secrets. (Consider the case of DuPont chemist Gary Min, who, after accepting a job with a competitor in 2005, raided DuPont's electronic library for $400 million worth of technical documents. He was caught by the FBI last year.) If I had downloaded any large engineering drawings onto a removable hard drive, Oakley's software would have alerted Wilkinson. And employees bad-mouth the boss. I wrote an e-mail to Anne that mentioned my editor at Popular Mechanics, Glenn Derene. Wilkinson rigged the software to flag anything with Derene's name, and alarm bells rang. Sorry, Glenn.

Surveillance of this sort is common. A 2005 survey by the American Management Association and the ePolicy Institute found that 36 percent of companies monitor workers on a keystroke-by-keystroke basis; 55 percent review e-mail messages, and 76 percent monitor Web sites visited. "Total Behavioral Visibility" is Raytheon Oakley's motto. The vice president of marketing, Tom Bennett, knows that some people fear workplace monitoring. But the technology has many positive aspects. "We are not Big Brother," he insists.

Employees are sometimes lazy or dishonest, but often they're simply careless. A parent who has to leave the office at midday to care for a sick child might copy sensitive company information onto a USB drive so that he can work at home. An account manager might carelessly send customer credit card numbers over an unsecured wireless network where they can be stolen. Bennett says that his company's software helps companies understand and improve how workers use their computers. The Oakley monitoring application works like a TiVo, allowing an instant video replay: where you pointed the mouse, when you clicked, what you wrote. This can catch the guilty but also exonerate the innocent, because the replay puts your actions in context.

The debate over surveillance pits the tangible benefits of saving lives and dollars against the abstract ones of preserving privacy and freedom. To many people, the promise of increased security is worth the exchange. History shows that new technologies, once developed, are seldom abandoned, and the computer vision systems being adopted today are transforming America from a society that spies upon a small number of suspicious individuals to one that monitors everybody. The question arises: Do people exercise their perfectly legal freedoms as freely when they know they're being watched? As the ACLU's Stanley argues, "You need space in your life to live beyond the gaze of society."

Surveillance has become pervasive. It is also more enduring. As companies develop powerful archiving and search tools, your life will be accessible for years to come in rich multimedia records. The information about you may be collected for reasonable purposes—but as its life span increases, so too does the chance that it may fall into unscrupulous hands.

Several months after I stayed at the Talbott Hotel, Derene, my editor, called Troy Strand to ask if he still had the security camera images of me at the hotel. He did. My niece Emma's Statue of Liberty shots are probably stored on a computer, as are the records of all my Pathmark purchases. Ramos could query my shopping trip of, say, Jan. 13, 2005, and replay video keyed precisely to any part of the register tape—from the fifth item scanned, pork chops, to the tenth, broccoli. That's innocuous and even humorous on the surface, but the more I thought about the store's power, the more it disturbed me.

"I would never do that," Ramos assured me. "But I could."

***James Vlahos** is a science, technology, and travel writer. He was a founding editor of *National Geographic Adventure* and is a regular contributor to the *New York Times Magazine, National Geographic Traveler, Popular Mechanics*, and *Scientific American*.

Vlahos, James. "Surveillance Society: New High Tech Cameras Are Watching You," *Popular Mechanics*, October 1, 2009. http://www.popularmechanics.com/technology/military/4236865.

Used by permission.

Cameras

Cameras are an important tool for crime prevention, criminal investigation, and monitoring interactions between law enforcement and the public. Participants in the PERF summit discussed their experiences with fixed surveillance cameras, in-car cameras, and officer body cameras.

by Police Executive Research Forum*

Fixed Surveillance Cameras

Jonathan Lewin, Managing Deputy Director
Chicago Police Department Office of Emergency Management and Communications·

CHICAGO'S 15,000 INTEGRATED CAMERAS HAVE CONTRIBUTED TO THOUSANDS OF ARRESTS

Our current camera program was introduced in June 2003. It's called POD, which stands for Police Observation Device, and is funded in a variety of ways, including through city funds, narcotics seizure funds, DOJ grants, state education funds, Housing Authority money, corporate funding, and funding by individual aldermen in the city. Every one of the 50 aldermen has access to "Neighborhood Menu" money that they can use, and, if they so choose, a portion of those funds can be used to buy cameras.

Camera locations are determined by a number of factors, including calls for service, public violence incidents, and community input. We developed an index score system which allows anyone to plug in any address in the city and instantly receive a crime index score based on crimes, calls for service, and arrests.

BANDWIDTH CONCERNS MUST BE A PRIORITY

We've gone through several different generations of cameras. As is the case with all technology, through the years they've become smaller and cheaper. Today, about 90 percent of them are wireless. Due to bandwidth limitations, we can currently only deliver about four simultaneous video streams to each district. We need to increase that bandwidth, and we're hoping that the D Block will be a way for us to do that. We now have so much content we want to disseminate to all our districts that it completely saturates our network and we can only deliver a few video streams at a time.

Our newest-generation camera, called an L-POD, is smaller, cheaper, lighter, and more versatile than previous models. All the components are built in, including an encoder and wireless radio.

Through an integration platform, we have connected close to 15,000 cameras. At our airports, the Department of Aviation has close to 3,000 cameras set up. Officers in our 80 public high schools can view video feeds from cameras set up inside and around the schools. City colleges, the Chicago Housing Authority, the Transit Authority, the private sector, and the Police Department all have cameras that feed into our integrated camera system.

We also have mobile video resources through several helicopters and other vehicles that can send video back to us. Video can be viewed at any of our 25 police districts, the Crime

Prevention and Information Center, and the Office of Emergency Management.

All our police officers receive First and Fourth Amendment training before they're allowed to access the system in any way, and all usage is supervised. All camera and operator actions are logged and can be tracked later.

The technology itself wasn't the biggest challenge in implementing this camera system. It was the intergovernmental agreements and memoranda of understanding that took us the longest to establish, especially with the schools, which have stricter privacy guidelines. We can't have surveillance in schools unless there's some kind of emergency event. Working out the details of that took months to hammer out.

Officers can conduct missions, which are proactive uses of cameras based on reasonable suspicion that crimes are likely to occur in a certain area. Officers track all missions they conduct. In 2009, we did over 18,000 of them, which led to over 4,000 arrests in which officers told us our cameras played a role in the arrests.

We don't currently have any automated facial recognition associated with this program. We're looking to incorporate an analytical system. We probably won't try to use facial recognition, but we would like to include analysis of patterns of behavior, objects left behind, and put license plate readers into the system. At any given time, we may have only 10 people actually watching the 15,000 cameras, so we need analytics that can alert those people to check the feed from certain cameras.

When we try to remove a camera from an area, there's an immediate outcry from the community. Our initial idea was to leave the cameras in place for 90 days at high-crime locations and then move them, but due to community objections we can't remove cameras now.

Minneapolis Assistant Chief Janeé Harteau:

CAMERAS AND SHOTSPOTTER HELPED US MAKE AN ARREST IN A HOMICIDE CASE

We now have a total of about 180 cameras. They have been extremely successful, and lately we have been working to expand our camera use and are testing another 34 around the university campus.

As we began installing cameras downtown, we found that we needed a way to communicate with the private security officers, who generally outnumber the police by about 13 to 1. We introduced the Radio Link system, which gives private security guards the ability to have direct communication with police by sharing a radio channel on their hand-held radios.

We've also started to place mobile cameras in other high-crime areas in the city and are incorporating our video system with other tools, such as Shot Spotter. For example, last September we had a homicide in the middle of a street. Shot Spotter immediately activated the camera, which captured a photo of a vehicle leaving the scene. We weren't able to capture the license plate number, but the vehicle had a silver stripe which was unique to the car, so it didn't take much time for officers to find a car matching that description. With that evidence we were able to make an arrest and get a conviction for the murder.

Initially cameras were monitored solely at the precincts, but they're now monitored centrally as well at our Strategic Information Center. In addition we are tied into the Department of

Transportation camera system, and we'd like to get access into other cameras, such as private businesses in downtown and outer areas to make it a regional system.

We now have the ability to send real-time information to officers while en route to a call or once they are on scene. If a shooting incident occurs, we don't want to just respond to the crime, we also want to prevent the next one. To do this we have to be able to get information to our officers about the shooting, the suspects who are involved, their hangouts, their associates, the vehicles they drive, and potential next victims.

We've been very successful with cameras, but the public assumes that these cameras are all being monitored 24 hours a day, 7 days a week, and that's not the reality. With predictive analytics, cameras can be more effective. We're going to start with loitering. We can set whatever parameters we want. For example, if somebody remains at a bus stop too long or sets down a backpack or suspicious package on our light rail system, the system can automatically alert the officers manning the desk. We'll have this technology at all our precincts and in our Strategic Information Center. When the system triggers an alert, we'll have the ability to back up the camera footage and see if there is anything we need to respond to.

We're also going to use the cameras to help us make resource deployment decisions. In downtown Minneapolis we have some very busy street corners. The cameras can provide us with accurate counts of the number of people at any given location, which helps us determine how many cops we should have there.

Detective Chief Inspector Jim Stokley, Metropolitan Police Service, London:

CAMERAS WERE CRITICAL IN HELPING US IDENTIFY 7/7 BOMBERS WITHIN FOUR DAYS

We have many different camera systems in place within London. Most of the camera systems we use are organized through our 32 individual boroughs, each of which has a different type of camera system in place. There are also different camera systems in all our transportation networks. Having so many different systems can be challenging, so today I've been interested to hear from the departments who avoid these difficulties by setting up their own cameras instead of using what's already in place.

Our first major investigation that involved the use of closed circuit cameras was our pursuit of a right-wing extremist who was randomly bombing diverse London communities. He was able to strike a couple times, but our cameras eventually captured an image of him, which led to his identification and arrest. Without this technology he might have gone on for quite a while longer before we caught him. Through cases like this, we saw the immediate benefits of the camera system.

Now I'd like to fast forward to the morning of July 7th, 2005. Three explosions occurred simultaneously on the London underground system and another occurred on a bus less than an hour later, killing a total of 52 people and injuring more than 700. We had no intelligence beforehand warning us of this attack. We had no immediate leads about the identity of the bombers, how they came into London, or what methods they had been using. In the past, bombing campaigns in London haven't been suicide bombing attacks, so we were looking for the bombers themselves.

Our first priority was to retrieve the video from those scenes. Using what we knew about the attacks, we tried to narrow down our video search to locations where it was likely the perpetrators were caught on video. We identified the King's Cross station and the Circle line as the hubs for the Underground bombings. We also knew which bus line the bomber was on and reasoned that he must have boarded the bus at one of those stops. By conducting interviews we were able to further narrow down the timeframe when the bomber could have boarded the bus. We also deployed officers to conduct local inquiries and look for additional useful video footage.

After examining the videos, we were able to find footage of the four bombers transferring from an above-ground train to the Underground system in King's Cross station. We traced their path back to discover they had boarded the train in a town about 40 miles north of London. We followed them on the cameras in that town to see the cars they had arrived in. These leads were the primary reason we were able to trace these bombings back to the perpetrators, and we identified the bombers four days after the attack.

Two weeks later, on July 21st, there were another four attempted bombings. The attempts were unsuccessful, so this situation was a manhunt to find criminals who we thought might try to strike again. The experience we had from conducting a similar investigation two weeks prior helped us use our video resources to find and distribute images of these suspects within about two hours.

Integrating technological and personnel resources was an essential part of these investigations, just as it is an essential part of any investigation. Technological advances can only help us do our job if we have capable people using and interpreting the information they bring in. And everyone needs to be capable of utilizing technology to do their part—from responding officers to investigators to lab technicians.

Atlanta Deputy Chief Shawn Jones:

ATLANTA HAS A COMPREHENSIVE PLAN TO GRADUALLY EXPAND CAMERAS ACROSS THE CITY

In 2007, the Atlanta Downtown Improvement District wanted to put cameras up in an area they call the "tourist triangle." We had the Peach Bowl coming to town, and they wanted to create a safe area for traveling between the hotels and the Georgia Dome, the World Conference Center and other destinations. They installed about 16 cameras in that area and monitored them with their own staff. Over the last year or so, they've turned those cameras over to us. We're trying to integrate the cameras into our 911 communication center, so we can have a video command center that will provide real-time crime information to our officers in the field. We are going to bring in our own staff so the cameras will be monitored by sworn police officers, with assistance from some analysts. We're in the planning process and recently visited Chicago, where we got some good information.

It will be an integrated network. We're thinking that we will cover about 3.5 square miles at first and only use these cameras in emergencies when 911 has been dialed. In the second phase of our plan, we'll move out to about 10 square miles and incorporate more of the cameras that aren't controlled by the police department. Other city agencies have cameras, and we'll want to pull them in. Simultaneously, we're going to explore some new intelligence analytics for our real-time crime center.

The third phase of our video plan is to cover about 72 of our city's 131 square miles. We've looked at all the crime that occurs within the city, and this phase will put us in range of capturing the hot-spot crime areas. We're also partnering with the Atlanta Public School System so that we'll have additional access to their cameras and can use our Atlanta police officers working in the schools, to be able to see in real time what's going on in the event of an emergency.

Phase four is to have the capability to send the video that comes in through dispatch to the patrol cars, so officers can see what type of situation they're responding to before they get there.

Finally, in phase five we're going to open it up to other commercial carriers, such as our Rapid Rail, bus, train, trolley cars, and commercial entities to be able to monitor what's going on if an emergency occurs. And in phase six, which is the last phase, we'll open it up to other municipalities in the event of an emergency where we have to respond.

We have different funding sources. Our police foundation is funding the video command center, and we have some trust account funds that we're going to be able to utilize to help fund the other parts. We're probably going to use some Urban Areas Security Initiative grants from DHS and some Georgia Emergency Management funds help us complete this process.

Bill Bratton, Chairman, Kroll:

AFTER INITIAL CONCERNS, RESIDENTS OF A HIGH-CRIME AREA SUPPORTED FIXED SURVEILLANCE CAMERAS

Jordan Downs is a neighborhood in Los Angeles that probably has the highest crime rates and the most gang influence in the city. While I was chief there, we tested a system that enabled officers in responding cars with computer terminals to see recordings from fixed surveillance cameras as calls came in. Fire trucks and ambulances could also be equipped with the devices to give them a visual when they had to respond to a dangerous area.

The reaction to this program was very favorable, and we saw significant decreases in crime. When cameras first went in, a lot of people were concerned about them. But after they saw the reductions in crime as a result of the cameras, the residents in the area supported the use of this technology.

In-Car Cameras

62% of responding agencies in the PERF survey said they plan to increase in-car recording capability so that that technology will be in 84% of cars on average.

Austin, TX Chief Art Acevedo:

IN-CAR VIDEOS CAN CLARIFY THE FACTS WHEN CONTROVERSIAL INCIDENTS OCCUR

We've had video systems in our cars for quite a while, but until recently they weren't digital systems. The older systems aren't ideal because officers have to press a button to turn them on, and they don't always have time to do this in the middle of a critical incident. I pushed for digital camera systems to be included in our budget, and we now have funding to put new systems in 550 police cars and 55 motorcycles. The most important feature of these cameras are the seven automatic recording triggers that start the cameras, for example when the driver's car door is opened or the lights are activated. And the system is always on and ready, so if there's a crash, it automatically starts recording and saves the video from the 30 seconds prior to the crash.

Our department averages about three officer-involved shootings a year, which of course receive close scrutiny from the public. We've found video recordings to be a useful way to see what happened and share our perspective on these incidents with the community.

Our most recent officer-involved shooting occurred last October. A 16-year-old burglary suspect was shot after aiming a gun at an officer while fleeing a store. Fortunately the camera in one of our police cars captured it all on video. We were able to tell the public that we had video that corroborated the officer's account of the incident. The citizens review panel, which typically requests an independent investigation after a shooting like this, didn't ask for one because they didn't see any policy violations. Once the investigation was completed, we released the video.

Body Cameras

Albuquerque Chief Ray Schultz:

AN OFFICER'S BODY CAM SHOWED THAT USE OF AN ELECTRONIC CONTROL WEAPON WAS APPROPRIATE

On March 1 of this year, we made it mandatory for our officers to wear a personal video camera. They cost $115 each and have upgraded memory cards to 8 GB. Officers are required to download the video from events to their laptops and then burn a DVD, and we tag the DVD into evidence. This is just an interim procedure until we're able to get a bigger server and do a direct download.

Fifteen days after we went to the mandatory wear policy for the cameras, we had an in-custody death after use of an Electronic Control Weapon. The officer's video camera captured the suspect apologizing for hitting the officer in the head with a crucifix. The suspect had gashed the officer's head open. Rescue personnel were at the scene taking care of the officer when the suspect fell over and had a medical episode. In this instance, the camera was able to exonerate the officers and show that they had done nothing wrong.

Indio, CA Former Chief Brad Ramos:

BODY CAMERAS CAPTURE VIDEO FOOTAGE THAT OTHER CAMERAS MISS

We put cameras into about 25 percent of our vehicle fleet. Unfortunately, outfitting the entire fleet would be very, very expensive. And I felt that most uses of force, officer-involved shootings, and complaints stemmed from incidents that occurred away from a police car, not right in front of it. We knew that car-mounted cameras wouldn't capture those incidents.

To deal with these issues, we started exploring the possibility of using body cameras when that technology first came out. We did a pilot program last summer, and we've decided to deploy them initially with officers in our motor units and then in our specialized units. In the next five years, we are going to try to have some sort of body camera on everybody in the department. So far we've been happy with the product and how it has tested in the field.

The cost is relatively inexpensive when compared to the amount of liability that police departments face. Thanks to quite a bit of risk management, including this technology, we haven't had many payouts as a result of our use-of-force investigations. I think when you look at the complete picture, it is a worthwhile investment.

Austin, TX Chief Art Acevedo:

BODY CAMERAS WILL BECOME STANDARD EQUIPMENT

We're going to be testing several body camera systems this month. I don't know if everyone in our field realizes how inexpensive this technology has become. We now have officers who buy pin cameras for themselves for $30 or $40. We were able to use the video footage from a $30 body camera that one of my corporals was wearing as part of our inquiry into an officer-involved shooting.

We didn't have a policy about retaining video footage from body cameras, so we're working with lawyers to draft a policy. We're going to say that officers are utilizing this equipment while on duty as part of their employment, so anything they record with evidentiary value will have to be kept with the department. Otherwise we can't let them use the body cameras.

I think that within the next five years, everyone will be wearing a body camera. This technology can help reduce mistrust in the government. Cameras are also becoming cheaper and cheaper. I see body cameras, as well as in-car digital video cameras, becoming standard equipment.

*The **Police Executive Research Forum** is a police research organization that provides management services, technical assistance, and executive-level education to support law enforcement agencies.

Police Executive Research Forum. "How Are Innovations in Technology Transforming Policing?—Cameras." Critical Issues in Policing Series. Washington, D.C., January 2012: 13–17; 20–21.

Used by permission.

PART 3:

Border Searches of Electronic Devices

The Fourth Amendment of the U.S. Constitution protects citizens from unreasonable government searches and seizures. Accordingly, in most instances, the government must show probable cause for suspecting a crime and obtain a warrant from a court before searching an area in which an individual has a reasonable expectation of privacy. Border searches are an important exception to these requirements. Government officials and law enforcement agents are legally authorized to perform searches at international borders without having a suspicion of wrongdoing or a warrant. This includes the search and seizure of electronic devices—such as laptops, Smartphones, and tablet computers. The scope of this "border search" exception is controversial, however.

From the government's perspective, maintaining control over U.S. borders is fundamental to national sovereignty. Providing for national security is inherent in national sovereignty; the Constitution expressly confirms that point by vesting in the president general power over foreign affairs. Today, border searches help protect against foreign invasion, criminals, and terrorists. They help keep contraband such as drugs and weapons out of the country, and they ensure that our national immigration system works according to law.

Despite the protection that border searches can offer, there are many reasons why the government should exercise restraint when conducting these searches. The border is the "front door" to the nation and the world's impression of and perspective on the United States are formed by the dignity afforded to every individual who enters the country. Unrestricted border searches are inconsistent with the values of a free nation. Most important, too much government power may lead to a breakdown in due process and lack of discretion in searches. Border agents may target political activists, minorities, and others for arbitrary and capricious reasons. Respect and equal treatment under the law require providing individuals with significant legal protections at the border.

Border searches in the digital age raise new and troubling issues. Laptops and other electronic devices can contain vast amounts of information. We store our personal photos, correspondence, financial documents, medical records, Internet browsing activity, and more on these devices. The fact that the government can take and search these devices, without a showing of wrongdoing, may feel very invasive. Yet, these searches have also prevented the entrance of child pornography into the United States and have been used in investigations of possible terrorist activity.

The following articles illustrate the complexities we face in preserving national security while also protecting individual privacy and dignity at the border. In this chapter, Nathan A. Sales reviews the policy and purposes behind border searches of digital devices, as well as the constitutional protections governing those searches. Stewart Baker argues that laptop searches at the border are effective at preventing crime and detecting terrorist plots, thus, requiring officials to prove reasonable suspicion before such searches would not be an effective method of protecting privacy and national security. Similarly, Jayson P. Ahern contends that U.S. Customs and Border Protection policies and practices do not violate privacy rights and that border searches of electronic devices are critical to the safety and welfare of our nation. Farhana Y. Khera, however, points out that border searches without oversight are frequently used to target and harass ethnic minority groups. Finally, Glenn Greenwald argues that without a legal framework, border searches can be used to target and intimidate filmmakers, activists, and journalists.

As you read the articles in this section, consider the following questions:

1. Should the government be able to search your electronic devices at the border without suspicion of wrongdoing? Are such searches an invasion of privacy or are they necessary to protect our national security?

2. Should we have laws regulating government searches of electronic devices at the border? If so, what limits should these laws impose? Will these limits help keep our borders safe or will they hinder such efforts?

3. To what extent should border officials be able to profile or target certain individuals based on their national origin, race, ethnicity, or profession? Do certain individuals deserve greater scrutiny at the border than others?

Statement of Nathan A. Sales

STATEMENT OF NATHAN A. SALES*
BEFORE THE UNITED STATES SENATE COMMITTEE ON
THE JUDICIARY, SUBCOMMITTEE ON THE CONSTITUTION,
CIVIL RIGHTS AND PROPERTY RIGHTS

"Laptop Searches and Other Violations of Privacy Faced by Americans Returning from Overseas Travel"

June 25, 2008

Chairman Feingold, Ranking Member Brownback, and Members of the Subcommittee, thank you for inviting me to testify on this important issue. My name is Nathan Sales, and I am a law professor at George Mason University School of Law, where I teach national-security law and administrative law. Previously, I served at the United States Department of Homeland Security as the Deputy Assistant Secretary for Policy Development. Please understand that the views I will express are mine alone, and should not be ascribed to any past or present employer or client.

The gist of my testimony is as follows. Border searches of laptop computers and other electronic devices implicate a range of compelling, and sometimes competing, interests. Those interests include the government's paramount need to detect terrorists crossing our borders and to combat child pornography, as well as law-abiding travelers' equally weighty interest in maintaining their personal privacy. A series of Supreme Court cases has held that "routine" border searches—i.e., searches of property—need not be preceded by any individualized suspicion whatsoever. These searches satisfy the Fourth Amendment's reasonableness requirement simply by virtue of the fact that they occur at the border. The consensus among lower federal courts is that a laptop search counts as "routine"; officers therefore don't need to have reasonable suspicion before inspecting a particular traveler's computer. Finally, while the Fourth Amendment imposes few restrictions on laptop searches, policymakers might wish to implement other safeguards that supplement these relatively modest constitutional protections.

I. The Competing Interests of Laptop Searches.

The government has an interest of the highest order in incapacitating terrorists who may be trying to enter this country. The 9/11 Commission reminded us that, for terrorists, the ability to travel is "as important as weapons."[1] Each time an al Qaeda operative boards a plane or crosses a border represents an opportunity to detect and capture him. One way to do so is to inspect the belongings travelers are carrying when they land, including their computers.

Consider Zacarias Moussaoui, the convicted 9/11 conspirator and al Qaeda operative. Moussaoui evidently stored incriminating data on his laptop computer, including information about crop-dusting aircraft and wind patterns.[2] If investigators had found this data on Moussaoui's laptop when he arrived in the United States, it's possible they might have begun to unravel his ties to al Qaeda.[3] More recently, in 2006, a laptop search at Minneapolis-St. Paul airport helped U.S. Customs and Border Protection officers detect a potentially risky traveler. Once he was referred to secondary inspection, CBP discovered that he had a manual on how to make improvised explosive devices, or

IEDs—a weapon of choice for terrorists in Afghanistan and Iraq. Inspecting the passenger's computer, officers also found video clips of IEDs being used to kill soldiers and destroy vehicles, as well as a video on martyrdom.[4]

Terrorism is not the only threat laptop searches can detect. Inspections of international travelers' computers also have proven instrumental in the government's efforts to combat child pornography and even ghastlier forms of child exploitation. In fact, there have been eleven federal decisions examining the scope of CBP's authority to search laptops at the border, and every single one has involved child pornography.

United States v. Irving[5] is chillingly representative. The defendant in that case, Stefan Irving, used to be the chief pediatrician for a school district in New York, but his license to practice medicine was stripped after a 1983 conviction for "attempted sexual abuse in the first degree of a seven-year old boy."[6] On May 27, 1998, Irving flew from Mexico to Dallas-Fort Worth International Airport. The purpose of his trip to Mexico had been to visit "a guest house that served as a place where men from the United States could have sexual relations with Mexican boys"; the defendant "preferred prepubescent boys, under the age of 11."[7] After Irving's flight arrived, customs officers searched his luggage and found "children's books and drawings that appeared to be drawn by children," as well as "a disposable camera and two 3.5 inch computer diskettes." The disks were analyzed and found to contain "[i]mages of child erotica."[8]

Unfortunately, Stefan Irving is far from an anomaly. A 2000 search at the U.S.-Canada border uncovered a computer and some 75 disks containing child pornography. One of the disks included "a home-movie of [the defendant] fondling the genitals of two young children. The mother of the two children later testified that [the defendant] was a family friend who had bab-ysat her children several times in their Virginia home."[9] In 2006, a border search of a vehicle at Bar Harbor, Maine turned up a laptop with numerous images of child pornography; officers also found "children's stickers, children's underwear, children's towels or blankets with super heroes printed on them," as well as "12–15 condoms" and "a container of personal lubricant."[10] Last year, at Del Rio, Texas, a border search of an external hard drive revealed "101,000 still images depicting child pornography" and "890 videos depicting pornographic images of children."[11]

While the government's interest in combating terrorism and child exploitation are significant indeed, the other side of the ledger has weighty interests of its own. Border searches of law-abiding travelers' laptop computers and other electronic devices have the potential to intrude on legitimate privacy inter-ests in unprecedented ways. "Individuals have a basic interest in withdrawing into a private sphere where they are free from government observation."[12] Privacy concerns are particularly acute when the traveler is a United States citizen, since courts generally recognize that Americans have stronger privacy inter-ests under the Constitution than aliens who are only visiting this country temporarily.[13]

Laptops can contain vast amounts of information. An 80-giga-byte hard drive is capable of storing the equivalent of 40 million printed pages. That's equal to "the amount of information con-tained in the books on one floor of a typical academic library."[14] Moreover, the type of data stored on a laptop can be intensely personal. A computer might contain digital photographs from the owner's vacation, an address book listing all of the owner's contacts, thousands of emails sent and received over the course of years, and so on; a laptop can function simultaneously as a photo album, Rolodex, and correspondence file. In addition to personal data, business travelers may keep trade secrets and other proprietary information on their laptops. And lawyers' computers might have materials covered by the attorney-client privilege. For these reasons, Professor David Cole of Georgetown University Law Center has likened computers to houses: "What a laptop records is as personal as a diary but much more extensive. It records every Web site you have searched. Every email you have sent. It's as if you're crossing the border with your home in your suitcase."[15]

II. The Supreme Court's Border-Search Precedents.

The Fourth Amendment's prohibition on unreasonable searches and seizures applies differently at the border than it does within the United States. While the government ordinarily must establish probable cause and obtain a warrant from a judge before conducting a search, the Supreme Court has carved out an exception for border searches. "Since the founding of our Republic," the government has had "plenary authority to conduct routine searches and seizures at the border, without probable cause or a warrant, in order to prevent the introduction of contraband into this country."[16] In fact, just two months before it sent what would become the Fourth Amendment to the states for ratification, Congress enacted legislation granting customs officials "full power and authority" to search "any ship or vessel, in which they shall have reason to suspect any goods, wares or merchandise subject to duty shall be concealed."[17] This power to "require that whoever seeks entry must establish the right to enter and to bring into the country whatever he may carry"[18] derives from the "inherent authority" of the United States "as sovereign" to "protect . . . its territorial integrity."[19]

There are two kinds of border searches: "routine" and "non-routine." Routine searches—i.e., searches of cargo, luggage, and other property—"are not subject to any requirement of reasonable suspicion, probable cause, or warrant."[20] For routine inspections, officers don't need to have any suspicion whatsoever, reasonable or otherwise. The Fourth Amendment permits them to conduct *"suspicionless"* searches.[21] This is not to suggest that the Fourth Amendment's reasonableness requirement doesn't apply at the border. It does. But border searches are deemed "reasonable simply by virtue of the fact that they occur at the border."[22]

Non-routine border searches are subject to the somewhat more exacting reasonable-suspicion standard. Before conducting this kind of inspection, officers must have some particularized basis for suspecting that the person to be searched is engaged in wrongdoing, such as carrying contraband.[23] So what counts as a non-routine search? The Supreme Court has indicated that invasive searches of the body are non-routine—for example, strip searches, body-cavity searches, and involuntary x-ray searches.[24] The reasons for requiring at least "some level of suspicion" before performing "highly intrusive searches of the person" are the "dignity and privacy interests of the person being searched."[25] Searches of the body are more invasive than searches of belongings, and the Court therefore insists that officers have a measure of individualized suspicion before conducting them.

III. Laptop Searches Under the Fourth Amendment.

The question then becomes whether a border laptop inspection is a routine search that can be performed without any particularized suspicion at all, or a non-routine search that must be justified by reasonable suspicion. The Supreme Court has never addressed the question. But a consensus is emerging among the lower federal courts that laptop inspections are routine searches for which reasonable suspicion is unnecessary.

By my count, there have been eleven federal decisions applying the Supreme Court's border-search precedents to laptop computers and other electronic storage devices. Seven of the eleven hold or imply that CBP may search laptops at the border with no particularized suspicion at all: The Ninth Circuit (twice), Fourth Circuit, Eastern District of Pennsylvania, Western District of Texas, District of Maine, and Southern District of Texas.[26] (The Third Circuit has hinted, in a case involving an inspection of a traveler's videotape, that it takes the same view.[27]) Three courts—the Second Circuit, Fifth Circuit, and District of Minnesota—dodged the question. The officers in those cases had reasonable suspicion to search the laptops and the courts therefore found it unnecessary to decide whether suspicionless searches were permissible.[28] Other than a single California district court that was reversed on appeal,[29] no court has held that customs officers must have reasonable suspicion before they search a laptop. No court has held that probable cause is needed to conduct a laptop search at the border. And no court has held that customs must obtain a warrant before examining a laptop.

My sense is that the Supreme Court is unlikely to disturb this lower-court consensus. For starters, the Court on at least two prior occasions has declined invitations to extend the more rigorous standards for invasive body searches into the realm of property searches. In *United States v. Ramsey*, the Court upheld a suspicionless border search of international mail, rejecting the notion that "whatever may be the normal rule with respect to border searches, different considerations, requiring the full panoply of Fourth Amendment protections, apply to international mail."[30] Likewise, in *United States v. Flores-Montano*, a unanimous Court denied that border searches involving the disassembly of vehicles required reasonable suspicion.[31] The Court appears to be drawing something of a bright-line rule: Invasive searches of the body might require reasonable suspicion, but searches of property—even quite sensitive types of property, like letters—do not.[32] As property, a laptop falls on the other side of the line.

The Court might be disinclined to establish a reasonable-suspicion requirement for laptop searches for another reason: Doing so would mean that the level of legal protection for messages, photos, and other data would vary based on whether they are kept in digital or physical format. Governing caselaw permits customs officers to conduct suspicionless border searches of mail,[33] address books,[34] photo albums,[35] and similar items, even though each can contain personal information of extreme sensitivity. A laptop computer is essentially a digitized version of a correspondence file, address book, and photo album, all in a single container. I suspect the Supreme Court would be reluctant to hold that data stored electronically is entitled to stronger privacy protections than the very same data would be if stored on paper.

Indeed, *Ramsey* hinted as much. In that case, the Court stressed that "there is nothing in the rationale behind the border-search exception which suggests that [a letter's] mode of entry will be critical." It went on to conclude that "no different constitutional standard should apply simply because the envelopes were mailed not carried. The critical fact is that the envelopes cross the border and enter this country, not that they are brought in by one mode of transportation rather than another."[36] Just as the manner in which envelopes are transported is irrelevant to the privacy protections their owners enjoy, so too the scope of privacy at the border should not depend on the fortuity that a traveler happens to store his personal information in the digital world and not the analog one. The mere fact of computerization shouldn't make a difference.[37]

Finally, I don't anticipate that the Court will be persuaded by efforts to liken laptop computers to homes. The reason the home has enjoyed uniquely robust privacy protections in the Anglo-American legal tradition is because it is a sanctuary into which the owner can withdraw from the government's watchful eye. "[A] man's house is his castle," and "'[t]he poorest man may in his cottage bid defiance to all the forces of the Crown.'"[38] Crossing an international border is in many ways the opposite of this kind of withdrawal. Rather than concealing oneself from the government, one is voluntarily presenting oneself to the government for inspection and permission to enter the country. One's expectation of privacy is considerably lower in those circumstances than when one is at one's residence. "[A] port of entry is not a traveler's home."[39]

Practically speaking, it ultimately may not matter whether courts allow suspicionless laptop searches or insist on reasonable suspicion. Secretary of Homeland Security Michael Chertoff has indicated that, regardless of whether the Fourth Amendment allows suspicionless searches, "as a matter of practice, we only do it where there's a reasonable suspicion."[40] To see why that might be so, it helps to have a basic understanding of how CBP processes travelers when they arrive in the United States. An inbound traveler will undergo a brief interview with a CBP officer to establish identity and entitlement to enter the country; this is known as "primary" inspection. Most people are admitted without further scrutiny, but suspicious travelers are referred to "secondary" inspection for more detailed questioning and searches. Sometimes people are sent to secondary because officers think they look nervous. Sometimes they're referred because their answers are evasive. Sometimes they're referred because of a hit in CBP's Automated Targeting System—a computerized system that matches travelers' personal information against government databases of known and suspected terrorists, criminals, and so on. A referral to secondary conceivably could be enough to establish reasonable suspicion, especially a referral based on an ATS hit.[41] If so, whether a laptop search is routine or non-routine might not matter much at all.

IV. Policy Considerations.

The Fourth Amendment imposes relatively weak constraints on the ability of CBP officers to perform laptop searches at the border, but the Constitution is not the only possible source of privacy protections. Policymakers at the Department of Homeland Security might consider implementing a number of safeguards that go beyond what the Fourth Amendment requires.

As a matter of first principles, CBP should provide the public with as much information about its laptop searches as is consistent with operational necessity. "[I]n the American constitutional system, transparency and openness is the general rule to which secrecy is the occasional exception."[42] Transparency would help ensure that any abuses of CBP's laptop-search powers are corrected, and thus contribute to the searches' perceived legitimacy. Of course, certain operational details may need to be kept under wraps to prevent the sources and methods the government uses to gather information from being compromised.[43] In those cases, CBP could provide classified briefings to the appropriate Members of Congress in lieu of full public disclosure.

CBP also might formalize the standards it uses to pick travelers for laptop searches. For instance, are people selected randomly? On the basis of previous travel history? The manner in which they paid for their airline tickets? Tips from other government agencies about particular passengers? CBP officers' observations about travelers' demeanor? Some combination of factors? These standards would help provide assurances to people who are asked to undergo laptop inspections that they were selected due to legitimate law-enforcement or intelligence considerations, and not on the basis of impermissible criteria such as race or religion. Again, it must be stressed that CBP should not reveal too much about the factors it uses to select passengers for laptop searches. Doing so could provide terrorists, child pornographers, and other criminals with a roadmap for avoiding detection.[44]

Third, the government should consider guidelines to govern the amount of time it takes to complete a laptop search. The longer an inspection lasts, the more it inconveniences the laptop's owner. Lengthier searches also increase the likelihood that officers who are hunting for contraband will, whether deliberately or by accident, start browsing through entirely innocent (and sensitive) computer files. It may not be practicable to establish a hard and fast rule that all laptop searches must be completed within, say, ninety minutes. But at a minimum, CBP could set goals to encourage effective yet speedy searches.

Fourth, the government ought to adopt standards on the retention and use of data gathered from laptop searches. If a search fails to uncover any criminal activity, CBP would be hard pressed to justify retaining any data from the passenger's computer. When, on the other hand, the government has an obvious need to keep copies of files—for example, if the data itself is contraband or is evidence of crime—it should strictly enforce policies that limit employees' access to the data and punish those who retrieve it without permission. A related point: CBP should take special care to see that trade secrets, privileged correspondence, and other sensitive business information are handled with appropriate discretion, and that there are harsh penalties for employees who access or disclose such data without authorization.

Finally, CBP should make and maintain detailed audit trails to ensure that any officer misconduct can be detected and punished. As Justice Breyer emphasized in a recent case involving border searches of automobiles, "Customs keeps track of the border searches its agents conduct, including the reasons for the searches. This administrative process should help minimize concerns that gas tank searches might be undertaken in an abusive manner."[45] It would have the same beneficial effect for laptop searches.

* * *

Mr. Chairman, thank you again for the opportunity to testify today. I would be happy to answer any questions you or the other Members of the Subcommittee might have.

NOTES

1. THE 9/11 COMMISSION REPORT 384 (2004).

2. *See* Philip Shenon, *Threats and Responses: The Judiciary; Congress Criticizes F.B.I. and Justice Department Over Actions Before Secret Wiretap Court,* N.Y. Times, Sept. 11, 2002, at A18.

3. For a discussion of the FBI's failure to obtain judicial authorization to search Moussaoui's laptop after his August 16, 2001 arrest, see Craig S. Lerner, *The Reasonableness of Probable Cause,* 81 Tex. L. Rev. 951, 957–72 (2003).

4. *See* Remarks of Stewart A. Baker, Assistant Secretary for Policy, United States Department of Homeland Security, at the Center for Strategic and International Studies, Dec. 19, 2006.

5. 452 F.3d 110 (2d Cir. 2006).

6. *Id.* at 114.

7. *Id.* at 115.

8. *Id.*

9. United States v. Ickes, 393 F.3d 501, 503 (4th Cir. 2005).

10. United States v. Hampe, Crim. No. 07-3-B-W, 2007 WL 1192365, at *2 (D. Me. April 18, 2007).

11. United States v. McAuley, No. DR-07-CR-786(1)-AML, 2008 WL 2387979, at *2 (W.D. Tex. June 6, 2008).

12. Nathan Alexander Sales, *Secrecy and National Security Investigations,* 58 Ala. L. Rev. 811, 823 (2007).

13. *See, e.g.,* United States v. Verdugo-Urquidez, 494 U.S. 259, 261-65 (1990) (holding that a Mexican national could not invoke the Fourth Amendment's guarantee against unreasonable searches and seizures to challenge a warrantless search by federal agents of his residences in Mexico, in part because he was not within the "class of persons who are part of a national community or who have otherwise developed sufficient connection with this country to be considered part of that community").

14. Orin S. Kerr, *Searches and Seizures in a Digital World,* 119 Harv. L. Rev. 531, 542 (2005).

15. *Quoted in* Ellen Nakashima, *Clarity Sought on Electronics Searches,* Wash. Post, Feb. 7, 2008, at A01.

16. United States v. Montoya de Hernandez, 473 U.S. 531, 537 (1985).

17. Act of July 31, 1789, c. 5, § 24, 1 Stat. 29, *quoted in* United States v. Ramsey, 431 U.S. 606, 616 & n.12 (1977). The Act's modern descendent is 19 U.S.C. § 1581(a). It provides:

    > Any officer of the customs may at any time go on board of any vessel or vehicle at any place in the United States or within the customs waters . . . and examine the manifest and other documents and papers and examine, inspect, and search the vessel or vehicle and every part thereof and any person, trunk, package, or cargo on board, and to this end may hail and stop such vessel or vehicle, and use all necessary force to compel compliance.

18. Torres v. Puerto Rico, 442 U.S. 465, 473 (1979).

19. United States v. Flores-Montano, 541 U.S. 149, 153 (2004).

20. *Montoya de Hernandez,* 473 U.S. at 538; *see also id.* at 551 (Brennan, J., dissenting) (agreeing that "thorough searches of [travelers'] belongings . . . do not violate the Fourth Amendment").

21. *Flores-Montano,* 541 U.S. at 154 (emphasis added).

22. *Ramsey,* 431 U.S. at 616; *see also id.* at 619 ("Border searches . . . have been considered to be 'reasonable' by the single fact that the person or item in question had entered into our country from outside."); *id.* at 620 ("It is their entry into this country from without it that makes a resulting search 'reasonable.'").

23. *See, e.g.,* United States v. Irving, 452 F.3d 110, 123 (2d Cir. 2006); United States v. Rivas, 157 F.3d 364, 367 (5th Cir. 1998).

24. *See Montoya de Hernandez,* 473 U.S. at 541 n.4.

25. *Flores-Montano,* 541 U.S. at 152.

26. *See* United States v. Arnold, 523 F.3d 941, 948 (9th Cir. 2008); United States v. Ickes, 393 F.3d 501, 505 & n.1 (4th Cir. 2005); United States v. Bunty, Crim. No. 07-641, 2008 WL 2371211, at *3 (E.D. Pa. June 10, 2008); United States v. McAuley, No. DR-07-CR-786(1)-AML, 2008 WL 2387979, at *4-6 (W.D. Tex. June 6, 2008); United States v. Hampe, Crim. No. 07-3-B-W, 2007 WL 1192365, at *4 (D. Me. April 18, 2007); United States v. Roberts, 86 F. Supp. 2d 678, 688-89 (S.D. Tex. 2000), *aff'd,* 274 F.3d 1007 (5th Cir. 2001); cf. United States v. Romm, 455 F.3d 990, 997 n.11 (9th Cir. 2006) (reading Supreme Court caselaw as "suggest[ing] that the search of a traveler's property at the border will always be deemed 'routine,'" but declining to resolve the issue since the defendant waived his argument).

27. *See* United States v. Linarez-Delgado, 259 Fed. Appx. 506, 507-08 (3d Cir. 2007) (emphasizing that customs officials may "conduct routine searches and seizures for which the Fourth Amendment does not require a warrant, consent, or reasonable suspicion," including searches of "[d]ata storage media and electronic equipment, such as films, computer devices, and videotapes").

28. *See* United States v. Irving, 452 F.3d 110, 124 (2d Cir. 2006); United States v. Roberts, 274 F.3d 1007, 1012 (5th Cir. 2001); United States v. Furukuwa, Crim. No. 06-145 (DSD/AJB), 2006 WL 3330726, at *1 (D. Minn. Nov. 16, 2006).

29. *See* United States v. Arnold, 454 F. Supp. 2d 999 (C.D. Cal. 2006), *rev'd*, 523 F.3d 941 (9th Cir. 2008).

30. 431 U.S. 606, 619-20 (1977).

31. 541 U.S. 149, 154-55 (2004).

32. Of course, the Court has indicated that some searches of property are so destructive that they require particularized suspicion, and that a search might be unreasonable because it is carried out in a particular offensive manner. *See id.* at 155-56, 155 n.2. Neither of those exceptions seems applicable to an ordinary laptop search.

33. *See, e.g.,* United States v. Ramsey, 431 U.S. 606, 619-23 (1977).

34. *See, e.g.,* United States v. Soto-Teran, 44 F. Supp. 2d 185, 191-92 (E.D.N.Y. 1996), *aff'd*, 159 F.3d 1349 (2d Cir. 1998).

35. *See, e.g.,* United States v. Ickes, 393 F.3d 501, 503 (4th Cir. 2005).

36. *Ramsey*, 431 U.S. at 620.

37. *See* United States v. McAuley, No. DR-07-CR-786(1)-AML, 2008 WL 2387979, at *5 (W.D. Tex. June 6, 2008) ("The fact that a computer may take such personal information and digitize it does not alter the Court's analysis.").

38. Miller v. United States, 357 U.S. 301, 307 (1958) (citations omitted); *see also* Wilson v. Layne, 526 U.S. 603, 610 (1999) (invoking the "centuries-old principle of respect for the privacy of the home"); Minnesota v. Carter, 525 U.S. 83, 99 (1998) (Kennedy, J., concurring) ("[I]t is beyond dispute that the home is entitled to special protection as the center of the private lives of our people.").

39. United States v. Thirty-seven Photographs, 402 U.S. 363, 376 (1971); *cf. Ickes*, 393 F.3d at 502 (upholding a suspicionless border search of a

vehicle even though "Ickes's van appeared to contain 'everything he own[ed]'" (alteration in original)).

40. Testimony of Michael Chertoff, Secretary, United States Department of Homeland Security, Before the United States Senate Committee on the Judiciary, Apr. 2, 2008.

41. *See, e.g.,* United States v. Bunty, Crim. No. 07-641, 2008 WL 2371211, at *3 & n.7 (E.D. Pa. June 10, 2008) (suggesting that an ATS hit established reasonable suspicion); *McAuley,* No. DR-07-CR-786(1)-AML, 2008 WL 2387979, at *5 n.7 (same); United States v. Furukuwa, Crim. No. 06-145 (DSD/AJB), 2006 WL 3330726, at *5 (D. Minn. Nov. 16, 2006) (same).

42. Sales, *supra* note 12, at 816.

43. *See, e.g.,* CIA v. Sims, 471 U.S. 159, 167 (1985) (describing sources and methods as "the heart of all intelligence operations"); United States v. Duggan, 743 F.2d 59, 73 (2d Cir. 1984) (emphasizing the "need to maintain the secrecy of lawful counterintelligence sources and methods" (quoting S. REP. NO. 95-701, at 15 (1978), *reprinted in* 1978 U.S.C.C.A.N. 3973, 3983 (internal quotation marks omitted)).

44. *Cf.* Detroit Free Press v. Ashcroft, 303 F.3d 681, 706 (6th Cir. 2002) ("This information could allow terrorist organizations to alter their patterns of activity to find the most effective means of evading detection.").

45. United States v. Flores-Montano, 541 U.S. 149, 156 (2004) (Breyer, J., concurring) (citation omitted).

*Nathan A. Sales is assistant professor of law at George Mason University School of Law.

Statement of Nathan A. Sales. "Laptop Searches and Other Violations of Privacy Faced by Americans Returning from Overseas Travel." U.S. Congress. Senate. Hearing before the United States Senate Committee on the Judiciary, Subcommittee on the Constitution, Civil Rights and Property Rights, 110th Congress, 2008.

Privacy for the Real World

by Stewart A. Baker*

By now you may be asking, "Okay, Mister-I'm-a-privacy-advocate-too, what's *your* solution to the tension between information technology and our current sense of privacy?"

That's a fair question. The short answer is that we should protect privacy, but not by defying the course of technology or by crippling government when it investigates crimes. We can do it by working with technology, not against it. In particular, we can use information technology to make sure that government officials lose *their* privacy when they misuse data that has been gathered for legitimate reasons. Information technology now makes it easier to track every database search made by every user, and then to follow any distribution of that data outside the system. In other words, it can make misuse of the data in government files much more difficult and much more dangerous.

But before talking about what might work, let's take a closer look at some of the ideas that don't. Privacy campaigners have a limited repertoire; they usually roll out one of three basic solutions to the privacy problem. Unfortunately, these three solutions either don't protect our privacy in any meaningful way or they make it so hard to catch terrorists and criminals that they will end up getting thousands of us killed. Or both.

[. . .]

The second way of protecting privacy is to require what's called a "predicate" for access to information. That's a name only a lawyer could love. In fact, the whole concept is one that only lawyers love.

Simply put, the notion is that government shouldn't get certain private information unless it satisfies a threshold requirement—a "predicate" for access to the data. Lawyers have played a huge role in shaping American thinking about privacy, and the predicate approach has been widely adopted as a privacy protection. But its value for that purpose is quite doubtful.

The predicate approach to privacy can be traced to the Fourth Amendment, which guarantees that "no Warrants shall issue, but upon probable cause." Translated from legalese, this means that the government may not search your home unless it has a good reason to do so. When the government asks for a search warrant, it must show the judge "probable cause"—evidence—that the search will turn up criminal evidence or contraband. Probable cause is the predicate for the search.

Lawyers spend a lot of time thinking about the Fourth Amendment. Every law student spends weeks exploring its intricacies. Evidence from an illegal search cannot be used in a criminal prosecution. So millions of defendants have made claims under the Fourth Amendment after being convicted, giving the courts many opportunities to apply the amendment. All problems look like a nail to someone who has only a hammer. And all privacy problems tend to look like the Fourth Amendment to lawyers who have grown up parsing its protections.

It's been applied to cops on the beat, for example. A traffic stop is pretty close to an arrest, and a pat-down is even closer to a full-fledged search. But requiring warrants and probable cause would make it impossible to pat down rough customers in a bad part of town or to stop drivers just to check license and registration. So the courts came up with a new predicate for such intrusions on our freedom—"reasonable suspicion."

When a flap arose in the 1970s over the FBI practice of assembling domestic security dossiers on Americans who had not broken the law, the attorney general stepped in to protect their privacy. He issued new guidelines for the FBI. He was a lawyer, so he declared that the FBI could not do domestic security investigations of Americans without a predicate.

The predicate wasn't probable cause; that was too high a standard. Instead, the attorney general allowed the launching of a domestic security investigation only if the bureau presented "specific and articulable facts giving reason to believe" that the subject of the investigation may be involved in violence.

Actually, the story of the FBI guidelines shows why the predicate approach often fails. The dossiers being assembled by the FBI were often just clippings and other public information. They usually weren't the product of a search in the classic sense; no federal agents had entered private property to obtain the information. Nonetheless, the FBI guidelines treated the gathering of the information itself as though it were a kind of search.

In so doing, the guidelines were following in Brandeis's footsteps—treating information as though it were physical property. The collection of the information was equated to a physical intrusion into the home or office of the individual. Implicitly, it assumes that data can be locked up like property.

But that analogy has already failed. It failed for Brandeis and it failed for the RIAA. It failed for the FBI guidelines, too. As clippings became easier to retrieve, clippings files became easier to assemble. Then Google made it possible for anyone to assemble an electronic clips file on anyone. There was nothing secret about the clippings then. They were about as private as a bus terminal.

But the law was stuck in another era. Under the guidelines, the FBI and the FBI alone needed a predicate to print out its Google searches. You have to be a pretty resilient society to decide that you want to deny to your law enforcement agencies a tool that is freely available to nine-year-old girls and terrorist gangs. Resilient but stupid. (Not surprisingly, the guidelines were revised after 9/11.)

That's one reason we shouldn't treat the assembling of data as though it were a search of physical property. As technology makes it easier and easier to collect data, the analogy between doing that and conducting a search of a truly private space will become less and less persuasive. No one thinks government agencies should have a predicate to use the White Pages. Soon, predicates that keep law enforcement from collecting information in other ways will become equally anachronistic, leaving law enforcement stuck in the 1950s while everyone else gets to live in the twenty-first century.

I saw this lawyerly affinity for predicates up close at DHS. The issue was laptop searches at the border. The government has always had the right to search anything crossing the border without probable cause. Smugglers are smart and highly motivated; they would find a way to exploit any limitations on the authority to conduct searches. The first Congress knew that quite well, and in 1789, two months before it sent the Fourth Amendment to the states for approval, Congress gave the customs service "full power and authority" to search "any ship or vessel, in which they shall have reason to suspect any goods, wares or merchandise subject to duty shall be concealed."[3]

Obviously, DHS and its border predecessors didn't search laptops in 1789. But they did search books, papers, correspondence, and anything else that could store information. That was the law for two hundred years, with one exception. The Supreme Court has ruled that a few extraordinarily intrusive techniques—body cavity searches and forced x-rays—require a "reasonable suspicion."[4]

Laptops are treated like books and papers. They are searched whenever border officials think that such a search is likely to be productive. And even the famously liberal ninth Circuit, the court of appeal that includes California, has had no trouble approving that practice.[5]

For good reason. Laptop searches pay off.

Take *United States v. Hampe*, triggered by a 2006 border search at Bar Harbor, Maine. The search turned up a laptop with numerous images of child pornography; officers also found "children's stickers, children's underwear, children's towels or blankets with super heroes printed on them," as well as "12–15 condoms" and "a container of personal lubricant." The law-books are full of unsuccessful appeals by convicted pedophiles and child porn smugglers, claiming that the laptops holding the evidence against them should not have been searched without a predicate.[6]

After 9/11, we used laptop searches to find possible terrorists. That's in part because investigators famously failed to inspect the laptop of one of the 9/11 conspirators, Zacarias Moussaoui, when it might have done some good. Found early enough, the information on his laptop might have helped uncover Moussaoui's ties to al Qaeda. Having learned that lesson, we began using laptop searches more often when terrorism was a risk.

In 2006, for example, border officials at the Minneapolis-St. Paul airport referred a suspect traveler to secondary inspection. There they found that his computer contained video clips of IEDs being used to kill soldiers and destroy vehicles and a video on martyrdom. He was also carrying a manual on how to make improvised explosive devices, or IEDs—a weapon of choice for terrorists in Afghanistan and Iraq.

Despite two hundred years of history and precedent, as well as the proven value of searching electronic media, privacy groups launched a campaign against laptop searches toward the end of the Bush administration. This was a strange and unhappy era in the debate over privacy. By 2005, privacy advocates had found a growing audience for claims that the Bush administration had abandoned all limits in pursuing terrorism—that it had swung the pendulum violently away from privacy and in favor of government authority.

By attacking alleged privacy violations in the war on terror, the privacy groups found that they could tap a passionate core of support. But apart from adoption of the USA PATRIOT Act, there hadn't been that many domestic legal changes after 9/11. But the privacy groups weren't about to stop shooting just because they were running out of targets. Instead, the rights groups started attacking security practices that had been established in the 1990s or earlier. I watched the return to pre-September 11 thinking with dismay. But even I was surprised to find groups seriously proposing to swing the pendulum back, not to September 10, 2001, but to July of 1789. (Perhaps I didn't realize, said one colleague, just how long the ACLU thought the Bush administration had been in power.)

The privacy advocates' solution to the laptop issue was the lawyer's favorite—a predicate requirement. Laptops should not be searched at the border, they argued, unless the border official could articulate some specific reason for conducting the search. That argument was rejected by both the Bush and the Obama administrations after careful consideration.

We rejected it for two reasons. It wouldn't have protected privacy in any meaningful way. And it would have helped pedophiles and terrorists defeat our border defenses. Other than that, it was jim-dandy.

Why wouldn't it help protect privacy? Because as a practical matter, no border official today searches a laptop without some reasonable suspicion about the traveler. The exponential increase in commercial jet travel and the unforgiving thirty-second rule mean that only one traveler in two hundred is sent to secondary inspection for a closer look. Once there, many travelers quickly satisfy the officials that they don't deserve more detailed inspection.

Everyone at the border is busy; there's another jet or another bus arriving in minutes. Border officers don't have the luxury of hooking up the laptops of random travelers for inspection without a good reason. Officers who waste their time and DHS's resources that way are going to hear from their supervisors long before they hear from the travelers' lawyers.

Okay, you may say, the rule wouldn't do much good. But surely it can't hurt, can it? If border officials only search laptops today when they have a good reason to do so, why not make that a requirement? What harm can it do to make reasonable suspicion a predicate for laptop searches at the border?

Plenty. Requiring reasonable suspicion before a laptop search will open every border search to litigation. And in court, it may be hard to justify even some very reasonable judgments.

Sometimes, the primary inspector will send the traveler to secondary simply because the inspector is not comfortable with the traveler. Remember Mohamed al Kahtani—the twentieth hijacker? He was sent to secondary inspection on the basis of intuition—there was no evidence of illegality in the fact that he did not speak English and hadn't filled out his arrival forms. But the inspector's intuition was dead right. Kahtani deserved all the scrutiny he got, and more. Still, if the inspector had opened the terrorist's laptop on the basis of his intuition, could he have been sure the courts would agree that he had a reasonable suspicion? That uncertainty would undermine the effectiveness of border procedures, perhaps giving a free ride to wealthy travelers or those who threaten legal action if they are delayed.

Inevitably, enforcement of a predicate requirement for border searches will produce litigation. The litigation will focus on the motives of the border officials. The courts will tell those officials that some reasons are not good enough. Defense lawyers will want to see the personnel records of border officials, hoping to show that they've inspected a disproportionate number of laptops belonging to minorities, or to Saudis, or to men, or any other pattern that might get the case thrown out. Border officials will have to start keeping detailed records justifying each laptop search. New paperwork and new procedures will clog the inspection process, backing up travelers and penalizing any inspector who searches a laptop.

A predicate requirement would mean that every official who inspects a laptop will get to spend quality time on the stand with a defense counsel dedicated to questioning the officer's motives and painting the officer as a racist, sexist, or whatever else the lawyer thinks might work. In close cases, it's inevitable that border officials will be slow to conduct a search that brings with it a host of paperwork and the chance to be cross-examined. And that inevitably means that we'll catch fewer criminals and terrorists.

Wait a minute, you might ask, what if those officials really are racists or sexists? Shouldn't we do something about that? Surely my laptop shouldn't be searched because of prejudice?

A lot of academics and lawyers are too quick to assume that law enforcement is full of racists or sexists; disliking cops is about the only form of prejudice that is still respectable in their circles.

But let's assume that their prejudice is right, at least sometimes, and that there are biased officials at work on the border. Surely there's a better way to find them and get them off the job than to count on criminal defense lawyers exposing them on the witness stand years after the event.

By now, notice, we're not even talking about privacy anymore. The "predicate" solution has, in effect, changed the subject. We're talking about the motives of border officials, or ethnic profiling, or something; but it isn't privacy. We're also moving the whole discussion into territory that lawyers find comfortable but that ordinary people might question.

The Fourth Amendment approach to privacy assumes that privacy is best protected by letting criminals challenge the search that produced the evidence against them. But before adopting that solution, we ought to be pretty sure that we're going to get benefits that match the cost of letting guilty defendants go free, something that isn't obvious here.

The predicate solution also creates more litigation and gives lawyers new power to discomfit officials. It's easy to see why that would appeal to lawyers, but American litigation is surely the most costly policymaking process on the planet—and not exactly democratic, either. Again, we'd need to foresee real benefits that can't be achieved in some other fashion before buying into that approach. And, for all the reasons I've given, there are very few benefits to be gained from the "predicate" approach to most privacy problems.

[. . .]

NOTES

[. . .]

3. An Act to Regulate the Collection of Duties, 1st Con. 1st Sess., Stat. 1, Ch. V, Sec. 24 at 43 (July 31,1789), online at http://books.google.com (search "Act to regulate collection of duties and July 31,1789").

4. U.S. v. Flores-Montano, 541 U.S. 149 (2004).

5. U.S. v. Arnold, 523 F.3d 941 (9th Cir. 2008).

6. U.S. v. Hampe, 2007 WL 1192365 (D. Maine).

[. . .]

*__Stewart A. Baker__ is a partner in the law firm of Steptoe & Johnson in Washington, D.C. From 2005 to 2009, he was the first assistant secretary for policy at the Department of Homeland Security. He served as general counsel of the National Security Agency from 1992 to 1994.

Baker, Stewart A. "Privacy for the Real World." Chapter 24 in *Skating on Stilts: Why We Aren't Stopping Tomorrow's Terrorism,* 321–331. Palo Alto: Hoover Institution Press, 2010. The publisher has made an online version of this work available under a Creative Commons Attribution-NoDerivs license 3.0. To view a copy of this license, visit http://creativecommons.org/licenses/by-nd/3.0/legalcode or send a letter to Creative Commons, 171 Second St., Suite 300, San Francisco, CA 94105 USA.

Statement of Jayson P. Ahern

STATEMENT OF JAYSON P. AHERN*
BEFORE THE SENATE COMMITTEE ON THE JUDICIARY,
CONSTITUTION SUBCOMMITTEE

"Laptop Searches and Other Violations of Privacy Faced By Americans Returning from Overseas Travel"

June 25, 2008

Chairman Feingold, Ranking Member Brownback, distinguished Members of the Subcommittee, I am pleased to submit this testimony to you to discuss U.S. Customs and Border Protection (CBP) policies and practices with regard to searching the contents of laptops and other digital devices at our nation's ports of entry. My testimony today will provide you with specific information that the subcommittee has requested on how CBP inspects these items.

At the outset, I want to emphasize that CBP disagrees with the premise contained in this hearing's title: CBP's efforts do not infringe on Americans' privacy. It is important to keep in mind that CBP is responsible for enforcing over 600 laws at the border, including those that relate to narcotics, intellectual property, child pornography and other contraband, and terrorism. CBP's ability to examine what is coming into the country is crucial to its ability to enforce U.S. law and keep the country safe from terrorism. This notion is not novel. As the U.S. Supreme Court has stated, "since the beginning of our Government," the Executive Branch has enjoyed "plenary authority to conduct routine searches and seizures at the border, without probable cause or a warrant, in order to regulate the collection of duties and to prevent the introduction of contraband into this country."

More recently, federal courts throughout the country have recognized that CBP's efforts at the border with respect to digital devices—like our efforts with respect to vehicles, suitcases, backpacks, containers of hard-copy documents, and other conveyances—are consistent with long-standing constitutional authority at the U.S. border and other laws. This past April, in United States v. Arnold, the U.S. Court of Appeals for the Ninth Circuit upheld the suspicionless search of an international traveler's laptop computer that uncovered child pornography, stating that "[c]ourts have long held that searches of closed containers and their contents can be conducted at the border." Likewise, in 2006 a U.S. citizen was convicted following the discovery of child pornography on his laptop during a border search. The Ninth Circuit refused to vacate the conviction. And a similar conclusion was reached by the U.S. Court of Appeals for the Fourth Circuit in United States v. Ickes, which also involved a conviction for possession of child pornography.

In addition to several successes in arresting individuals possessing child pornography, CBP border searches also have been helpful in limiting the movement of terrorists, individuals who support their activities and threats to national security. During border searches of laptops CBP officers have found violent jihadist material, information about cyanide and nuclear material, video clips of Improvised Explosive Devices (IEDs) being exploded, pictures of various high-level Al-Qaida officials and other material associated with people seeking to do harm to the U.S. and its citizens. These materials have led to the refusal of admission and the removal of these dangerous people from the United States.

Another example of how a border search led to disruption of a national security threat is the case of Xuedong Sheldon MENG. In November 2004, ICE agents learned that MENG, a Canadian national, allegedly stole proprietary software programs from a U.S. company and attempted to sell the software to the People's Republic of China (PRC). Two of the software programs are both controlled items for export under the AECA and the International Traffic in Arms Regulations (ITAR). On December 6, 2004, MENG traveled from China to Orlando, FL, to attend a defense conference. ICE agents coordinated with CBP to conduct a border search of MENG and his belongings when he entered the United States at Minneapolis, MN. During the search, CBP officers identified a laptop computer and portable hard drive belonging to MENG. A preliminary search of the laptop revealed that it contained software belonging to the American company which is a controlled item for export under ITAR.

On June 18, 2008, MENG was sentenced in the Northern District of California to two years incarceration for violations of 18 USC 1831, the Economic Espionage Act; and 22 USC 2778, the Arms Export Control Act. MENG also received a $10,000 fine and 3 years probation. Additionally, this is the first ICE case involving a conviction under 18 USC 1831. This is also the first conviction and sentencing for violations of 22 USC 2778 involving computer software. This joint ICE and FBI investigation was made possible by information gained by the initial CBP border search of his laptop and portable hard drive.

CBP and Immigration and Customs Enforcement (ICE) continue to carry out border searches within their legal authorities and have been able to arrest criminals and limit the entrance of dangerous people to the U.S. as a result. To treat digital media at the international border differently than CBP has treated documents and other conveyances historically would provide a great advantage to terrorists and others who seek to do us harm. As the U.S. Court of Appeals for the Second Circuit stated in the case United States v. Irving, which upheld the border search of luggage and a subsequent search of a camera and computer diskettes, treating the computer diskettes differently than other closed containers "would allow individuals to render graphic contraband, such as child pornography, largely immune to border search simply by scanning images onto a computer disk before arriving at the border." The same could be said for terrorist communications. Indeed, the Fourth Circuit in United States v. Ickes rejected an argument that additional protections should apply to certain material contained on computers, stating that this logic "would create a sanctuary at the border" for all such material, "even for terrorist plans."

As America's frontline border agency, CBP employs highly trained and professional personnel, resources, expertise, and law enforcement authorities to meet our twin goals of improving security and facilitating the flow of legitimate trade and travel. CBP is responsible for preventing terrorists and terrorist weapons from entering the United States, for apprehending individuals attempting to enter the United States illegally, and stemming the flow of illegal drugs and other contraband. We also are protecting our agricultural and economic interests from harmful pests and diseases and safeguarding American businesses from theft of their intellectual property. Finally, we are regulating and facilitating international trade, collecting import duties, and enforcing United States trade laws.

One goal of the CBP inspection process is to establish that a person attempting to enter the United States does not pose a threat to the safety and welfare of our nation. Our ability to search information contained in documents and electronic devices, including laptops, is just one enforcement tool aimed at defending against these threats. As you know, all persons, baggage, and other merchandise arriving in or departing from the United States are subject to inspection and search by CBP officers. As part of the inspection process, officers verify the identity of persons, determine the admissibility of aliens, and look for possible terrorists, terrorist weapons, controlled substances, and a wide variety of other prohibited and restricted items. Every person seeking to enter the United States must be examined by a CBP officer at a designated port of entry. This may include checking names and conveyances in law enforcement databases; examining entry and identity documents; examining belongings and conveyances; collecting biometric information where applicable; and questioning the traveler.

Aliens have the burden of establishing that they are admissible to the U.S., or are entitled to the immigration status they seek. U.S. citizens also have to establish their citizenship to the satisfaction of the officer and may be subject to further inspection if they are the subject of a lookout record, if there are indicators of possible violations (such as the possible possession of prohibited items, narcotics, or other contraband), or if they have been selected for random compliance examination.

At the Senate Judiciary Committee's hearing on the oversight of the Department of Homeland Security (DHS), held on April 2, 2008, a question was asked about the inspection of individuals with connections to countries associated with significant terrorist activity. At that hearing, Secretary Chertoff stated that,

"U.S. citizens are not treated differently based upon their ethnic background, but their individualized behavior could be a basis for singling them out, or if they matched a physical description it could be a basis for singling them out." One of the primary objectives of the CBP inspection process is to establish that a person is lawfully entering the United States, and does not pose a threat to the safety and welfare of our nation. Thus, an individual's frequent travel to countries associated with significant terrorist activity, narcotics smuggling, or sexual exploitation of minors, may give our officers reason to question that person's reasons for travel. When officers are satisfied that the person has valid reasons for the frequent travel, and there are no other areas of concern or potential violations, the person may be cleared to enter the United States. There are no special rules for personal belongings or documents. However, CBP does enforce numerous laws concerning material in paper or electronic form, both of which are treated the same conceptually and constitutionally. For example, U.S. laws prohibit the importation of child pornography, [as well as items] that constitute pirated intellectual property, or that contain any threat to take the life of or inflict bodily harm upon any person.

In regards to the privacy of these searches, CBP officers conduct their work in a manner designed to adhere to all constitutional and statutory requirements, including those that are applicable to privileged, personal, and business confidential information. The Trade Secrets Act prohibits federal employees from disclosing, without lawful authority, business confidential information to which they obtain access as part of their official duties. Moreover, CBP has strict policies and procedures that implement constitutional and statutory safeguards through internal policies that compel regular review and purging of information that is no longer relevant. CBP will protect information that may be discovered during the examination process, as well as private information of a personal nature that is not in violation of any law.

One example of an instance where CBP determined it necessary to conduct a search of a laptop computer and other electronic equipment occurred on July 17, 2005, when a Michael Arnold arrived at Los Angeles International Airport on a flight from Manila, Philippines. Mr. Arnold was selected for a secondary examination, and exhibited nervous behavior when questioned about the purpose of travel to Manila. After failing to provide consistent answers about the individual's occupation and purpose of travel, a declaration was obtained and the individual's luggage was inspected. Upon the inspection of the laptop and CDs found in the individual's luggage, officers found images of adults molesting children. U.S. Immigration and Customs Enforcement (ICE) then conducted an interview of the individual and searched the contents of the individual's laptop, CDs, and memory stick. These items were detained, and turned over to ICE for investigation. During his subsequent prosecution, the district court suppressed the evidence on the ground that the search violated the constitution. The government appealed, and the lower court's decision was overturned by the Ninth Circuit, which held that "reasonable suspicion is not needed for customs officials to search a laptop or other personal electronic storage devices at the border." As the U.S. Supreme Court noted in the Flores-Montano decision in 2004, the Government's interest in preventing the entry of unwanted persons and effects—and the corresponding search authority of the sovereign—is at its zenith at the international border.

It is important to understand that CBP typically encounters well over a million travelers every day and is responsible for enforcing over 600 federal laws at the border. CBP does not have the resources to conduct searches on every laptop or cell phone that pass through our ports of entry, nor is there a need to do so. When we do conduct a search, it is often premised on facts, circumstances, and inferences which give rise to individualized suspicion, even though the courts have repeatedly confirmed that such individualized suspicion is not required under the law.

CBP's frontline officers and agents will continue to protect America from terrorist threats and accomplish our traditional enforcement missions in immigration, customs, and agriculture, while balancing the need to facilitate legitimate trade and travel. As I mentioned, the initiatives discussed today are only a portion of CBP's efforts to secure our homeland, and we will continue to provide our men and women on the frontlines with the necessary tools to help them gain effective control of our Nation's borders.

I would like to thank the Subcommittee, for the opportunity to present this testimony today, and for your continued support of DHS and CBP.

*Jayson P. Ahern** is the former acting commissioner of the U.S. Customs and Border Patrol. He is currently a principal at The Chertoff Group, a security consulting company based in Washington, D.C.

Statement of Jayson P. Ahern. "Laptop Searches and Other Violations of Privacy Faced By Americans Returning from Overseas Travel." U.S. Congress. Senate. Hearing before the Senate Committee on the Judiciary, Constitution Subcommittee, 110th Congress, 2008.

Testimony of Farhana Y. Khera

TESTIMONY OF FARHANA Y. KHERA*
BEFORE THE UNITED STATES SENATE COMMITTEE ON THE
JUDICIARY, SUBCOMMITTEE ON THE CONSTITUTION

"Laptop Searches and Other Violations of Privacy Faced by
Americans Returning from Overseas Travel"

June 25, 2008

Introduction

On behalf of Muslim Advocates, I welcome the opportunity to
testify before the U.S. Senate Committee on the Judiciary, Subcommittee on the Constitution regarding invasive searches and
interrogations at the nation's borders.

Muslim Advocates (www.muslimadvocates.org) is a national
legal advocacy and educational organization dedicated to promoting and protecting freedom, justice and equality for all,
regardless of faith, using the tools of legal advocacy, policy
engagement and education and by serving as a legal resource
to promote the full participation of Muslims in American civic
life. Founded in 2005, Muslim Advocates is a sister entity to the
National Association of Muslim Lawyers, a network of over 500
Muslim American legal professionals. Muslim Advocates seeks
to protect the founding values of our nation and believes that
America can be safe and secure without sacrificing constitutional rights and protections.

Since September 11, 2001, the Muslim American community has been subjected to heightened scrutiny by law enforcement authorities, including "voluntary" interviews conducted extensively in the community by the FBI; the NSEERS registration program targeting males from primarily Muslim and Arab nations to comply with special registration requirements with the INS (and later DHS); and concerns about targeting the Muslim American community for data-gathering about where they live, their socioeconomic status, their interest in alternative forms of media, associations with ethnic organizations, where they worship, and other private information.

Muslim Advocates has received a number of complaints from U.S. citizens and legal residents in the Muslim, Arab and South Asian American communities who have experienced invasive questioning, searches and seizures at airports or land crossings upon their return to the U.S. after international travel. These activities include searches and seizures of laptops, cell phones, and digital cameras, as well as questioning about individuals' associations, or religious or political beliefs and activities. These incidents raise concerns about:

1. invasive questioning;

2. invasive searches and seizures, especially of data-carrying devices; and

3. discriminatory policing at the border.

The U.S. Department of Homeland Security (DHS) and Customs and Border Patrol (CBP) have a critical responsibility to protect our nation's borders, including barring entry to those who would seek to do our nation harm. At the same time, DHS and CBP officials, who have been granted enormous law enforcement power by the American people, have an obligation to wield that power consistent with the rights and protections guaranteed by the Constitution to all Americans, regardless of religion, ethnicity or race.

My testimony presents a number of incidents from across the country that suggest that the First and Fourth Amendment rights of innocent Americans are being violated. The circumstances of these incidents also suggest that racial, ethnic and/or religious profiling is taking place at the border. My testimony therefore concludes with recommendations for Congress to help protect the rights of law-abiding Americans returning home.

INTERROGATIONS AND SEARCHES AT THE NATION'S BORDERS ARE INVASIVE AND PERVASIVE.

Muslim Advocates and other civil rights groups have received numerous complaints from travelers who, upon re-entry to the U.S., are subjected to invasive questions and/or searches. Innocent Muslim, Arab and South Asian Americans from all walks of life have had their electronic devices searched by CBP agents, or have been interrogated by CBP agents about their political views and activities, religious beliefs and practices, and associations with organizations, friends and relatives—all without any reasonable suspicion that the individuals were engaged in unlawful activity.

Most of the complaints received involve experiences from 2007 to the present, at air and land ports of entry across the U.S., including Seattle, San Francisco, Houston, Detroit, Boston, and Newark. Although these complaints are not the result of a comprehensive study or a systematic collection of incidents, there is reason to believe that these cases are indicative of a pattern of similar cases at the border.

The following is a summary of some of the complaints received:

1. A corporate vice president of a major high-tech company based in the Seattle, WA area has been subjected to interrogations on at least eight separate occasions since Spring 2007. A business and community leader, he previously testified before the U.S. House of Representatives on measures to strengthen the American information technology industry and received the Walter Cronkite Faith and Freedom Award from the Interfaith Alliance Foundation in 2003. Since early 2007, he has traveled for business and personal reasons to a number of different countries, including Japan, Canada, United Kingdom (and other parts of Europe), and Turkey. Upon his return, CBP agents have interrogated him about the names, birth dates and addresses of family members living abroad and in the U.S., the identities of business and personal contacts with whom he met during his travels, his religious practices (e.g., which mosque he attends), and his activities on behalf of a Muslim charitable organization in the Greater Seattle area he helped establish, as well as the organization's activities. (This charity, which has never been designated as a terrorist organization, has worked closely with other faith communities in the Pacific Northwest as part of multi-faith efforts, including collaborative community service projects such as building homes for the needy.) CBP officials have searched his cell phone, made copies of various documents on several occasions, and extensively searched his belongings, as well as those of family members who traveled with him. This U.S. citizen has filed complaints with DHS, as well as the FBI and his members of Congress, but he has yet to receive a meaningful reply. One CBP agent told him that to avoid such interrogations he would have to cease international travel.

2. An American Muslim of Pakistani descent, who is a graduate of Georgetown University Law Center and now practicing with a major law firm on the west coast, was interrogated by CBP agents at San Francisco International Airport after visiting relatives overseas in Spring 2008. Upon confirming her citizenship status, she thoroughly answered initial questions about her travels and identity. Nevertheless, without any reason to believe that this U.S. citizen was carrying prohibited items or was otherwise engaged in unlawful activity, the CBP agent arbitrarily insisted on searching her luggage, seized her digital camera and reviewed the images—reflecting pictures from her travel with her family, as well as various photos taken in the United States prior to her travel. The agent interrogated her about the identities of the people in her travel photos, their location, and her relationships to them. Upon seeing a book in her bag about a presidential candidate, the CBP agent then posed questions about her political views of candidates in the 2008 presidential election.

3. A firefighter, 20-year former member of the National Guard, Gulf War veteran, and current member of the local Homeland Security Emergency Response Team in Toledo, OH has been questioned on numerous occasions since 2006 at the Detroit Ambassador Bridge while trying to visit family members in Ontario, Canada.[1] He was detained at times for up to four hours. CBP agents have searched his car and his cell phone and have asked about why he chose to convert to Islam. In one encounter, CBP officials confronted him with a letter to the editor he wrote in a local Toledo newspaper criticizing U.S. foreign policy. CBP agents asked what inspired him to write it and whether he personally knew anyone mentioned in the piece. On at least ten occasions, he has been asked

about any foreign associates he or his wife, who is of Lebanese descent, may have and his financial transactions.

This military veteran has persistently sought redress for this scrutiny, but has only been told by DHS that his "records have been modified." After receiving this response, he has been detained at the border three additional times, during the most recent of which he was handcuffed in front of his children as a CBP agent said, "look at what you have got yourself into." He has also been intimidated at the border by a CBP agent who emptied and reloaded a gun while interrogating him.

4. An American Muslim graduate student at Yale University is frequently subjected to scrutiny when returning from international travel. This U.S. citizen is currently pursuing a doctoral degree in Islamic studies, has been cited by press outlets including *The Houston Chronicle* and *The Washington Post* as an expert on mainstream Islam and the integration of Muslims in the U.S., and has been consulted as an expert by federal government agencies, including the National Counterterrorism Center and the Department of State. The scrutiny appears to have begun in 2005 and continues to the present. CBP agents at Newark International Airport have interrogated him several times about the contents of his lectures, the places where he has lectured, and even the mosques in which he has prayed. In addition, CBP agents at Houston Intercontinental Airport also interrogated him in Spring 2005 about his views of particular religious doctrines. CBP agents at various locations have photocopied his lecture notes on several occasions, and agents at the Niagara Falls border crossing in late 2005 seized and recorded data from his cell phone before interrogating him about his

relationships with individuals who appeared in it. He has asked authorities both informally and formally about the basis for the apparent suspicion he has received. Citing national security concerns, however, authorities have denied him any explanation or guidance about how to relieve it.

5.   A Muslim American of South Asian descent who is an engineer in the information technology sector was detained for several hours, searched and interrogated at San Francisco International Airport in Summer 2007 after returning from an overseas business trip that included a visit with family members. CBP agents searched and seized his checkbook and asked questions about his donations to specific charitable and religious organizations and his associations with specific Muslim community leaders in the San Francisco Bay Area. The agent demonstrated familiarity with the Muslim organizations and their leaders—none of whom have been designated by the federal government as entities or individuals with whom Americans are prohibited from doing business. After seizing (and ultimately confiscating) the traveler's cell phone, the agent advised him that he "would be in big trouble" if a search of its contents revealed the names of particular leaders of charitable organizations to which he had donated. This traveler's cell phone was ultimately returned, in a broken and inoperable condition, five months after this incident—around the same time that he became a naturalized U.S. citizen.

6.   A San Francisco Bay Area software engineer reported being questioned for almost 20 hours after three international trips, despite hearing a CBP agent explain to another agent that he was not an actual match to a watch list. This U.S. citizen was asked about his religion, whether he hated the U.S.

government, [and] whether he had visited mosques, and [was] even told that he should "pray more." When he offered to give one agent his wife's phone number so the agent could verify his identity, he was asked, "Isn't it rude in Islamic culture to give a man a woman's phone number?" Customs agents inspected his company laptop computer, examined all the books in his luggage, recorded information on one book about the Quran, and interfered when he attempted to take notes about the screening. Despite sending complaint letters to multiple federal agencies, he has been unable to resolve his situation.[2]

7. A California businessman has been detained, interrogated, and searched numerous times upon his return to the United States. He has been asked what he thinks of Iran's president, whether he supports terrorism, whether he met any terrorists during the Hajj pilgrimage to Saudi Arabia, and what he thinks about Jews and the state of Israel. This U.S. citizen's laptop computer was removed from his presence for over two hours, and he was told that officers were examining all the files, including letters from his wife and children.[3]

8. A software engineer in Northern California has been subjected to scrutiny beginning in January 2007 at San Francisco International Airport after returning from a religious pilgrimage to Saudi Arabia. His digital camera was searched and CBP agents made him identify other people accompanying him on the pilgrimage who appeared in the pictures. In June and July 2007, this U.S. citizen was scrutinized during consecutive weekend trips to Canada for a self-development workshop organized by a Muslim organization. On each occasion his cell phone was searched and was used to search another SIM card he had. The interrogations lasted up to two hours,

and his attempt to return from Ottawa, Canada in June 2007 was impeded by a detention, interrogation and laptop and cell phone search that forced him to miss his flight. [4] CBP agents posed questions about the particular conference he attended, its host, and the host's religious views. CBP agents questioned him at length about whether he believed the founder of the conference has ties to terrorists, and whether the traveler himself could have encountered terrorists, or terrorist sympathizers, at mosques he attends.

Citing concerns about CBP agents recording his family members' information, this traveler chose to suspend international travel and has resumed only after purchasing an extra cell phone and laptop with no stored data. After the most recent interrogation in Toronto, Canada in July 2007, a CBP agent affirmatively apologized for posing such invasive questions and suggested that he was required to do so.

9   An American Muslim has been detained, questioned and searched at Logan International Airport on several occasions from 2002 to the present upon returning home from pursuing graduate studies abroad. CBP agents have searched his laptop computer on at least two occasions and have taken his flash drives and CD's to a back room where he presumes that the information has been copied. After confirming his citizenship, he has been asked about his religious practices, beliefs, and even directly challenged about why he is a Muslim.

Invasive Interrogations and Searches Offend Several Core Constitutional Rights.

CBP practices described herein burden substantive constitutional rights, including the Fourth Amendment guarantee against unreasonable searches and seizures and the First Amendment freedom to maintain political views, religious practice and personal associations without inviting government scrutiny. The recent decision of the U.S. Court of Appeals for the Ninth Circuit in *U.S. v. Arnold*, 2008 U.S. App. LEXIS 8590 (9th Cir., Apr. 21, 2008), holding that CBP can conduct searches of laptops without reasonable suspicion, magnifies these concerns. That decision effectively grants CBP the authority to conduct searches of Americans returning home arbitrarily and without cause.

The privacy, security and liberty interests of law-abiding Americans are at stake. In the wake of the *Arnold* decision, a broad array of over 20 civil libertarian, civil rights, interfaith and community organizations from across the ideological spectrum recently called on Congress to conduct oversight of CBP's investigatory activities at the border and to consider legislation to protect the constitutional rights of Americans returning home from international travel.[5]

Invasive questioning at the border about individuals' political opinions, religious views, or individuals' houses of worship, pilgrimage or other religious practice significantly burdens First Amendment rights to religious freedom and free expression. Invasive questioning about individuals' participation in charitable organizations or conferences or relationships with family and friends also significantly burdens the First Amendment right of association. Similarly, intrusive searches of digital cameras, cellular phones and handwritten notes place at risk of potential scrutiny the various subjects of a traveler's photos, cell phone contacts, or even people merely referenced in a traveler's private personal diary.

The statute creating DHS charged the new agency with securing the borders and preventing the entry of terrorists and instruments of terrorism into the United States. In the incidents described above, however, CBP appears to be asking questions about First Amendment protected activities and expression that are unrelated to specific criminal activity or border security. [6] Instead, these questions, as well as the invasive searches and seizures of electronic data, seem to be part of a general data-gathering activity by CBP. If so, a general data-gathering activity raises significant privacy and civil liberties concerns, including why this data is being gathered, who is being targeted, what data is being gathered, and how the data is being stored, shared and used.

CBP's Conduct Raises Concerns About Racial, Ethnic and Religious Profiling and Runs Counter to Equal Protection Guarantees.

The complaints received from Muslim, Arab and South Asian Americans suggest that racial, ethnic or religious profiling is taking place at the borders and airports.

With the CBP asserting a broad authority to engage in searches, seizures and questioning, it raises legitimate concerns about how this authority is being carried out and whether there is an unfair and disparate impact on certain racial, ethnic or religious communities.[7] If, especially after the *Arnold* decision, a CBP agent is not required to have particularized suspicion to search or question, then there is an even greater likelihood that bias or impermissible factors can influence a CBP agent.

Such conduct would be wrong and in violation of the equal protection rights guaranteed by the Constitution. The administration has taken steps to end race- or ethnic-based profiling by federal law enforcement agencies. In 2001 during his first address to Congress, President Bush pledged to end racial profiling.[8] The U.S. Department of Justice (DOJ) later issued guidance purporting to ban racial and ethnic profiling by federal law enforcement agencies.[9] That DOJ Guidance stated:

> "Racial profiling in law enforcement is not merely wrong, but also ineffective. Race-based assumptions in law enforcement perpetuate negative racial stereotypes that are harmful to our rich and diverse democracy, and materially impair our efforts to maintain a fair and just society."

The DOJ Guidance then set forth the following principles:

> "In making routine or spontaneous law enforcement decisions, such as ordinary traffic stops, Federal law enforcement officers may not use race or ethnicity to any degree, except that officers may rely on race and ethnicity in a specific suspect description. This prohibition applies even where the use of race or ethnicity might otherwise be helpful."
>
> "In conducting activities in connection with a specific investigation, Federal law enforcement officers may consider race and ethnicity only to the extent that there is trustworthy information, relevant to the locality or time frame, that links persons of a particular race or ethnicity to an identified criminal incident, scheme, or organization. This standard applies even where the use of race or ethnicity might otherwise be lawful."

The DOJ Guidance then set forth two exceptions—for national security and border integrity. In these contexts, the DOJ Guidance states that federal law enforcement officers may not consider race or ethnicity except to the extent permitted by the Constitution or federal law.

The Department of Homeland Security subsequently adopted the DOJ Guidance:

> "It is the policy of the Department of Homeland Security to prohibit the consideration of race or ethnicity in our daily law enforcement activities in all but the most exceptional instances, as defined in the DOJ Guidance. DHS personnel may use race or ethnicity only when a compelling governmental interest is present. Rather than relying on race or ethnicity, it is permissible and indeed advisable to consider an individual's connections to countries that are associated with significant terrorist activity."[10]

At a hearing before the Senate Judiciary Committee on April 2, 2008, responding to a question from Senator Feingold, Homeland Security Secretary Michael Chertoff denied that ethnic profiling is taking place and explained that CBP agents consider factors such as individualized behavior and travel patterns in determining whether a U.S. citizen's connections to high risk countries merit further questioning and search.

While we welcome Secretary Chertoff's rejection of racial and ethnic profiling, DHS guidance allows him to do so. In addition, his response leaves unresolved the questions of how "individualized behavior" is defined and what factors are used by CBP agents to determine whether reasonable suspicion exists. For example, does CBP consider a traveler's appearance (e.g., wearing a beard or headscarf (hijab)) or nature of travel (e.g., religious pilgrimage) the basis for subjecting the traveler to secondary search and/or questioning? Similarly, is the country from which someone has traveled a proxy for religion or ethnicity? If so, these factors would be either discriminatory on their face, or so imprecise as to lead to a disparate impact on travelers who are Muslim or of Arab or South Asian descent.

Furthermore, the DHS guidance and Chertoff's assertions do not address concerns about religious or national origin profiling, which, like racial and ethnic profiling, should have been addressed by DOJ and DHS. Indeed, the fact that a number of complainants have noted that they have been asked about their religious practice and views underscores the need for clear federal authority—and ideally a federal law—on this issue.

Moreover, if CBP is found to be wielding its authority broadly, targeting Americans based on their religion or ethnicity, then CBP is not only engaging in discriminatory conduct, but has too much discretion, and the result is a waste of resources. Training and more rigorous scrutiny and oversight of CBP would improve security.

Finally, we note that DHS has rebuffed prior public requests to disclose its actual practices. Despite informal requests, as well as formal requests under the Freedom of Information Act filed by the Electronic Frontier Foundation and the Asian Law Caucus, DHS has refused to disclose meaningful information about any potential policies and procedures for interrogations, searches or seizures at the border.

RECOMMENDATIONS

Muslim Advocates urges the Committee to examine CBP and DHS border search and interrogation practices, and to consider legislative action to protect law-abiding Americans from arbitrary and invasive interrogations and searches when returning home from abroad.

1. Muslim Advocates recommends that Congress consider legislation that incorporates the following elements:

- Clarifies that searching data and electronic devices goes beyond a routine border search and requires reasonable suspicion.

- Clarifies that seizing data and electronic devices requires probable cause.

- Clarifies that questions about an individual's political or religious views or activities or lawful associations with individuals or groups are impermissible.

- Clarifies that the country from which an individual travels cannot be a pretext for religious, national origin or ethnic based investigatory activities.

- Clarifies that race, ethnicity, national origin or religion should not be considered in deciding upon the scope and substance of investigatory or other law enforcement activity, except where race, ethnicity, national origin or religion, along with other factors, is part of a suspect's description based on specific, credible information linking that suspect to a criminal incident.

- Requires CBP to report to Congress its policies and procedures on searches and questioning, including the standards for determining whether someone is sent to secondary inspection and whether to search or seize data or electronic devices, and the training that CBP agents receive to engage in questioning and electronic data searches and seizures, including copies of training materials and guidance.

- Requires CBP agents to collect data on border searches and interrogations and report this information to the public and to Congress, allowing Congress to monitor whether CBP policies are having a disparate impact on individuals based on their race, ethnicity, national origin, or religion. The data collected should include the CBP agent's basis for reasonable suspicion (or probable cause, if a seizure of data or electronic devices) in flagging the individual for secondary inspection; the race, religion, ethnicity and national origin of the individuals stopped; whether data was searched; whether data or property was seized; and what kind of law enforcement action was taken based on the data seized or questions asked.

2. Muslim Advocates urges Congress to request that the General Accountability Office (GAO) conduct a thorough investigation and review of CBP policies and procedures, as well as actual practices, for selecting individuals for secondary inspection.

3. Muslim Advocates urges Congress to pass the *End Racial Profiling Act* (S.2481/H.R. 4611) ("ERPA"). As discussed above, there is need for a clear prohibition of racial, ethnic, national origin and religious profiling by federal law enforcement. The current DOJ guidance, and its adoption by DHS, does not explicitly prohibit profiling based on religion or national origin and contains overly broad exceptions for border security. In addition, data collection to allow the relevant federal agencies, Congress and the public to understand the scope of the problem and to monitor improvements in the application of solutions is critically needed. ERPA would address these concerns.

Congress must ensure that innocent, law-abiding Americans are able to travel freely, visit friends and relatives abroad, and engage in commerce, without fear that federal law enforcement will use the inherently coercive context of a border crossing to engage in violations of their privacy and First Amendment–protected beliefs and activities. Congress must ensure that CBP both protects our nation and respects our nation's constitutional rights and protections.

NOTES

1. *See U.S. Citizens Question Terror Watch Lists, CBS News (December 8, 2007), available at* http://www.cbsnews.com/stories/2007/12/08/eveningnews/main3595024.shtml. *See also* Ellen Nakashima, *Collecting of Details on Travelers Documents*, WASHINGTON POST (September 22, 2007).

2. This individual was identified through the Asian Law Caucus, a San Francisco-based civil rights organization.

3. This individual was identified through the Asian Law Caucus.

4. See Ellen Nakashima, *Clarity Sought on Electronic Searches*, WASHINGTON POST (February 7, 2008).

5. *See* Letter from Muslim Advocates, et al. to U.S. House of Representatives, Committee on Homeland Security, et al. (June 20, 2008), *available at* http://www.muslimadvocates.org/more.php?id=43_0_1_0_M; Letter from ACLU, Electronic Frontier Foundation et al. to U.S. House of Representatives, Committee on Homeland Security Committee (May 1, 2008), *available at* http://www.eff.org/press/archives/2000/05/01/border-search-open-letter; *U.S. v. Arnold*, 2008 U.S. App. LEXIS 8590 (9th Cir., April 21, 2008).

6. We note that, to the extent the questioning is taking place without a tie to specific criminal activity, the nature of the setting—secondary questioning at a port of entry when an American, probably tired from a long flight, is seeking to get home—is coercive and would not be permissible in other settings within the U.S. For example, an FBI agent cannot detain a citizen within the country in order to interrogate him or her about religious practices, political views, or participation in local houses of worship or charitable organizations.

7. The Association of Corporate Travel Executives, law firms, high tech companies and other businesses that conduct international travel have also reported that electronic devices have been searched and seized. It appears, however, that intrusive questioning on First Amendment–protected activities have focused primarily on travelers who are Muslim or of Arab or South Asian descent.

8. *See* President George W. Bush, *Memorandum for the Attorney General* (Feb. 27, 2001), *available at* http://www.whitehouse.gov/news/releases/2001/02/20010228-1.html; The White House, *Record of Achievement: Fighting Crime* (noting that "Less than six weeks after taking office, President Bush called for an end to racial profiling in Federal law enforcement."), *available at* http://www.whitehouse.gov/infocus/achievement/chap16.html.

9. *See* Dep't of Justice, *Justice Department Issues Policy Guidance to Ban Racial Profiling* (June 17, 2003), *available at* http://www.usdoj.gov/opa/pr/2003/June/03_crt_355.htm ("The racial profiling guidance bars federal law enforcement officials from engaging in racial profiling . . . has been adopted by the President as executive policy for federal law enforcement, and governs all federal law enforcement activities . . . ."); *see also* Exec. Order No. 12,333, §2.4 ("Agencies within the Intelligence Community shall use the least intrusive collection techniques feasible within the United States or directed against United States persons abroad.").

10. *See* U.S. Dep't of Homeland Security, *The Department of Homeland Security's Commitment to Race Neutrality in Law Enforcement Activities* (June 1, 2004), *available at* http://www.dhs.gov/xlibrary/assets/CRCL_MemoCommitmentRaceNeutrality_June04.pdf.

*Farhana Y. Khera is president and executive director of Muslim Advocates.

Testimony of Farhana Y. Khera. "Laptop Searches and Other Violations of Privacy Faced by Americans Returning from Overseas Travel." U.S. Congress. Senate. Hearing before the United States Senate Committee on the Judiciary, Subcommittee on the Constitution, 110th Congress, 2008.

U.S. Filmmaker Repeatedly Detained at Border

by Glenn Greenwald*

Laura Poitras makes award-winning controversial films, and is targeted by the U.S. government as a result.

One of the more extreme government abuses of the post-9/11 era targets U.S. citizens re-entering their own country, and it has received far too little attention. With no oversight or legal framework whatsoever, the Department of Homeland Security routinely singles out individuals who are suspected of no crimes, detains them and questions them at the airport, often for hours, when they return to the U.S. after an international trip, and then copies and even seizes their electronic devices (laptops, cameras, cellphones) and other papers (notebooks, journals, credit card receipts), forever storing their contents in government files. No search warrant is needed for any of this. No oversight exists. And there are no apparent constraints on what the U.S. Government can do with regard to whom it decides to target or why.

In an age of international travel—where large numbers of citizens, especially those involved in sensitive journalism and activism, frequently travel outside the country—this power renders the protections of the Fourth Amendment entirely illusory. By virtue of that amendment, if the government wants to search and seize the papers and effects of someone on U.S. soil, it must (with some exceptions) first convince a court that there is probable cause to believe that the objects to be searched relate to criminal activity and a search warrant must be obtained. But now, none of those obstacles—ones at the very heart of the design of the Constitution—hinders the U.S. Government: now, they can just wait until you leave the country, and then, at will, search, seize and copy all of your electronic files on your return. That includes your emails, the websites you've visited, the online conversations you've had, the identities of those with whom you've communicated, your cell phone contacts, your credit card receipts, film you've taken, drafts of documents you're writing, and anything else that you store electronically: which, these days, when it comes to privacy, means basically everything of worth.

This government abuse has received some recent attention in the context of WikiLeaks. Over the past couple of years, any American remotely associated with that group—or even those who have advocated on behalf of Bradley Manning—have been detained at the airport and had their laptops, cellphones and cameras seized: sometimes for months, sometimes forever. But this practice usually targets people having nothing to do with WikiLeaks.

A 2011 FOIA request from the ACLU revealed that just in the 18-month period beginning October 1, 2008, more than 6,600 people—roughly half of whom were American citizens—were subjected to electronic device searches at the border by DHS, all without a search warrant. Typifying the target of these invasive searches is Pascal Abidor, a 26-year-old dual French-American citizen and an Islamic Studies Ph.D. student who was traveling from Montreal to New York on an Amtrak train in 2011 when he was stopped at the border, questioned by DHS agents, handcuffed, taken off the train and kept in a holding cell for several hours before being released without charges; those DHS agents seized his laptop and returned it 11 days later when, the ACLU explains, "there was evidence that many of his personal files, including research, photos and chats with his girlfriend, had been searched." That's just one case of thousands, all without any oversight, transparency, legal checks, or any demonstration of wrongdoing.

*****

But the case of Laura Poitras, an Oscar-and Emmy-nominated filmmaker and intrepid journalist, is perhaps the most extreme. In 2004 and 2005, Poitras spent many months in Iraq filming a documentary that, as *The New York Times* put it in its review, "exposed the emotional toll of occupation on Iraqis and American soldiers alike." The film, "My Country, My Country," focused on a Sunni physician and 2005 candidate for the Iraqi Congress as he did things like protest the imprisonment of a 9-year-old boy by the U.S. military. At the time Poitras made this film, Iraqi Sunnis formed the core of the anti-American insurgency and she spent substantial time filming and reporting on the epicenter of that resistance. Poitras' film was released in 2006 and nominated for the 2007 Academy Award for Best Documentary.

In 2010, she produced and directed "The Oath," which chronicled the lives of two Yemenis caught up in America's War on Terror: Salim Hamdan, the accused driver of Osama bin Laden whose years-long imprisonment at Guantanamo led to the 2006 Supreme Court case, bearing his name, that declared military commissions to be a violation of domestic and international law; and Hamdan's brother-in-law, a former bin Laden bodyguard. The film provides incredible insight into the mindset of these two Yemenis. The *NYT* feature on "The Oath" stated that, along with "My Country, My Country," Poitras has produced "two of the most searching documentaries of the post-9/11 era, on-the-ground chronicles that are sensitive to both the political and the human consequences of American foreign policy." At the 2010 Sundance film festival, "The Oath" won the award for Best Cinematography.

Poitras' intent all along with these two documentaries was to produce a trilogy of War on Terror films, and she is currently at work on the third installment. As Poitras described it to me, this next film will examine the way in which The War on Terror has been imported onto U.S. soil, with a focus on the U.S. Government's increasing powers of domestic surveillance, its expanding covert domestic NSA activities (including construction of a massive new NSA facility in Bluffdale, Utah), its attacks on whistleblowers, and the movement to foster government transparency and to safeguard Internet anonymity. In sum, Poitras produces some of the best, bravest and most important filmmaking and journalism of the past decade, often exposing truths that are adverse to U.S. Government policy, concerning the most sensitive and consequential matters (a 2004 film she produced for PBS on gentrification of an Ohio town won the Peabody Award and was nominated for an Emmy).

But Poitras' work has been hampered, and continues to be hampered, by the constant harassment, invasive searches, and intimidation tactics to which she is routinely subjected whenever she re-enters her own country. Since the 2006 release of "My Country, My Country," Poitras has left and re-entered the U.S. roughly 40 times. Virtually every time during that six–year period that she has returned to the U.S., her plane has been met by DHS agents who stand at the airplane door or tarmac and inspect the passports of every deplaning passenger until they find her (on the handful of occasions where they did not meet her at the plane, agents were called when she arrived at immigration). Each time, they detain her, and then interrogate her at length about where she went and with whom she met or spoke. They have exhibited a particular interest in finding out for whom she works.

She has had her laptop, camera and cellphone seized, and not returned for weeks, with the contents presumably copied. On several occasions, her reporter's notebooks were seized and their contents copied, even as she objected that doing so would invade her journalist-source relationship. Her credit cards and receipts have been copied on numerous occasions. In many instances, DHS agents also detain and interrogate her in the foreign airport before her return, on one trip telling her that she would be barred from boarding her flight back home, only to let her board at the last minute. When she arrived at JFK Airport on Thanksgiving weekend of 2010, she was told by one DHS agent—after she asserted her privileges as a journalist to refuse to answer questions about the individuals with whom she met on her trip—that he "finds it very suspicious that you're not willing to help your country by answering our questions." They sometimes keep her detained for three to four hours (all while telling her that she will be released more quickly if she answers all their questions and consents to full searches).

Poitras is now forced to take extreme steps—ones that hamper her ability to do her work—to ensure that she can engage in her journalism and produce her films without the U.S. Government intruding into everything she is doing. She now avoids traveling with any electronic devices. She uses alternative methods to deliver the most sensitive parts of her work—raw film and interview notes—to secure locations. She spends substantial time and resources protecting her computers with encryption and password defenses. Especially when she is in the U.S., she avoids talking on the phone about her work, particularly to sources. And she simply will not edit her films at her home out of fear—obviously well-grounded—that government agents will attempt to search and seize the raw footage.

That's the climate of fear created by the U.S. Government for an incredibly accomplished journalist and filmmaker who has never been accused, let alone convicted, of any wrong doing whatsoever. Indeed, documents obtained from a FOIA request show that DHS has repeatedly concluded that nothing incriminating was found from its border searches and interrogations of Poitras. Nonetheless, these abuses not only continue, but escalate, after six years of constant harassment.

*****

Poitras has been somewhat reluctant to speak publicly about the treatment to which she is subjected for fear that doing so would further impede her ability to do her work (the *NYT* feature on "The Oath" included some discussion of it). But the latest episode, among the most aggressive yet, has caused her to want to vociferously object.

On Thursday night, Poitras arrived at Newark International Airport from Britain. Prior to issuing her a boarding pass in London, the ticket agent called a Customs and Border Patrol (CBP) agent (Yost) who questioned her about whom she met and what she did. Upon arriving in Newark, DHS/CBP agents, as always, met her plane, detained her, and took her to an interrogation room. Each time this has happened in the past, Poitras has taken notes during the entire process: in order to chronicle what is being done to her, document the journalistic privileges she asserts and her express lack of consent, obtain the names of the agents involved, and just generally to cling to some level of agency.

This time, however, she was told by multiple CBP agents that she was prohibited from taking notes on the grounds that her pen could be used as a weapon. After she advised them that she was a journalist and that her lawyer had advised her to keep notes of her interrogations, one of them, CBP agent Wassum, threatened to handcuff her if she did not immediately stop taking notes. A CBP Deputy Chief (Lopez) also told her she was barred from taking notes, and then accused her of "refusing to cooper-ate with an investigation" if she continued to refuse to answer their questions (he later clarified that there was no "investiga-tion" per se, but only a "questioning"). Requests for comment from the CBP were not returned as of the time of publication.

Just consider the cumulative effect of this six years of harass-ment and invasion. Poitras told me that it is "very traumatizing to come home to your own country and have to go through this every time," and described the detentions, interrogations and threats as "infuriating," "horrible" and "intimidating." She told me that she now "hates to travel" and avoids international travel unless it is absolutely necessary for her work. And as she pointed out, she is generally more protected than most people subjected to similar treatment by virtue of the fact that she is a known journalist with both knowledge of her rights and the ability to publicize what is done to her. Most others are far less able to resist these sorts of abuses. But even for someone in Poitras' position, this continuous unchecked government inva-sion is chilling in both senses of the word: it's intimidating in its own right, and deters journalists and others from challenging government conduct.

*****

As is true for so many abuses of the Surveillance State and assaults on basic liberties in the post-9/11 era, federal courts have almost completely abdicated their responsibility to serve as a check on these transgressions. Instead, federal judges have repeatedly endorsed the notion that the U.S. Government can engage in the most invasive border searches of citizens, including seizures and copying of laptops, without any reasonable suspicion of wrongdoing whatsoever, let alone probable cause.

That has happened in part because federal courts have become extremely submissive to assertions of Executive authority in the post-9/11 era, particularly when justified in the name of security. It's also in part because anyone with a record of antiauthoritarianism or a willingness to oppose unrestrained government power, with very rare exception, can no longer get appointed to the federal bench; instead, it's an increasingly homogeneous lot with demonstrated fealty to institutional authority. And it's also in part because many life-tenured federal judges have been cloistered on the bench for decades, are technologically illiterate, and thus cannot apprehend the basic difference between having your suitcase searched at the airport and having the contents of your laptop and cellphone copied and stored by the U.S. Government.

One potentially important and encouraging exception to this trend was a ruling two weeks ago by U.S. District Judge Denise Casper, an Obama-appointed judge in the District of Massachusetts. As I've reported previously, David House, an activist who helped found the Bradley Manning Support Network, was detained by DHS when returning from a vacation in Mexico and had all of his electronic devices, including his laptop, seized; those devices were returned to him after almost two months only after he retained the ACLU of Massachusetts to demand their return. The ACLU then represented him in a lawsuit he commenced against the U.S. Government, alleging that his First and Fourth Amendment rights were violated by virtue of being targeted for his political speech and advocacy.

The DOJ demanded dismissal of the lawsuit, citing the cases approving of its power to search without suspicion, and also claimed that House was targeted not because of his political views but because of his connection to the criminal investigation of Manning and WikiLeaks. But the court refused to dismiss House's lawsuit, holding that if he were indeed targeted by virtue of his protected activities, then his Constitutional rights have been violated:

> Before even questioning House, the agents seized his electronic devices and in seizing them for forty-nine days, reviewed, retained, copied and disseminated information about the Support Network. Although the agents may not need to have any particularized suspicion for the initial search and seizure at the border for the purpose of the Fourth Amendment analysis, it does not necessarily follow that the agents, as is alleged in the complaint, may seize personal electronic devices containing expressive materials, target someone for their political association and seize his electronic devices and review the information pertinent to that association and its members and supporters simply because the initial search occurred at the border. . . .
>
> When agents Santiago and Louck stopped House while he was en route to his connecting flight, they directed him to surrender the electronic devices he was carrying. They questioned him for an extended period of time only after seizing his devices. When the agents questioned House, they did not ask him any questions related to border control, customs, trade, immigration, or terrorism and did not suggest that House had broken the law or that his computer may contain illegal material or contraband. Rather, their questions focused solely on his association with Manning, his work for the Support Network, whether he

had any connections to WikiLeaks, and whether he had contact with anyone from WikiLeaks during his trip to Mexico. Thus, the complaint alleges that House was not randomly stopped at the border; it alleges that he was stopped and questioned solely to examine the contents of his laptop that contained expressive material and investigate his association with the Support Network and Manning. . . .

That the initial search and seizure occurred at the border does not strip House of his First Amendment rights, particularly given the allegations in the complaint that he was targeted specifically because of his association with the Support Network and the search of his laptop resulted in the disclosure of the organizations, members, supporters, donors as well as internal organization communications that House alleges will deter further participation in and support of the organization. Accordingly, the Defendants' motion to dismiss House's First Amendment claim is DENIED. [emphasis added]

As Kevin Gosztola notes in an excellent report on this ruling, the court—although it dubiously found that "the search of House's laptop and electronic devices is more akin to the search of a suitcase and other closed containers holding personal information travelers carry with them when they cross the border which may be routinely inspected by customs and require no particularized suspicion"—also ruled that the length of time DHS retained House's laptop (six weeks) may render the search and seizure unreasonable in violation of the Fourth Amendment.

But thus far, very few efforts have been made to restrain this growing government power. More than a year ago, Democratic Rep. Loretta Sanchez described to me legislation she proposed just to impose some minimal rules and safeguards governing what DHS can do at the airport, but it's gone nowhere. A much stronger bill, proposed by then–Sen. Feingold, would have barred laptop seizures entirely without a search warrant, but it suffered the same fate. Apparently, the Small Government faction calling itself the "Tea Party" has no greater interest in restraining this incredibly invasive government power than the Democratic Party which loves to boast of its commitment to individual rights.

It's hard to overstate how oppressive it is for the U.S. Government to be able to target journalists, filmmakers and activists and, without a shred of suspicion of wrong doing, learn the most private and intimate details about them and their work: with whom they're communicating, what is being said, what they're reading. That's a radical power for a government to assert in general. When it starts being applied not randomly, but to people engaged in activism and journalism adverse to the government, it becomes worse than radical: it's the power of intimidation and deterrence against those who would challenge government conduct in any way. The ongoing, and escalating, treatment of Laura Poitras is a testament to how severe that abuse is.

If you're not somebody who films the devastation wrought by the U.S. on the countries it attacks, or provides insight into Iraqi occupation opponents and bin Laden loyalists in Yemen, or documents expanding NSA activities on U.S. soil, then perhaps you're unlikely to be subjected to such abuses and therefore perhaps unlikely to care much. As is true for all states that expand and abuse their own powers, that's what the U.S. Government counts on: that it is sending the message that *none of this will affect you as long as you avoid posing any meaningful challenges to what they do.* In other words: you can avoid being targeted if you passively acquiesce to what they do and refrain from interfering in it. That's precisely what makes it so pernicious, and why it's so imperative to find a way to rein it in.

*Glenn Greenwald** is a former constitutional and civil rights litigator and current contributing writer at Salon.com. He is the author of three *New York Times* best-selling books: *How Would a Patriot Act?*; *A Tragic Legacy*; and *With Liberty and Justice for Some*.

Greenwald, Glenn. "U.S. Filmmaker Repeatedly Detained at Border." Salon. com, April 8, 2012. http://www.salon.com/2012/04/08/u_s_filmmaker_repeatedly_detained_at_border/singleton.

This article first appeared in Salon.com, at http://www.Salon.com An online version remains in the archives.

Reprinted with permission.

PART 4:

Backdoor Surveillance

Sometimes the police conduct a search by first knocking on a person's front door. They then enter with the resident's consent or enter using the authority of a search warrant signed by a judge. Other times, however, the police might use a "backdoor"—a clandestine search done without the resident's knowledge or permission.

One common method police use to gather information is wiretapping. To use a wiretap, police must first get a court order by demonstrating probable cause. Police are typically required to exhaust other, less intrusive methods of investigation before requesting a wiretap order. Once the wiretap investigation is concluded, the police must notify the people who were wiretapped.

This section explores arguments for how wiretaps should work with new electronic communication technology. The debate about wiretapping in the electronic age began in the mid-1990s, when the Internet was just becoming popular. In 1994, Congress passed the Communications Assistance for Law Enforcement Act (CALEA), which requires telephone systems to be made wiretap-ready with built-in "backdoor" surveillance capability. CALEA was passed in response to concerns of law enforcement that emerging telephone technology was making it far too difficult to carry out traditional wiretaps. Congress decided, however, *not* to require backdoor access under CALEA for software and hardware connected to the Internet.

Since CALEA's passage, however, the Internet has grown to dominate modern communications. Today, law enforcement officials fear that the proliferation of online communication tools creates new channels for criminal activity that sophisticated criminals can use to plan and coordinate illicit activities. With technology evolving at such a fast rate, law enforcement officials fear that they are "going dark"—losing the technical ability to conduct certain types of electronic surveillance. If this is true, gathering evidence of crime and wrongdoing could become increasingly difficult. Law enforcement officials contend that the scope of CALEA should extend to cover online communication services such as social networks, web email services, and online multi-player gaming systems. They believe that backdoors to these services are essential for national security.

A range of groups opposes the expansion of CALEA to make the Internet and new technology wiretap-ready. Cybersecurity experts argue that backdoors result in systems with intentional flaws and vulnerabilities, which terrorists and criminals can exploit to their advantage. They point out that an apparatus built to let the good guys in can create an opening for the malicious as well. Those concerned about civil liberties raise the issue of the potential for government abuse of backdoor access, arguing that law enforcement is not disabled by technology but is actually enjoying a "golden age of surveillance" in which they have access to an unprecedented amount of information. Private sector e-commerce companies worry that increased regulation will involve costly new (and complex) wiretap requirements, while inhibiting innovation.

In this section, journalist Declan McCullagh reviews the FBI's plan to expand CALEA so it can use backdoors to monitor online communication systems. Valerie Caproni then argues that law enforcement is increasingly unable to conduct certain types of surveillance, which makes it difficult to employ court-authorized wiretaps because new web communications technologies do not have built-in backdoors. On the opposing side, Susan Landau contends that extending CALEA to web-based communications will result in decreased innovation and threaten national security. Finally, Peter Swire and Kenesa Ahmad argue that we are in a "golden age of surveillance" in which law enforcement surveillance capabilities are actually far greater than ever before.

As you read the articles in this section, think about the following questions:

1. Why is it important for law enforcement to have secret access to our communications? Is "backdoor" access to communications an effective way to protect national security?

2. Why is it important to restrict the extent to which law enforcement can secretly gain access to (and monitor) our communications? For what reasons should law enforcement be limited in its "backdoor" access?

3. How can we maintain law enforcement surveillance capability of new technologies while ensuring oversight of and safeguards to individual privacy?

FBI: We Need Wiretap-ready Web sites — Now

by Declan McCullagh*

CNET learns the FBI is quietly pushing its plan to force surveillance backdoors on social networks, VoIP, and Web e-mail providers, and that the bureau is asking Internet companies not to oppose a law making those backdoors mandatory.

The FBI is asking Internet companies not to oppose a controversial proposal that would require firms, including Microsoft, Facebook, Yahoo, and Google, to build in backdoors for government surveillance.

In meetings with industry representatives, the White House, and U.S. senators, senior FBI officials argue the dramatic shift in communication from the telephone system to the Internet has made it far more difficult for agents to wiretap Americans suspected of illegal activities, CNET has learned.

The FBI general counsel's office has drafted a proposed law that the bureau claims is the best solution: requiring that social-networking Web sites and providers of VoIP, instant messaging, and Web e-mail alter their code to ensure their products are wiretap-friendly.

"If you create a service, product, or app that allows a user to communicate, you get the privilege of adding that extra coding," an industry representative who has reviewed the FBI's draft legislation told CNET. The requirements apply only if a threshold of a certain number of users is exceeded, according to a second industry representative briefed on it.

The FBI's proposal would amend a 1994 law, called the Communications Assistance for Law Enforcement Act, or CALEA, that currently applies only to telecommunications providers, not Web companies. The Federal Communications Commission extended CALEA in 2004 to apply to broadband networks.

FBI Director Robert Mueller is not asking companies to support the bureau's CALEA expansion, but instead is "asking what can go in it to minimize impacts," one participant in the discussions says. That included a scheduled trip this month to the West Coast—which was subsequently postponed—to meet with Internet companies' CEOs and top lawyers.

A further expansion of CALEA is unlikely to be applauded by tech companies, their customers, or privacy groups. Apple (which distributes iChat and FaceTime) is currently lobbying on the topic, according to disclosure documents filed with Congress two weeks ago. Microsoft (which owns Skype and Hotmail) says its lobbyists are following the topic because it's "an area of ongoing interest to us." Google, Yahoo, and Facebook declined to comment.

In February 2011, CNET was the first to report that then-FBI general counsel Valerie Caproni was planning to warn Congress of what the bureau calls its "Going Dark" problem, meaning that its surveillance capabilities may diminish as technology advances. Caproni singled out "Web-based e-mail, social-networking sites, and peer-to-peer communications" as problems that have left the FBI "increasingly unable" to conduct the same kind of wiretapping it could in the past.

In addition to the FBI's legislative proposal, there are indications that the Federal Communications Commission is considering reinterpreting CALEA to demand that products that allow video or voice chat over the Internet—from Skype to Google Hangouts to Xbox Live—include surveillance backdoors to help the FBI with its "Going Dark" program. CALEA applies to technologies that are a "substantial replacement" for the telephone system.

"We have noticed a massive uptick in the amount of FCC CALEA inquiries and enforcement proceedings within the last year, most of which are intended to address 'Going Dark' issues," says Christopher Canter, lead compliance counsel at the Marashlian and Donahue law firm, which specializes in CALEA. "This generally means that the FCC is laying the groundwork for regulatory action."

Subsentio, a Colorado-based company that sells CALEA compliance products and worked with the Justice Department when it asked the FCC to extend CALEA seven years ago, says the FBI's draft legislation was prepared with the compliance costs of Internet companies in mind.

In a statement to CNET, Subsentio President Steve Bock said that the measure provides a "safe harbor" for Internet companies as long as the interception techniques are "'good enough' solutions approved by the attorney general."

Another option that would be permitted, Bock said, is if companies "supply the government with proprietary information to decode information" obtained through a wiretap or other type of lawful interception, rather than "provide a complex system for converting the information into an industry standard format."

A representative for the FBI told CNET today that: "(There are) significant challenges posed to the FBI in the accomplishment of our diverse mission. These include those that result from the advent of rapidly changing technology. A growing gap exists between the statutory authority of law enforcement to intercept electronic communications pursuant to court order and our practical ability to intercept those communications. The FBI believes that if this gap continues to grow, there is a very real risk of the government 'going dark,' resulting in an increased risk to national security and public safety."

Next Steps

The FBI's legislation, which has been approved by the Department of Justice, is one component of what the bureau has internally called the "National Electronic Surveillance Strategy." Documents obtained by the Electronic Frontier Foundation show that since 2006, Going Dark has been a worry inside the bureau, which employed 107 full-time equivalent people on the project as of 2009, commissioned a RAND study, and sought extensive technical input from the bureau's secretive Operational Technology Division in Quantico, Va. The division boasts of developing the "latest and greatest investigative technologies to catch terrorists and criminals."

But the White House, perhaps less inclined than the bureau to initiate what would likely be a bruising privacy battle, has not sent the FBI's CALEA amendments to Capitol Hill, even though they were expected last year. (A representative for Sen. Patrick

Leahy, head of the Judiciary committee and original author of CALEA, said today that "we have not seen any proposals from the administration.")

Mueller said in December that the CALEA amendments will be "coordinated through the interagency process," meaning they would need to receive administration-wide approval.

Stewart Baker, a partner at Steptoe and Johnson who is the former assistant secretary for policy at Homeland Security, said the FBI has "faced difficulty getting its legislative proposals through an administration staffed in large part by people who lived through the CALEA and crypto fights of the Clinton administration, and who are jaundiced about law enforcement regulation of technology—overly jaundiced, in my view."

On the other hand, as a senator in the 1990s, Vice President Joe Biden introduced a bill at the FBI's behest that echoes the bureau's proposal today. Biden's bill said companies should "ensure that communications systems permit the government to obtain the plain text contents of voice, data, and other communications when appropriately authorized by law." (Biden's legislation spurred the public release of PGP, one of the first easy-to-use encryption utilities.)

The Justice Department did not respond to a request for comment. An FCC representative referred questions to the Public Safety and Homeland Security Bureau, which declined to comment.

From the FBI's perspective, expanding CALEA to cover VoIP, Web e-mail, and social networks isn't expanding wiretapping law: If a court order is required today, one will be required tomorrow as well. Rather, it's making sure that a wiretap is guaranteed to produce results.

But that nuanced argument could prove radioactive among an Internet community already skeptical of government efforts in the wake of protests over the Stop Online Piracy Act, or SOPA, in January, and the CISPA data-sharing bill last month. And even if startups or hobbyist projects are exempted if they stay below the user threshold, it's hardly clear how open-source or free software projects such as Linphone, KPhone, and Zfone—or Nicholas Merrill's proposal for a privacy-protective Internet provider—will comply.

The FBI's CALEA amendments could be particularly troublesome for Zfone. Phil Zimmermann, the creator of PGP who became a privacy icon two decades ago after being threatened with criminal prosecution, announced Zfone in 2005 as a way to protect the privacy of VoIP users. Zfone scrambles the entire conversation from end to end.

"I worry about the government mandating backdoors into these kinds of communications," says Jennifer Lynch, an attorney at the San Francisco-based Electronic Frontier Foundation, which has obtained documents from the FBI relating to its proposed expansion of CALEA.

As CNET was the first to report in 2003, representatives of the FBI's Electronic Surveillance Technology Section in Chantilly, Va., began quietly lobbying the FCC to force broadband providers to provide more-efficient, standardized surveillance facilities. The FCC approved that requirement a year later, sweeping in Internet phone companies that tie into the existing telecommunications system. It was upheld in 2006 by a federal appeals court.

But the FCC never granted the FBI's request to rewrite CALEA to cover instant messaging and VoIP programs that are not "managed"—meaning peer-to-peer programs like Apple's

Facetime, iChat/AIM, Gmail's video chat, and Xbox Live's in-game chat that do not use the public telephone network.

If there is going to be a CALEA rewrite, "industry would like to see any new legislation include some protections against disclosure of any trade secrets or other confidential information that might be shared with law enforcement, so that they are not released, for example, during open court proceedings," says Roszel Thomsen, a partner at Thomsen and Burke who represents technology companies and is a member of an FBI study group. He suggests that such language would make it "somewhat easier" for both industry and the police to respond to new technologies.

But industry groups aren't necessarily going to roll over without a fight. TechAmerica, a trade association that includes representatives of HP, eBay, IBM, Qualcomm, and other tech companies on its board of directors, has been lobbying against a CALEA expansion. Such a law would "represent a sea change in government surveillance law, imposing significant compliance costs on both traditional (think local exchange carriers) and nontraditional (think social media) communications companies," TechAmerica said in e-mail today.

Ross Schulman, public policy and regulatory counsel at the Computer and Communications Industry Association, adds: "New methods of communication should not be subject to a government green light before they can be used."

"Going Dark" timeline

June 2008: FBI Director Robert Mueller and his aides brief Sens. Barbara Mikulski, Richard Shelby, and Ted Stevens on "Going Dark."

June 2008: FBI Assistant Director Kerry Haynes holds "Going Dark" briefing for Senate Appropriations Subcommittee and offers a "classified version of this briefing" at Quantico.

August 2008: Mueller briefed on Going Dark at strategy meeting.

September 2008: FBI completes a "high-level explanation" of CALEA amendment package.

May 2009: FBI Assistant Director Rich Haley briefs Senate Intelligence Committee and Mikulsi staffers on how bureau is "dealing with the 'Going Dark' issue.'" Mikulski plans to bring up "Going Dark" at a closed-door hearing the following week.

May 2009: Haley briefs Rep. Dutch Ruppersberger, currently the top Democrat on House Intelligence, who would later co-author CISPA.

September 2008: FBI staff briefed by RAND, which was commissioned to "look at" Going Dark.

November 2008: FBI Assistant Director Marcus Thomas, who oversees the Quantico-based Operational Technology Division, prepares briefing for President-Elect Obama's transition team.

December 2008: FBI intelligence analyst in Communications Analysis Unit begins analysis of VoIP surveillance.

February 2009: FBI memo to all field offices asks for anecdotal information about cases where "investigations have been negatively impacted" by lack of data retention or Internet interception.

March 2009: Mueller's advisory board meets for a full-day briefing on Going Dark.

April 2009: FBI distributes presentation for White House meeting on Going Dark.

April 2009: FBI warns that the Going Dark project is "yellow," meaning limited progress, because of "new administration personnel not being in place for briefings."

April 2009: FBI general counsel's office reports that the bureau's Data Interception Technology Unit has "compiled a list of FISA dockets... that the FBI has been unable to fully implement." That's a reference to telecom companies that are already covered by the FCC's expansion of CALEA.

May 2009: FBI's internal Wikipedia-knockoff Bureaupedia entry for "National Lawful Intercept Strategy" includes section on "modernize lawful intercept laws."

May 2009: FBI e-mail boasts that the bureau's plan has "gotten attention" from industry, but "we need to strengthen the business case on this."

June 2009: FBI's Office of Congressional Affairs prepares Going Dark briefing for closed-door session of Senate Appropriations Subcommittee.

July 2010: FBI e-mail says the "Going Dark Working Group (GDWG) continues to ask for examples from Cyber investigations where investigators have had problems" because of new technologies.

September 2010: FBI staff operations specialist in its

Counterterrorism Division sends e-mail on difficulties in "obtaining information from Internet Service Providers and social-networking sites."

---

*Declan McCullagh is the chief political correspondent for CNET. Previously, he was a senior correspondent for CBS News' website. From 1998 to 2002, he was *Wired*'s Washington bureau chief.

McCullagh, Declan. "FBI: We need wiretap-ready web sites—now." CNET. com, May 4, 2012. http://news.cnet.com/8301-1009_3-57428067-83/ fbi-we-need-wiretap-ready-web-sites-now/.

Used with permission of CBS Interactive Copyright © 2012. All rights reserved.

Statement of Valerie Caproni

STATEMENT OF VALERIE CAPRONI*
BEFORE THE HOUSE JUDICIARY COMMITTEE,
SUBCOMMITTEE ON CRIME, TERRORISM AND HOMELAND
SECURITY

"Going Dark: Lawful Electronic Surveillance in the Face of
New Technologies"

February 17, 2011

Good morning, Chairman Sensenbrenner, Ranking Member
Scott, and members of the subcommittee. Thank you for the
opportunity to testify before you today about how new technology and a rapidly changing communications landscape are
eroding the ability of the government to conduct court-ordered
intercepts of wire and electronic communications.

Introduction

In order to enforce the law and protect our citizens from threats
to public safety, it is critically important that we have the ability
to intercept electronic communications with court approval. In
the ever-changing world of modern communications technologies, however, the FBI and other government agencies are facing
a potentially widening gap between our legal authority to intercept electronic communications pursuant to court order and
our practical ability to actually intercept those communications.

We confront, with increasing frequency, service providers who do not fully comply with court orders in a timely and efficient manner. Some providers cannot comply with court orders right away but are able to do so after considerable effort and expense by the provider and the government. Other providers are never able to comply with the orders fully.

The problem has multiple layers. As discussed below, some providers are currently obligated by law to have technical solutions in place prior to receiving a court order to intercept electronic communications but do not maintain those solutions in a manner consistent with their legal mandate. Other providers have no such existing mandate and simply develop capabilities upon receipt of a court order. In our experience, some providers actively work with the government to develop intercept solutions while others do not have the technical expertise or resources to do so. As a result, on a regular basis, the government is unable to obtain communications and related data, even when authorized by a court to do so.

We call this capabilities gap the "Going Dark" problem. As the gap between authority and capability widens, the government is increasingly unable to collect valuable evidence in cases ranging from child exploitation and pornography to organized crime and drug trafficking to terrorism and espionage—evidence that a court has authorized the government to collect. This gap poses a growing threat to public safety.

Two examples illustrate the Going Dark problem.

Over a two year period ending in late 2009, the Drug Enforcement Administration (DEA) investigated the leader of a major international criminal organization that was smuggling multi-ton shipments of cocaine between South America, the

United States, Canada and Europe, and was trafficking arms to criminal organizations in Africa. A confidential source informed the DEA that the leader of the organization was a former law enforcement officer who went to great lengths to utilize communications services that lacked intercept solutions. Through the hard work of the agents and with the assistance of a confidential human source, DEA managed to dismantle the drug trafficking portion of the organization. Unfortunately, it was unable to prosecute the arms trafficking portion of the organization, which operated beyond the reach of law enforcement's investigative tools. In that case, the communications provider lacked intercept capabilities for the target's electronic communications, and the government's other investigative techniques were ineffective in gathering the necessary evidence. As a result, elements of this organization continue to traffic weapons today.

In another example, in 2009, the FBI investigated a child prostitution case involving a pimp who was trafficking in underage girls and producing child pornography. The target used a social networking site to identify victims and entice them into prostitution. The provider of the social networking site did not have a technical intercept solution. Although the agents had sufficient evidence to seek court authorization to conduct electronic surveillance, they did not do so because the service provider did not have the necessary technological capability to intercept the electronic communications. In this case, the FBI was able to build a case against the target and secure his conviction using other investigative techniques, but our inability to intercept certain electronic communications resulted in a weaker case and a lighter sentence than might otherwise have occurred. It also impeded the agents' ability to identify additional potential victims and co-conspirators.

While these examples illustrate the nature of the Going Dark problem, it is important to emphasize a few relevant points.

- The Going Dark problem is not about the government having inadequate legal authority—the legal authorities we have for intercepting electronic communications are adequate. Rather, the Going Dark problem is about the government's practical difficulties in intercepting the communications and related data that courts have authorized it to collect.

- Going Dark has been used to refer to law enforcement's ability to [collect] different types of investigative data. As we discuss the Going Dark problem today, we are not focusing on access to stored data. Rather, we are focusing on the interception of electronic communications and related data in real or near-real time. Without the ability to collect these communications in real or near-real time, investigators will remain several steps behind, and leave us unable to act quickly to disrupt threats to public safety or gather key evidence that will allow us to dismantle criminal networks.

- Addressing the Going Dark problem does not require a broadly applicable solution to every impediment that exists to the government's ability to execute a court order for electronic surveillance. There will always be very sophisticated criminals who use communications modalities that are virtually impossible to intercept through traditional means. The government understands that it must develop individually tailored solutions for those sorts of targets. However, individually tailored solutions have to be the exception and not the rule.

- Addressing the Going Dark problem does not require fundamental changes in encryption technology. We understand that there are situations in which encryption will require law enforcement to develop individualized solutions.

- Finally, addressing the Going Dark problem does not require the Internet to be re-designed or re-architected for the benefit of the government. Within the current architecture of the Internet, most of our interception challenges could be solved using existing technologies that can be deployed without re-designing the Internet and without exposing the provider's system to outside malicious activity.

Any solution to the Going Dark problem should ensure that when the government has satisfied a court that it has met the legal requirements to obtain an order to intercept the communications of a criminal, terrorist or spy, the government is technologically able to execute that court order in a timely fashion that is isolated to the individual subject to the order. At the same time, efforts to address this problem must do so in a way that strikes a fair balance between the needs of law enforcement and other important interests and values, such as cybersecurity, civil liberties, innovation, and U.S. global competitiveness.

Legal Framework

The government conducts court-ordered electronic surveillance of the content of communications pursuant to Title III of the Omnibus Crime Control and Safe Streets Act of 1968, as amended, and the Foreign Intelligence Surveillance Act of 1978 (FISA), as amended. Title III authorizes the government to obtain a court order to conduct surveillance of wire, oral or electronic communications when it is investigating certain serious, enumerated crimes. FISA similarly relies upon judicial authorization, through the Foreign Intelligence Surveillance Court, to approve similar surveillance directed at foreign intelligence and international terrorism threats. The government obtains court authorization to install and use pen registers and trap and trace devices pursuant to chapter 206 of Title 18, United States Code, and FISA. Such devices reveal dialing, routing, addressing, and signaling information but not the substance, purport, or meaning of communications.

These authorities address privacy and civil liberties interests, commercial interests, and the government's interest in intercepting communications necessary to protect public safety. Indeed, Title III and FISA orders are among the most difficult investigative authorities to obtain and use. Focusing on intercepting phone calls in a criminal case, the investigator must establish, to the satisfaction of a federal district court judge, that there is probable cause to believe the person whose communications are targeted for interception is committing, has committed or is about to commit one of the specific enumerated felonies, that alternative investigative procedures have failed, are unlikely to succeed or are too dangerous, and that there is probable cause to believe that evidence of the specified felony will be obtained through the surveillance. The application can only be submitted to the court with the approval of a high-ranking official of the Department of Justice. After obtaining an intercept order, the investigator is required to minimize the interception of non-pertinent and privileged communications, and to provide the Court with regular progress updates. The court order expires after 30 days. If the government wishes to extend the period of surveillance, it must submit a new application with a fresh showing of probable cause. In short, Title III imposes a rigorous set of requirements designed to ensure that this investigative tool is used only against the most serious criminals and only when other, less intrusive techniques will not be effective to protect the public safety.

From the outset, the government has required some assistance from communications service providers to implement court orders for electronic surveillance. Both Title III and FISA include provisions mandating technical assistance so that the government will be able to carry out activities authorized by the court. For example, Title III specifies that a "service provider, landlord . . . or other person shall furnish [the government]. . . forthwith all . . . technical assistance necessary to accomplish the interception . . ." As the communications environment has grown in volume and complexity, technical assistance has proven to be essential for interception to occur. These provisions alone, however, have not been sufficient to enable the government to conduct surveillance in a timely and effective manner.

In the early 1990s, the telecommunications industry was undergoing a major transformation and the government faced an earlier version of this problem. At that time, law enforcement agencies were experiencing a reduced ability to conduct intercepts of mobile voice communications as digital, switch-based telecommunications services grew in popularity. In response, Congress enacted the Communications Assistance for Law Enforcement Act (CALEA) in 1994. CALEA requires "telecommunications carriers" to develop and deploy intercept solutions in their networks to ensure that the government is able to intercept electronic communications when lawfully authorized. Specifically, it requires carriers to be able to isolate and deliver particular communications, to the exclusion of other communications, and to be able to deliver information regarding the origination and termination of the communication (also referred to as "pen register information" or "dialing and signaling information"). CALEA regulates the capabilities that covered entities must have and does not affect the process or the legal standards that the government must meet in order to obtain a court order to collect communications or related data.

While CALEA was intended to keep pace with technological changes, its focus was on telecommunications carriers that provided traditional telephony and mobile telephone services; not Internet-based communications services. Over the years, through interpretation of the statute by the Federal Communications Commission, the reach of CALEA has been expanded to include facilities-based broadband Internet access and Voice over Internet Protocol (VoIP) services that are fully inter-connected with the public switched telephone network. Although that expansion of coverage has been extremely helpful, CALEA does not cover popular Internet-based communications modalities such as webmail, social networking sites or peer-to-peer services.

At the time CALEA was enacted, the focus on traditional telecommunications services made sense because Internet-based and wireless communications were in a fairly nascent stage of development and digital telephony represented the greatest challenge to law enforcement. However, as discussed below, due to the revolutionary expansion of communications technology in recent years, the government finds that it is rapidly losing ground in its ability to execute court orders with respect to Internet-based communications that are not covered by CALEA. Also, experience with CALEA has shown that certain aspects of that law sometimes make it difficult for the government to execute orders even for providers that are covered by CALEA.

Challenges Associated with New Technologies

From a time when there were a handful of large companies that serviced the vast majority of telephone users in the country using fairly standard technology (the situation that existed when CALEA was enacted in 1994), the environment in which court-authorized surveillance now occurs is exponentially more complex and difficult. Since 1994, there has been a dramatic increase in the volume of communications, the types of services that are offered, and the number of service providers. It is no longer the case that the technology involved in communications services is largely standard. Now, communications occur through a wide variety of means, including cable, wireline, and wireless broadband, peer-to-peer and VoIP services, and third party applications and providers—all of which have their own technology challenges. Today's providers offer more sophisticated communications services than ever before, and an increasing number of the most popular communications modalities are not covered by CALEA.

Methods of accessing communications networks have similarly grown in variety and complexity. Recent innovations in hand-held devices have changed the ways in which consumers access networks and network-based services. One result of this change is a transformation of communications services from a straight-forward relationship between a customer and a single CALEA-covered provider (e.g., customer to telephone company) to a complex environment in which a customer may use several access methods to maintain simultaneous interactions with multiple providers, some of whom may be based overseas or are otherwise outside the scope of CALEA.

As a result, although the government may obtain a court order authorizing the collection of certain communications, it often serves that order on a provider who does not have an obligation under CALEA to be prepared to execute it. Such providers may not have intercept capabilities in place at the time that they receive the order. Even if they begin actively attempting to engineer a solution immediately upon receipt of the order and work diligently with government engineers, months and sometimes years can pass before they are able to develop a solution that complies with the applicable court order. Some providers never manage to comply with the orders fully.

Even providers that are covered by CALEA do not always maintain the required capabilities and can be slow at providing assistance. Indeed, as with non-CALEA providers, for some CALEA-covered entities, months can elapse between the time the government obtains a court order and surveillance begins. In the interim period, potentially critical information is lost even though a court has explicitly authorized the surveillance.

This failure of some CALEA-covered providers to be able to comply fully with court orders is due in part to the process in CALEA for establishing standards for intercept capabilities that law enforcement agencies have found to be ineffective in practice. CALEA accords industry "safe harbor" from a CALEA enforcement action when they build their solution consistent with published industry standards, regardless of whether or not the standards satisfy CALEA's technical capability requirements or meet the needs of law enforcement. That reality can result in providers developing and maintaining intercept capabilities that do not achieve the goal of actually providing the government the information it is lawfully authorized to collect.

To compound matters, CALEA's enforcement requirements make it very difficult for the government to bring an enforcement action in court against a covered provider. CALEA's enforcement provisions are written in a manner that leaves the government with the choice of pursuing a CALEA enforcement action against a provider or developing the solution that provides us the ability to collect the evidence we need to further our investigation. Placing the mission first, we invariably develop the intercept capability ourselves. Once a solution is developed, we cannot satisfy CALEA's standards for enforcement.

The enforcement mechanisms in Title III and FISA are also difficult to use as an effective lever to encourage providers to develop and maintain lawful intercept solutions. With respect to both providers that are covered by CALEA and providers that are not, the judicial remedy for non-compliance with the technical assistance requirements in Title III and FISA is contempt. A contempt action is practically and legally difficult to pursue and is unlikely to succeed absent a total refusal of cooperation.

Challenges Facing State and Local Law Enforcement

State and local law enforcement agencies also face a serious intercept capabilities gap. For the most part, our state and local counterparts do not enjoy the resources, facilities, experience, technical expertise, and relationships with industry that federal agencies utilize to effectuate electronic surveillance. With a few exceptions, they are largely unable to conduct electronic surveillance of any Internet-based communications services.

The challenge facing our state and local counterparts is exacerbated by the fact that there is currently no systematic way to make existing federally developed electronic intercept solutions widely available across the law enforcement community. Federal, state and local law enforcement agencies have varying degrees of technical expertise regarding electronic surveillance and lack an effective mechanism for sharing information about existing intercept capabilities. This leads to the inefficient use of scarce technical resources and missed opportunities to capitalize on existing solutions. In addition, there are significant communication gaps between law enforcement and the communications industry: law enforcement often lacks information about new communications services offered by providers while providers often lack understanding of the needs of law enforcement. The absence of effective coordination and information sharing impedes the development of timely, cost-effective intercept capabilities that are broadly available to law enforcement across the country.

To help address these issues, the President's fiscal year 2012 Budget requests $15 million to establish a Domestic Communications Assistance Center (DCAC). The DCAC will leverage the research and development efforts of federal, state, and local law enforcement with respect to electronic surveillance capabilities, facilitate the sharing of technology between law enforcement agencies, advance initiatives to implement solutions complying with CALEA, and seek to build more effective relations with the communications industry. Due to the immediacy of these issues, DOJ is identifying space and building out the facility now.

Conclusion

The government's consideration of its electronic surveillance challenges must account for the complexity and variety of today's emerging communications services and technologies. This complexity and variety creates a range of opportunities and challenges for law enforcement. On the one hand, increased communications affords law enforcement potential access to more information relevant to preventing and solving crime. On the other hand, the pace of technological change means that law enforcement must update or develop new electronic surveillance techniques on a far more frequent basis, as existing tools will become obsolete quicker than ever before. In this setting, federal law enforcement faces new challenges on an ongoing basis. At the same time, state and local law enforcement agencies, who traditionally have fewer technical resources necessary to perform lawful electronic surveillance, increasingly need to rely upon the federal government to serve as a central source of expertise.

At this time, the Administration does not have a formal position on whether any legislative changes are necessary. However, it is examining a variety of potential solutions that would address various aspects of the Going Dark problem. We look forward to working with Congress to find a solution that restores and maintains the ability of law enforcement agencies to intercept communications and collect related data pursuant to court orders in a manner that protects public safety, promotes innovation, and safeguards civil liberties. Chairman Sensenbrenner, Ranking Member Scott, and members of the Subcommittee, thank you for the opportunity to address this Subcommittee. I look forward to answering your questions.

*Valerie Caproni** served as general counsel for the FBI from 2003 to 2011. She is currently vice president and deputy general counsel, litigation and investigations, for Northrop Grumman Corporation.

Statement of Valerie Caproni. "Going Dark: Lawful Electronic Surveillance in the Face of New Technologies." U.S. Congress. House of Representatives. Hearing before the House Judiciary Committee, Subcommittee on Crime, Terrorism and Homeland Security, 112th Congress, 2011.

Testimony of Susan Landau

TESTIMONY OF SUSAN LANDAU*
BEFORE THE COMMITTEE OF THE JUDICIARY,
SUBCOMMITTEE ON CRIME, TERRORISM AND HOMELAND
SECURITY

"Going Dark: Lawful Electronic Surveillance in the Face of New Technologies."

February 17, 2011

Mr. Chairman and Members of the Committee:

Thank you very much for the opportunity to testify today on "Going Dark: Lawful Electronic Surveillance in the Face of New Technologies." My name is Susan Landau, and I am currently a fellow at the Radcliffe Institute for Advanced Study at Harvard University. For the last half dozen years I have studied the risks that occur when wiretapping capabilities are embedded in communications infrastructures, and written about them in the *Washington Post, Scientific American,* and elsewhere. My book detailing these dangers, *Surveillance or Security? The Risks Posed by New Wiretapping Technologies,* has just been published by MIT Press. I am also co-author of *Privacy on the Line: The Politics of Wiretapping and Encryption* (MIT Press, 1998).[1]

My comments represent my own views, and not those of any of the institutions with which I am affiliated.

Today I want to speak to you about the security threats raised by extending the Communications Assistance for Law

Enforcement Act to IP-based communications. The intent of proposals to extend CALEA to IP-based communications is to secure the nation. Rather than doing so, surveillance mechanisms built into communications infrastructure threaten to create serious vulnerabilities for national security and present threats to innovation.

A Genuine Problem

Law enforcement is entirely correct that it faces a problem. Rapidly changing communications technologies have created complex challenges to legally authorized interception. This problem began with the break-up of AT&T. Rapid innovation coincided with a soaring number of service providers and suppliers of communications technology. Legally authorized interception has only become more complex with the Internet and the rapid innovation in IP-based communications.

At the same time, it is important to realize that advanced telecommunications provide capabilities to law enforcement unexpected at the time the original wiretap statutes were passed. Both CallerID and cell phones have proved remarkably useful to investigators. Location information from cell phones found the main plotter of the terrorist acts on September 11th, Khalid Shaikh Mohammed, one of the July 21st London bombers when he fled to Rome, and has enabled, for example, the U.S. Marshals Service to drop the average time to find a fugitive from forty-two days to two. Transactional data—the who, when, where—of a communication is a very rich source of information for investigators, and can likely be used even more to even greater value. While there is a genuine problem with intercepting some communications, the FBI now has access to more communications, and more metadata about communications, than ever before in history.

Building in Intercept Capability Creates New Security Risks

But if law enforcement has a problem, a solution that expands the Communications Assistance for Law Enforcement Act (CALEA) to new IP-based communications is one that creates new security risks. Building wiretapping into communications infrastructure creates serious risk that the communications system will be subverted either by trusted insiders or skilled outsiders, including foreign governments, hackers, identity thieves and perpetrators of economic espionage. This risk is not theoretical.

For a period of ten months in 2004–2005, over one hundred senior officials of the Greek government, including the prime minister and the heads of the ministries of interior, justice, and national defense, were eavesdropped upon as a result of a breach in wiretapping capability built into a switch.[2] We know how it was done.

Vodafone Greece had purchased switches from the Swedish manufacturer Ericcson; these switches are designed to allow lawful interception. Vodafone Greece had not purchased the wiretapping capability. But in an update to the switch, the wiretapping capability was automatically added, though a user interface to allow Vodafone Greece to easily access that capability—and the capability to audit the interception—was not. Intruders modified twenty-nine different blocks of computer code to initiate the wiretapping of the targets, and this added software included a capability for further surreptitious updating. The breach was discovered when some texts had gone awry. But while we know how the breach occurred, we do not know who did it.

Meanwhile between 1996–2006, Telecom Italia appears to have suffered an insider attack in which six thousand people were the target of unauthorized wiretaps.[3] The number of people wiretapped is so large that it means at least one in ten thousand Italians was wiretapped—and that no large business or political deal was ever truly private. Massive dossiers were collected on politicians, financiers, businesspeople, bankers, journalists and judges. It appears that the motivation for the interception was monetary, that is, bribes and blackmail, and was instigated by authorized users of the system. The case is still in trial.

In 2010, an IBM researcher, Tom Cross, discovered that a Cisco architecture for IP networks based on standards published by the European Telecommunications Standards Institute for law-enforcement interception was not sufficiently specified and that is was possible to spoof the system.[4] In particular, criminals could fool the system into allowing them to install unauthorized wiretaps. Just as in the Greek Vodafone case, it was possible to bypass the audit mechanisms. Systems based on these standards were already in use.

The FBI itself has not been immune from problems with implementing wiretap systems. The DCS3000 system (previously known as Carnivore) was an FBI system for delivering ISP wiretap and pen register data to bureau investigators. Because the information was to be used both in investigations and prosecutions, the chain of evidence had to be unimpeachable. But DCS3000 used an auditing system that shared user logins and could easily be spoofed. In addition, system auditing depended on an easily forged manual log sheet. The system was highly vulnerable to insider attacks. It was exactly poor auditing mechanisms that allowed Robert Hanssen to check what the FBI knew about him—and here were poor auditing systems being built into FBI wiretapping systems in the mid 2000s.

The problems at Vodafone Greece, Telecom Italia, with the Cisco interception architecture, and at the FBI all occurred against the wider background of increasing national concern over cybersecurity. Wiretapping built into a communications application or switch is an architected security breach. Rather than securing us, such capabilities endanger us.

What Cybersecurity Risks Does the U.S. Face?

At the time, CALEA's passage was sought because of wiretapping's value in fighting against "drug trafficking, organized crime, violent crime, kidnapping, crimes against children, and public corruption."[5] Since then, we have witnessed a dramatic change in both the nature of communication and the nature of the threats against the United States. It is worth taking a small step back in time to put these shifts in context.

In the early days of the Cold War, the Soviet Union spied on the U.S. military, but over time shifted to spying on defense contractors and other parts of U.S industry, and other nations did also. Not only do enemies of the U.S spy on us, but our friends do as well and they share the information with companies in their own countries. For example, as a result of an unknown insider supplying secret corporate research and business plans to the Japanese consulate in San Francisco, Fairchild Semiconductor was badly weakened, and needed U.S government help to survive a takeover bid by Fujitsu. A 2003 FBI study estimated an annual $200 billion cost to the U.S. economy as a result of economic espionage.

Beginning in this decade, the world shifted in two fundamental ways that substantively changed the nature of this type of industrial espionage; it was made cheaper, and there was a very large customer [base] for the information. The growth of the Internet and computing technology has greatly simplified the ability of spies, especially those at a distance, to get "inside" a company. The other change is China. Well aware of the information infrastructure asymmetry between China and the U.S., China is seeking to use the asymmetry to its advantage. Other nations also exploit our heavy dependence on cyber infrastructure, but China seems particularly active in doing so.

The first public notice of Chinese intrusions into U.S. computers came with the 2004 "Titan Rain" infiltrations of four U.S defense installations that occurred in the space of eight hours. Using unpatched software to access the military sites, the intruders, who had obviously been "inside" their targets previously, rapidly packed up files of interest and exfiltrated them, first to Taiwan and Korea, then to southern China. Sensitive helicopter and flight-planning software were among the files removed.

Since that time, such cyber exploitations have become constant occurrences, and many U.S. companies and government sites have been targeted. The modus operandi is always the same. Some software vulnerability—unpatched software, a user opening a targeted mail that contains malware (or that directs the user to a site with malware)—allows the intruder in. The intruder spends time carefully studying the site and finding the files of interest. At some point, the intruder efficiently ships out copies. This is carefully done. By the time the corporate or government site becomes aware that there has been an intrusion, it is often too late. The data has been shipped to China. Organizations that have been exploited in this way cut across large swaths of American industry and government, including such leading members as Google, Lockheed Martin, NASA,

Northrup Grumman, and Oak Ridge National Laboratory. Nor is the Department of Defense immune. Major General William Lord, the air force's chief information officer, reported that "China has downloaded 10 to 20 terabytes of data from the NIPRNet, DoD's non-classified IP Router Network."

How serious is this threat? In September 2010, U.S. Deputy Secretary of Defense William Lynn wrote in *Foreign Affairs* that, "Although the threat to intellectual property is less dramatic than the threat to critical national infrastructure, it may be the most significant cyberthreat that the United States will face over the long term. Every year, an amount of intellectual property many times larger than all the intellectual property contained in the Library of Congress is stolen from networks maintained by U.S. businesses, universities, and government agencies."

It is likely that the cost of economic espionage is many times higher than the number reported in 2003. U.S. national strength depends not only on military capabilities, but even more fundamentally on economic strength. Cyberexploitations now constitute a very serious national-security threat. Mandating surveillance capabilities in new communications technologies could greatly exacerbate that threat. As Congress considers how to respond to wiretapping needs of law enforcement, it is instructive to consider how the U.S. handled the related cryptography issue in the 1990s.

Mistakes the U.S. Made in the 1990s

The 1990s were the times of the "Crypto Wars," in which the U.S. government[6] effectively controlled the use of strong encryption domestically through export-control regulations. These regulations required an export license for products with strong cryptography[7] if the cryptography was being used to provide confidentiality. The regulations sharply dampened—if not completely closed off—the market for products with strong forms of cryptography. Few companies wanted to produce products that could not be exported, or that could be exported only if they were admittedly less secure than the version sold within the United States. The fear, uncertainty, and doubt surrounding the use of cryptography in systems—and the ability to export the resulting product—meant that developers often eschewed cryptographic solutions. And sometimes products that fell within the regulations could not be exported anyway.

An egregious example was a DNSSEC implementation. DNSSEC is an Internet protocol that helps ensure a user is getting to the right website (e.g., a real Bank of America website and not a spoofed one). The U.S. government thinks the security this provides is a good thing, and has pushed for adoption. Since 2009 all federal civilian agencies are required to deploy it (and the military intends to do the same). But in the 1990s the U.S. policy was confused.

Although export-control regulations were clear that products that used cryptography for authentication purposes—this was the case for DNSSEC—could be exported, when it was pointed out that the same cryptography could also be used for confidentiality purposes, permission to export the DNSSEC product was rescinded. U.S. government actions actively prevented the technology from shipping—a move counterproductive to U.S. security. Such actions meant that engineers and managers were unsure whether products using strong cryptography would be permitted for export—even if they met the rules. Rather than risk wasting time and money, the products were developed without the security measures. The result is that we're still paying for that weak security eleven years after the U.S. government changed its posture on cryptographic export controls, and, with some exceptions, permitted the export of products with strong cryptography. When that change occurred, it happened with the support of the National Security Agency (NSA).

The ultimate result of the export-control policies of the 1990s was a delayed deployment of security measures. The policy was very short sighted, buying the U.S. additional security during part of that decade, but at the cost of long-term insecurity for U.S. computer and communications infrastructure. Let's not repeat it.

It is essential that legal extensions of CALEA to IP-based communications not cause the same problems as the misguided cryptographic export-control regulations of the 1990s.

In this context, it is worth noting that in 2005 the NSA endorsed a full set of unclassified algorithms that may be used for securing a communications network. Clearly there is a conflict between communications intelligence and communications security—and the NSA is voting on the side of communications security.

Insecurities of Communications

When AT&T was the communications infrastructure, the communications network was centralized. Wiretaps were relatively easy to place—they went in the telephone central office, which held the switch closest to the subscriber—and also relatively easy to protect—for they were placed in the brick buildings that housed these switches. Turning on a wiretap meant having access to the switch. While one could wiretap an individual by placing alligator clips somewhere between the central office and the target's phone, one could not do wholesale wiretapping on a large group of people in that way.

The computer and communications revolution had a profound impact on communications surveillance. This revolution changed the paths through which communications traveled, changing how and where wiretaps could be placed, and changing the delivery mechanism for the surveillance. All of these changed the risks introduced by communications interception.

These same technological changes have also meant that communications surveillance itself creates insecurities. The switches that enable wiretapping allow remote access; this is standard operating procedure and is a CALEA requirement for phone networks. But such remote access can be used by others, and was, in fact, the basis for the illegal Greek Vodafone surveillance. One might expect that communications providers—ISPs, designers of new communications applications—could protect their systems even when wiretapping capabilities are built in, but this is unlikely to be the case. In the U.S., there are hundreds of communications providers, many of them very small (e.g., with fewer than one hundred employees). Companies producing new communications applications are similarly often small (e.g., start-ups with few employees). These providers lack the expertise and capability to fully secure their systems. Building secure software is hard.

Much more information traverses the network than when people communicated by point-to-point telephone calls. This exposure puts the nation at risk. Consider, for example, the fact that by studying the queries on influenza-like illnesses, Google Flu Trends was able to spot flu outbreaks two weeks ahead of the Center for Disease Control. However, unless we secure our communication nodes, others can look in too. In 1972, the Soviets were monitoring transmissions between the wheat traders and the U.S. Department of Agriculture, and were able to corner the wheat market because they knew more about our production than the U.S. government did. What if someone were monitoring communications to Google and determined that the U.S. was about to suffer a flu pandemic and used that information to corner the market for the flu vaccine? After all, communications to Google are not typically encrypted and could easily be wiretapped by rogue software at a communications switch.

Electronic Surveillance Policies That Hurt Competitiveness and National Security

As we contemplate new laws for enabling access to authorized surveillance, two things should be clear:

- Communications security should not be weakened by building in backdoors to facilitate surveillance;

- The computer and telecommunications environment should continue to support innovation.

The first is extremely difficult to achieve if laws require that methods be built into the system to accommodate authorized surveillance. By design, interception, legally authorized or not, breaks security. Ensuring that the interception architecture is correctly designed is very difficult. What makes the situation even worse is that failure has a high cost. If a Lockheed Martin or a Northrup Grumman fails to adequately secure its networks, the cost can be thousands of their proprietary files stolen. But if a communications switch or application is inadequately secured, that cost occurs for the millions of communications that utilize that switch or application.

Proposals have been floated that new Internet communications applications should be "wiretap vetted" prior to deployment. As I have already explained, building surveillance technologies into communications technology is a very risky business. It is very bad for competition. It is also very bad for innovation. One of the remarkable aspects of Internet innovation is how few resources are needed to develop a project. From Facebook, which started in 2004 with a handful of employees, to the newest Google communication application, speak-to-tweet—a combination of Twitter, Google, and SayNow that enables Twitter messages to be delivered through voicemail (and which was developed over a weekend in January to enable Egyptians to communicate during the time that Egypt cut connections to the Internet)—the Internet has enabled innovation to occur rapidly and with a minimum of resources. Two Stanford computer science graduate students with an idea on search, [and] a Harvard undergraduate with a thought about social networking—these are [innovators whose] ideas [. . .] rapidly and effectively launched technologies and companies in highly competitive environments.

It is important to realize that innovation is not exclusively an American phenomenon; it happens all across the planet. Skype was developed in Estonia for example. Requiring that Internet applications with communications systems—anything from speak-to-tweet to Second Life to software supporting music jam sessions—be vetted first will put American innovation at a global disadvantage. For American competitiveness it is critical that we preserve the ease and speed with which innovative new communications technologies can be developed. I do not need to tell you how crucial innovation is to our nation's long-term economic growth and security.

What is the Problem that Needs Solving?

Let me be clear. This is not an argument against wiretapping, which has proved invaluable in cases ranging from Aldrich Ames to Najibullah Zazi. This is an argument against building wholesale wiretapping capability into the core of our emerging and highly diverse communications infrastructure. To do so would be needlessly dangerous; it amounts to developing for our enemies capabilities they might not be able to build on their own—and capabilities that they may well use against us.

The critical national-security problem facing computers and telecommunications is not law enforcement's ability to conduct authorized surveillance; it is our lack of cybersecurity. It makes no sense to pursue wiretapping solutions that put U.S. cybersecurity at risk. This does not mean that we should not pursue solutions that enable legally authorized wiretaps, but that solutions to the current difficulties faced by law enforcement must not be solved in a manner that puts U.S. communications at serious risk of being eavesdropped upon by outside parties, whether criminals, non-state actors, or other nation states.

The issue is that the FBI and state and local enforcement have, on occasion, run into situations where new communications technologies have thwarted legally authorized wiretaps. The fundamental question is how we as a society should work to solve the problem. One solution proposed by law enforcement and implemented by CALEA for the public switched telephone network required that these technologies have wiretapping capabilities built into them. As the Greek Vodafone experience showed, that is a dangerous solution. Tom Cross showed how the same type of solution can also be dangerous for IP-based communications networks (such as those currently supporting Voice over IP).

CALEA applied to IP-based communications is a solution answering the wrong question. The issue is not how does law enforcement force the technology to provide wiretapping capability. The issue is how can law enforcement wiretap a communication using new technology? Changing focus enables us to see new solutions.

With the rapid technology innovation occurring in communications, the FBI needs to be entrepreneurial. Rather than making every component of the communications infrastructure vulnerable to intrusion, a lawful wiretapper could install carefully controlled equipment in select places for the specific duration and target of the wiretap—much like the physical taps that used to be placed on individual subscriber lines in a telephone central office.

In the new environment that law enforcement faces, law enforcement needs to be ahead of the game. Currently the FBI and local law enforcement are case-based agencies, and investigators tackle a new communications technology when it turns up in a case. It can be very difficult to develop the correct surveillance technology in time to aid an ongoing investigation. That approach is the wrong way to be doing things.

In particular, the bureau's surveillance skills need to be ahead technologically on new communications systems. The bureau is making these efforts in its "Going Dark" program. That is the right direction to pursue and it should be pursued with even greater vigor. I recommend that the bureau further augment its research arm so that it can learn about new communications technologies as they are being developed and deployed, and so it can determine ways to intercept communications over those technologies when there is legal authorization for an intercept. This is not a new recommendation. This was a recommendation made in 1996 by the National Research Council's report on cryptography policy[8]—a recommendation that was not followed at the time. It is good that the FBI has recently started the Going Dark program. I would like to see that program put a strong emphasis on technologists with advanced communications and communications surveillance training.

It is undoubtedly the case that proposing that the FBI expand a research branch studying new communications and surveillance technologies is a risky suggestion in these difficult economic times. But the fact is that communications interception costs, and if we don't pay one way, we will pay in another. If interception is imposed in a CALEA-like manner, the costs shift to communications providers. If interception is done by requiring that developers of new communications technologies work with the government to provide interception capabilities before deploying, the costs shift to the start-ups and developers—and will have high negative impact on innovation. So this proposal of a strengthened research arm may actually be in the end the most cost-effective way of accomplishing what needs to be done. More importantly, it is a way of enabling legally authorized surveillance capabilities without putting U.S. communications systems at risk by designing wiretapping capabilities into them.

Summing Up

Law enforcement has legitimate concerns about its continued ability to wiretap in the face of rapidly innovating communications technologies. But in an increasingly globalized and networked economy and with increasing cyberexploitations aimed at the U.S. government and U.S. industry, expanding surveillance capabilities into communications applications and infrastructure is a dangerous step. Rather than strengthening the

U.S., such a direction would create long-term national-security risks. It would provide for our enemies that which they might not be able to build for themselves: a ready-made system for wiretapping U.S. domestic communications.

By augmenting the FBI's research into interception technologies, the U.S. would accomplish several important societal goals:

- We would preserve law enforcement's capability to conduct legally authorized interceptions.

- We would continue to have the U.S. be a welcoming environment for computer and telecommunications innovation.

- We would work towards the goal of increased cybersecurity, rather than undermining it.

I agree that with the new communications technologies, there is a need for law-enforcement access to legally authorized surveillance. But it must be done in a way that does not undermine U.S. values or U.S. national security. If we take the approach that I am proposing, then not only will costs likely be lower—developing technology in a hurry is always likely to cost more—but the protection provided will be better, and most importantly, it will be without the risks coincident without further extending CALEA mandates to the Internet environment.

Thank you very much. I would be happy to take questions.

NOTES

1. Additional biographical information relevant to the subject matter to the hearing: Prior to being at the Radcliffe Institute, I was a distinguished engineer at Sun Microsystems. At Sun I was involved in issues related to cryptography and export control, security and privacy of federated identity management systems, and in developing our policy stance in digital rights management. I serve on the National Research

Council Computer Science and Telecommunications Board and on the advisory committee for the National Science Foundation's Directorate for Computer and Information Science and Engineering. I also served for six years on the National Institute of Standards and Technology's Information Security and Privacy Advisory Board and was a member of the Commission on Cyber Security for the 44th Presidency. I hold a PhD in theoretical computer science from MIT.

2. Vassilis Prevelakis and Diomidis Spinellis, "The Athens Affair," *IEEE Spectrum*, July 2007 at 18–25.

3. Piero Colaprico, "Da Telecom dossier sui Ds Mancini parla dei politici," *La Repubblica*, January 26, 2007.

4. Tom Cross, "Exploiting Lawful Intercept to Wiretap the Internet," Black Hat DC 2010, February 2010.

5. Louis Freeh, Testimony, Joint Hearing of the Technology and Law Subcommittee of the Senate Judiciary Committee and the Civil and Constitutional Rights Subcommittee of the House Judiciary Committee. Subject: wiretapping. Witness: FBI Director Louis Freeh. March 18, 1994.

6. In fact the effort to control encryption was entirely through the executive branch. Congress introduced a number of bills to liberalize the cryptographic export-control regulations, and the loosening that occurred in 2000 may have happened partially because of bills being considered in Congress at the time.

7. Strong cryptography is a sliding term meaning those types of cryptography that are difficult to break with current technology. In the early 1990s, 56-bit DES constituted strong cryptography, but by the end of the decade, a $250,000 special-purpose machine built by the Electronic Frontier Foundation was able to decode a message encrypted with 56-bit DES in a matter of hours, and the system was no longer considered strong.

8. Kenneth Damand Herbert S. Lin, eds., *Cryptography's Role in Securing the Information Society*, National Academy Press, at 333–335.

*Susan Landau is a fellow at the Radcliffe Institute for Advanced Study, Harvard University.

Testimony of Susan Landau. "Going Dark: Lawful Electronic Surveillance in the Face of New Technologies." U.S. Congress. House of Representatives. Hearing before the Committee of the Judiciary, Subcommittee on Crime, Terrorism and Homeland Security, 112th Congress, 2011.

'Going Dark' Versus a 'Golden Age for Surveillance'

by Peter Swire and Kenesa Ahmad*

This post is part of "CDT Fellows Focus,"[1] a series that presents the views of notable experts on tech policy issues. This week, Peter Swire, the C. William O'Neill Professor of Law at the Moritz College of Law of the Ohio State University, and Kenesa Ahmad, Legal and Policy Associate with the Future of Privacy Forum, are our guest contributors. This post is based on an excerpt from their paper "Encryption and Globalization," which is available online[2] and will be published in final form by the Columbia Science and Technology Law Review. Their full article analyzes developments in encryption law and policy since the United States permitted export of strong encryption in 1999. The article explains why strong encryption should be encouraged globally, in contrast to current regulatory limits on effective encryption in India, China, and other countries. Posts featured in "CDT Fellows Focus" don't necessarily reflect the views of CDT; the goal of the series is to present diverse, well-informed views on significant tech policy issues.

Law enforcement and national security agencies are worried that they are "going dark" due to new technology. Their fear is that they will not be able to wiretap and decode new forms of Internet and other communications. This concern is correct in certain respects. In some instances, agencies do lose access to categories of information they previously relied upon.

This post, however, argues that "going dark" is the wrong image. Instead, today should be understood as a "golden age of surveillance." Compared with earlier periods, surveillance capabilities have greatly expanded. Consider three areas where law enforcement has far greater capabilities than ever before: (1) location information; (2) information about contacts and confederates; and (3) an array of new databases that create "digital dossiers" about individuals' lives. This information about any individual suspect is made even more useful because of the way data mining can help identify suspects.

The battle between the images of darkness and light is important. If the overall truth were that agencies are "going dark," then legislatures and agencies would have an important argument for expanding surveillance powers. On the other hand, careful review of the facts shows that we do live in a "golden age of surveillance." Skepticism should accompany agency requests for new powers. Our current research, and this post, explains why we should be skeptical about the bad encryption rules being instituted in India, China, and other nations around the world. We are undertaking ongoing research on encryption, lawful access, and globalization. More broadly, the existence of a "golden age of surveillance" supports efforts such as the Digital Due Process Coalition[3], which is seeking to reinstitute protections for our communications and personal data in our modern networked environment.

The "Going Dark" Problem

Law enforcement and national security agencies object to the use of strong encryption in electronic communications for one main reason: The agencies are losing some surveillance capabilities they previously relied upon. Wiretaps and relatively easy access to stored records have historically been important tools for these agencies. When strong encryption is used to secure emails or mobile phone calls, agencies can access the communications but are unable to decipher their encrypted forms. If agencies gain access to encrypted laptops or other forms of encrypted data at rest, the lawful interception process is similarly frustrated.

In 2011 testimony, FBI General Counsel Valerie Caproni described the problem: "We call this capabilities gap the 'Going Dark' problem. As the gap between authority and capability widens, the government is increasingly unable to collect valuable evidence in cases ranging from child exploitation and pornography to organized crime and drug trafficking to terrorism and espionage—evidence that a court has authorized the government to collect."

"Going dark" is an evocative and compelling image. The phrase invites us to imagine communications shrouded in darkness—cloaked in encryption—so that the eyes of the agency are blind. Although we may want justice to be "blind" in order to achieve impartiality, we surely do not want our police to be blind.

In the 1990's, the "going dark" argument was often made by the FBI and NSA, although the term itself was not widely used. In 1994, the Communications for Law Enforcement Act was passed to address FBI concerns that the shift from copper wires to fiber optics made traditional phone wiretaps less useful. The NSA's ability to collect communications was threatened during this period as a greater proportion of international calls shifted from radio communications (often easy to intercept by the agency) to fiber optic cables (generally easy to intercept only at a switch controlled by a telecommunications company).

Coupled with the rapid development and widespread availability of strong encryption, the agencies faced the likelihood that many communications would not be as readily accessible as before.

Despite these risks, in 1999 the U.S. government decided to embrace the use of strong encryption. Arguments in favor of Internet security, civil liberties, and international trade prevailed over the surveillance agencies' objections. The government ultimately recognized the private sector's need for and dependence on strong encryption, and identified the inherent value in using strong encryption for law enforcement and national security purposes. Despite losing what were termed the "crypto wars," important agency concerns were addressed. The FBI received enhanced funding for its technical capabilities, and this funding has continued to grow over time. Together, government and industry leaders worked to develop the system of public-private partnership that continues today, in which industry experts meet with the government about encryption and technology for the carrying out of lawful intercepts.

Today as a "Golden Age for Surveillance"

The Internet and the advancement of IP-based communications present new obstacles to lawful interception. At the same time, these developments provide law enforcement and national security agencies with powerful new surveillance capabilities. The discussion here highlights three areas where law enforcement has far greater capabilities than ever before: (1) location information; (2) information about contacts and confederates; and (3) an array of new databases that create "digital dossiers" about individuals' lives. This information about any individual suspect is made even more useful because of the way data mining can help identify suspects.

We are in a new age where most people carry a tracking device, the mobile phone. Location information comes standard with a wireless network—the phone company needs to know where your phone is to send you the call. A specific cell handles the call, so the network knows what cell you are in. Location information is tremendously useful for law enforcement and national security agencies. It can put a suspect at the scene of a crime, or establish an alibi. It can act as a "bug" without the need for the agency to place a bug on the suspect's person or property.

The precise rules for storing this location data vary by jurisdiction and wireless carrier. In many instances, though, the routine practice is that location data is stored for a significant period of time. Carriers in the U.S. are subject to data preservation orders, so location information on known suspects is retained once a proper agency request has been made. The number of requests from law enforcement for such location information has climbed sharply in recent years according to statistics in the U.S.

It is true that the cautious suspect can try to avoid this location tracking by using a prepaid cellphone or not carrying the phone when doing criminal activities. Some countries have placed limits on non-identified mobile phones, however, and the suspect has to worry that his or her confederates will show up at a meeting carrying their regular mobile phones. More generally, a tremendous number of people now carry cell phones as they go through their daily lives. Location information thus becomes available for surveillance purposes in ways never before possible.

Information about a suspect['s] or witness' confederates is the second category of information newly available in rich detail to the agencies. For many investigations, *who* is called is at least as important as *what* is said in the call. The investigator gets leads on whom else to investigate and can follow those leads to the contact's contacts, and so on.

The importance of confederates has become famous in social networking. The term "social graph" was coined, in connection with social networks to describe the phenomenon of "the global mapping of everybody and how they're related."[4] For investigatory agencies, mapping everybody and how they are related is extremely useful. Social networking sites themselves will become an increasingly important source of investigatory material in coming years. The phenomenon is much broader, however:

- A generation ago, long-distance phone calls were expensive, and international calls a rare event in most people's lives. As costs have plummeted, the volume of local, long-distance, and international calls has grown dramatically. Calling records show the "to/from" information for calls already made, pen register orders reveal who a person is calling, and trap-and-trace orders show who is calling the person. The number of such orders in the U.S. has climbed sharply.

- The explosion of mobile phone use has supplemented the rise in wireline calls, and mobile use continues to increase rapidly. India, for instance, is showing an astonishing 17 million new wirelines per month in 2011.

- E-mails have become a pervasive feature of life for many people. The emergence of global web mail providers including Gmail and Hotmail gives investigatory agencies the convenience of serving many lawful requests to a small number of providers.

- The rise of unlimited text messaging plans in many jurisdictions provides numerous clues about a person's key confederates, and the time and date of their communications.

- VOIP (voice over Internet Protocol) calls are growing rapidly. Skype was sold to Microsoft for $8.5 billion in 2011. Even for calls whose content is encrypted, Skype connects the callers and the "to/from" information is subject to legal process.

These wireline calls, wireless calls, e-mails, texts, VOIP calls, and social networking records are treasure troves of information for investigatory agencies. In the bygone era of face-to-face communications, no trace was usually left regarding whom a suspect had talked with. Today, by contrast, an individual would need to abstain from many everyday activities to prevent the government from obtaining information about his or her contacts. The identity of those contacts helps lead investigators to additional targets of interest, thereby painting a broader and more precise picture of potential criminal or national security activity.

Information about location and a person's confederates, in turn, are simply examples of the larger trend towards detailed personal records. Consider the amount of information stored on an individual's personal computer. A standard laptop today often holds many gigabytes of data, more than a mainframe computer held 20 years ago. If the government obtains access to an individual's personal computer, it is highly likely that the computer will reveal detailed and diverse records about the person's life. The records retained on that computer, in turn, are only a small subset of the records stored on other computers—banks, hospitals, online advertisers, data brokers, government agencies, and other record holders possess exponentially more detailed data on individuals than in the past. Although a few people attempt to live "off the grid," this is not a feasible option for the vast majority of citizens in developed countries. Once an individual is identified as a target, the government—via lawful process—can access detailed information specific to that individual.

We live in a "golden age for surveillance" because investigatory agencies have unprecedented access to information about a suspect. In addition, data mining provides unprecedented tools for identifying suspects.

Choosing Between "Going Dark" and "A Golden Age for Surveillance"

This post argues that the big picture for agency access to data is mostly "golden." The loss of agency access to information, due to encryption, is more than offset by surveillance gains from computing and communications technology. In addition, government encryption regulation harms cybersecurity. These conclusions will not be easily accepted by investigatory agencies, however, so it is important to work through the analysis in more detail.

Communications that were previously subject to wiretap may now be shrouded in encryption. In place of the old monopoly telephone network, agencies have to contend with a confusing variety of communications providers, some of which have little experience in complying with legal process. It is no wonder agency officials strenuously object to the use of new technology that hinders their ability to employ traditional surveillance methods.

Implementing wiretaps and reading the plain text of communications are not the only goal, however. The computing and communications infrastructure are vital to economic growth, individual creativity, government operations, and numerous other goals. If there is a modest harm to investigatory agencies and an enormous gain, societies should choose the enormous gain. In 1999 the U.S. government concluded that strong encryption was precisely that sort of valuable technology—it was worth going at least slightly "dark" in order reap the many benefits of effective encryption. Not even the attacks of September 11, 2001 changed that judgment.

The evidence suggests, furthermore, that the degradation of wiretap capability has been modest at most, and—at least statistically—wiretaps have become more useful over time. The number of wiretap orders implemented in the U.S. has grown steadily the last two decades. According to publically available statistics, court-approved wiretaps are now at a record high: 3,194 wiretap court orders were issued for the interception of electronic, wire, or oral communications in 2010, a 34% increase from the 2,376 issued in 2009. In the six instances where encryption was encountered, it did not prevent law enforcement from retrieving the plain text forms of communication.

These numbers actually understate the expansion of wiretapping in the U.S., in part due to the shift to "roving" wiretaps. In earlier years, separate court orders were required for each device used by the target of an investigation. Over time, however, Congress authorized roving wiretaps so that one wiretap order could apply to all the devices used by a suspect. Additionally, wiretaps were authorized by investigation, rather than for each individual target within an investigation. This means that the statistics understate the growth in actual use of wiretaps.

What explains the agencies' sense of loss when the use of wiretaps has expanded, encryption has not been an important obstacle, and agencies have gained new location, contact, and other information? One answer comes from behavioral economics and psychology, which has drawn academic attention to concepts such as "loss aversion" and the "endowment effect." "Loss aversion" refers to the tendency to prefer avoiding losses to acquiring gains of similar value. This concept also helps explain the "endowment effect"—the theory that people place higher value on goods they own versus comparable goods they do not own. Applied to surveillance, the idea is that agencies feel the loss of one technique more than they feel an equal-sized gain from other techniques. Whether based on the language of behavioral economics or simply on common sense, we are familiar with the human tendency to "pocket our gains"—assume we deserve the good things that come our way, but complain about the bad things, even if the good things are more important.

A simple test can help the reader decide between the "going dark" and "golden age of surveillance" hypotheses. Suppose the agencies had a choice of a 1990-era package or a 2011-era package. The first package would include the wiretap authorities as they existed pre-encryption, but would lack the new techniques for location tracking, confederate identification, access to multiple databases, and data mining. The second package would match current capabilities: some encryption-related obstacles, but increased use of wiretaps, as well as the capabilities for location tracking, confederate tracking, and data mining. The second package is clearly superior—the new surveillance tools assist a vast range of investigations, whereas wiretaps apply only to a small subset of key investigations. The new tools are used far more frequently and provide granular data to assist investigators.

Conclusion

This post casts new light on government agency claims that we are "going dark." Due to changing technology, there are indeed specific ways that law enforcement and national security agencies lose specific previous capabilities. These specific losses, however, are more than offset by massive gains. Public debates should recognize that we are truly in a golden age of surveillance. By understanding that, we can reject calls for bad encryption policy. More generally, we should critically assess a wide range of proposals, and build a more secure computing and communications infrastructure.

[. . .]

LINKS

1. http://cdt.org/cdt-fellows-focus
2. http://papers.ssrn.com/sol3/papers.cfm?abstract_id=1960602
3. http://digitaldueprocess.org/index.cfm?objectid=37940370-2551-11DF-8E02000C296BA163
4. http://www.cbsnews.com/stories/2010/04/21/tech/main6418458.shtml
5. https://twitter.com/#%21/CenDemTech

*Peter P. Swire is the C. William O'Neill Professor of Law at the Moritz College of Law of The Ohio State University.

Kenesa Ahmad is a fellow at the Future of Privacy Forum.

Swire, Peter, and Kenesa Ahmad. "'Going Dark' Versus a 'Golden Age for Surveillance.'" November 28, 2011. Center for Democracy & Technology. https://www.cdt.org/blogs/2811going-dark-versus-golden-age-surveillance.

Copyright © 2012 by Center for Democracy & Technology.

Used by permission.

PART 5:

Locational Tracking

Advances in technology have led to a radical change in the ability to track the location of individuals. Ten or fifteen years ago, GPS technology was largely used by a few government agencies, not the general public. Today, a large portion of Americans own mobile phones with GPS capability. We carry these devices everywhere—they have become an integral part of our everyday lives. These devices can track our every movement. Although mobile phone location data at any given moment are not especially revealing, when linked with past location information, the data provide details of where we have been and, accordingly, what we may have been doing.

Both the Supreme Court and Congress have begun to address the issues surrounding locational tracking. In the 2012 case of

U.S. v. Jones, the Court ruled that law enforcement must obtain a search warrant before using a GPS device to track vehicles of criminal suspects. However, the decision did not address whether search warrants are necessary for tracking individuals in other ways, e.g., with cell phone location data. In response to these concerns, Congress considered passing the Geolocational Privacy and Surveillance Act (GPS Act) in 2011. Had it been passed, the bill would have governed the circumstances under which law enforcement, commercial entities, and private parties can lawfully access and obtain locational data about individuals.

Use of GPS tools makes the tracking of individuals suspected of criminal activity much more efficient and precise. Accordingly, locational tracking draws significant support from law enforcement officials. Formerly, suspect tracking required constant patrolling. Now officers can use a GPS device to monitor suspects, thus conserving manpower and reducing expenses. Locational information is especially important in time-sensitive cases, when getting a warrant can slow a criminal investigation. For an entirely different reason, prison reform advocates support the use of GPS to track criminals as an alternative to house arrest or prison. Such use helps keep costs of incarceration down.

Privacy advocates fiercely oppose the unwarranted and pervasive use of locational data. They contend that unrestricted government tracking threatens core civil liberties, including those protected by the Fourth Amendment. Without judicial oversight, individuals are afforded weak protection against extensive and prolonged government surveillance. The sensitive nature of locational information is especially susceptible to abuse. For example, without appropriate restrictions, the government could target minorities or other groups. Other issues include: Should parents be permitted to track their children?

Should administrators be able to track students on and off school premises?

In this section, Richard M. Thompson II provides an overview of *U.S. v. Jones* and explores how the ruling may apply to situations where law enforcement uses different forms of locational surveillance not addressed in the ruling. Judge Joseph I. Cassilly maintains that the standards of the proposed GPS Act requiring law enforcement to obtain a warrant for location tracking would slow criminal investigations. On the opposing side, Catherine Crump argues that warrant requirements under the GPS Act are necessary to protect our constitutional right to privacy. Graeme Wood maintains that locational surveillance is a useful, just, and cost-effective method to monitor convicted criminals. Finally, Andrew J. Blumberg and Peter Eckersley argue that the pervasive nature of new technology poses a serious threat to our locational privacy.

As you read the materials in this section, think about the following questions:

1. Under what circumstances is it acceptable for the government to track your location? Should the government be limited in its ability to do so and for what reasons?

2. Under what circumstances is it not acceptable for the government to track your location? Is locational tracking invasive of privacy or is it necessary for public safety?

3. Does the form of locational tracking matter? Should standards and limitations be the same regardless of what tracking technology is used?

United States v. Jones: GPS Monitoring, Property, and Privacy

by Richard M. Thompson II*

Summary

In *United States v. Jones*, 132 S. Ct. 945 (2012), all nine Supreme Court Justices agreed that Jones was *searched* when the police attached a Global Positioning System (GPS) device to the undercarriage of his car and tracked his movements for four weeks. The Court, however, splintered on what constituted the search: the attachment of the device or the long-term monitoring. The majority held that the *attachment* of the GPS device and an attempt to obtain information was the violation; Justice Alito, concurring, argued that the *monitoring* was a violation of Jones's reasonable expectation of privacy; and Justice Sotomayor, also concurring, agreed with them both, but would provide further Fourth Amendment protections. This report will examine these three decisions in an effort to find their place in the body of existing Fourth Amendment law pertaining to privacy, property, and technology.

In *Jones*, the police attached a GPS tracking device to the bottom of Jones's car and monitored his movements for 28 days. At trial, the prosecution relied on Jones's movements to a stash house to tie him to a drug conspiracy. Jones was convicted and given a life sentence. The United States Court of Appeals for the District of Columbia Circuit reversed, holding that the evidence was unlawfully obtained under the Fourth Amendment. The Supreme Court agreed. The majority, speaking through Justice Scalia, explained that a physical intrusion into a constitutionally protected area, coupled with an attempt to obtain information, can constitute a violation of the Fourth Amendment. Although the Court's landmark decision in *Katz v. United States*, 389 U.S. 347 (1967), supposedly altered the focus of the Fourth Amendment from property to privacy, the majority argued that it left untouched traditional spheres of Fourth Amendment protection—a person and his house, papers, and effects. Because the police had invaded Jones's property—his car, which is an *effect*—that was all the Court needed to hold that a constitutional search had occurred.

The majority's test, however, provides little guidance in instances where the government need not physically install a device to conduct surveillance, for instance, by using cell phones or preinstalled GPS devices in vehicles. To understand how the Court may rule on these technologies, one must look to the two concurrences, which provide a more global interpretation of the Fourth Amendment. Justice Alito, writing for a four-member concurrence, would have applied the *Katz* privacy formulation, asserting that longer-term monitoring constitutes an invasion of privacy, whereas short-term monitoring does not. He left it to future courts to distinguish between the two. Justice Sotomayor's concurrence appears to provide the most protection, finding that both the trespass approach and the privacy-based approach should be utilized. She also questioned the rule that any information provided to a third party, which occurs in many commercial transactions like banking or computing, should lose all privacy protections.

Although all three opinions concluded that the government's action in *Jones* was a search, none expressly required that police get a warrant in future GPS tracking cases. (The government forfeited the argument.) Further, there is no clear indication of the level of suspicion—probable cause, reasonable suspicion, or something less—that is required to attach a GPS unit and monitor the target's movements. Additionally, there have been several bills filed in the 112th Congress, including Senator Patrick J. Leahy's Electronic Communications Privacy Act Amendment Act of 2011 (S. 1011) and Senator Ron Wyden's and Representative Jason Chaffetz's identical legislation, S. 1212 and H.R. 2168, the Geolocational Privacy and Surveillance Act (GPS bill), that would require a warrant based upon probable cause to access geolocation information.

Introduction

There is little doubt that technology is fast becoming intertwined with our jobs, our social life, and even our most private interactions with each other. This phenomenon creates friction among many compelling interests. The first is a clash between two contrasting values: the desire for privacy and the longing to be connected through the newest and most advanced technology. To a certain extent, as one advances, the other must necessarily recede. Meanwhile, courts are tasked with determining the balance between government's law enforcement needs and the people's privacy. The Fourth Amendment to the U.S. Constitution provides the measuring stick to determine this balance. The amendment ensures "[t]he right of the people to be secure in their persons, houses, papers, and effects, against unreasonable searches and seizures, shall not be violated."[1] Its primary function is to prohibit government intrusion upon the privacy and property rights of the people. When new technology is involved, achieving this balance is not an easy undertaking.

United States v. Jones presented such a challenge to the Supreme Court. The question posed was whether the installation and month-long monitoring of a GPS device attached to Jones's car constituted a violation of the Fourth Amendment's prohibition against "unreasonable searches and seizures."[2] This usage of the Global Positioning System (GPS)[3] is not unusual in criminal investigations,[4] but up to that point longer-term monitoring had not been directly tested by the Court. Thus, many observers awaited the *Jones* ruling for its potential impact not only on government monitoring programs, but also on general Fourth Amendment cases involving prolonged government surveillance.

In prior government tracking cases,[5] the Court applied the test from *Katz v. United States*, which addresses whether the individual had a reasonable expectation of privacy in the area to be searched.[6] Because the police in *Jones* physically invaded his property to attach the GPS device—whereas in the previous cases they had not—the Court declined to apply *Katz*, but instead based its decision on a trespass theory.[7] The trespass theory asks whether there was a physical intrusion onto a constitutionally protected area coupled with an attempt to obtain information.[8] In *Jones*, there was, so the Court applied this more limited test and held that a search occurred. Though the majority bypassed the *Katz* approach, Justice Alito, concurring with Justices Breyer, Ginsburg, and Kagan, would have applied *Katz*.[9] Long-term surveillance, Justice Alito wrote, violated Jones's reasonable expectation of privacy under *Katz*. Justice Sotomayor agreed with both the majority and Alito's concurrence, but called for additional protection by questioning the viability of the third-party doctrine, which holds that any information voluntarily given to a third party loses all privacy protections.[10]

This report will analyze all three opinions in an attempt to determine how *Jones* might affect future use of GPS tracking and other government surveillance techniques. First, it will briefly recount the facts that led to Jones's prosecution, his appeal, and the Supreme Court's review. Next, it will analyze the majority's property-based test, evaluating it against similar Fourth Amendment case law. Additionally, this section will raise issues concerning the possible impact of this approach on similar search and seizure cases. Next, the report will examine both Justice Alito's and Justice Sotomayor's concurrences and their potential impact on cases involving technology. Because the Court did not express whether a warrant is required, the report will posit several theories on how this issue may be resolved in the future.

United States v. Jones: A Property-Based Approach to the Fourth Amendment

In 2004, a Joint Task Force of the FBI and the District of Columbia Metropolitan Police Department suspected Antoine Jones was part of a drug distribution ring.[11] Based on information obtained from wiretaps, a pen register,[12] and video surveillance, the task force obtained a warrant to monitor Jones's Jeep with a GPS tracking device. According to the terms of the warrant, the officers had 10 days to install it and were required to do it in the District of Columbia. The officers installed the device on the 11th day in Maryland while the Jeep was parked in a public parking lot.[13] For the next four weeks the device tracked Jones's every movement, creating 2,000 pages of monitoring data.[14] During this time, the device tracked Jones's movements to and from a known stash house.

Jones was indicted for conspiracy to distribute and possession with intent to distribute cocaine. At trial, the prosecution relied heavily on Jones's movements derived from the GPS to connect him with a larger drug ring.[15] He moved to dismiss this information as a warrantless search under the Fourth Amendment. The United States District Court for the District of Columbia excluded the data derived when his car was parked in his garage but allowed into evidence all of his public movements.[16] Jones was ultimately convicted and sentenced to life imprisonment.[17] The United States Court of Appeals for the District of Columbia Circuit reversed, holding that the GPS data were derived in violation of Jones's reasonable expectation of privacy under the Fourth Amendment.[18] The Supreme Court then granted a writ of certiorari, agreeing to review Jones's case.

Most observers assumed the Supreme Court would, like the D.C. Circuit Court of Appeals, apply the reasonable expectation of privacy test developed in *Katz v. United States* to determine if the tracking was a Fourth Amendment search. Under the *Katz* test, a search in the constitutional sense has occurred if the individual had an actual expectation of privacy in the area to be searched that society would deem reasonable.[19] Since 1967, when *Katz* was handed down, the Court had developed a body of case law applying this privacy-based formulation of the Fourth Amendment.[20]

The *Jones* majority, led by Justice Scalia, took a different route.[21] It held that the *attachment* of the GPS device, coupled with its use to monitor Jones's movements, was a constitutional search.[22] The Fourth Amendment ensures that "[t]he right of the people to be secure in their persons, houses, papers, and effects, against unreasonable searches and seizures, shall not be violated."[23] Because Jones's vehicle is an *effect*—listed in the text of the Fourth Amendment—the police's physical intrusion by attaching the GPS for tracking purposes constituted a *search*.[24] This theory hinges on common law trespass as it was known in 1791 (when the Fourth Amendment was adopted). It does not rely on *Katz*, nor any subjective conception of privacy. The majority contended that Jones's rights should not strictly depend on whether his reasonably expected zone of privacy was pierced.[25] Rather, the majority asserted, property rights also define an individual's right to be free from government intrusion.

[. . .]

The Implications of *Jones* and Technology

As more cell phones and cars are outfitted with GPS tracking technologies, police need not physically attach a device to track its movements. Because the *Jones* majority opinion is based on a *physical* trespass into a constitutionally protected area, it seemingly will not apply where GPS is preinstalled. Justices Alito, and his four-Justice concurrence, and Sotomayor, concurring separately, provide insight into how a future court may apply the Fourth Amendment to evolving technologies.[50] These opinions rely, to a certain extent, on the mosaic theory first discussed in the D.C. Circuit opinion, which says that tracking a person's public movements over a long duration is constitutionally unacceptable even if tracking each of the movements individually may be permitted. Whether this approach will garner a majority on the Court is unclear. However, at a minimum, these concurrences have engendered discussion in the lower courts, with several courts citing the mosaic theory as a viable alternative.[51]

The question then becomes how much weight should the Alito and Sotomayor concurring opinions be accorded?[52] There is no *one* rule to answer this question.[53] Generally, there are two types of concurrences in Supreme Court opinions. The first is the true concurrence, in which the Justice concurs in the judgment, but disagrees with the reasoning.[54] Justice Alito's opinion exemplifies that type of concurrence; he agreed that the surveillance constituted a Fourth Amendment search, but would have decided the case under the traditional reasonable expectation of privacy test instead of the trespass test. The second category is the simple concurrence, where the Justice agrees with the judgment and the reasoning of the majority,[55] but also poses possible new theories that may not be directly relevant to that particular case, but can be used later to move the law in a particular direction.[56] Justice Sotomayor's opinion seems to fit this latter category. Although these two concurrences chart somewhat different courses in their strategy and reasoning, when combined they appear to command five votes on the Court—a potential majority.[57]

[...]

Warrant Requirement after *Jones*

All nine Justices agreed that tracking a person for four months is a constitutional search. Where there is little agreement among Court observers, though, is what level of suspicion is required to conduct GPS monitoring or whether a warrant is required.[96]

Because the government failed to argue that a warrant was not required or that something less than probable cause would be enough to conduct this surveillance, the Court considered the arguments forfeited.[97] Thus, to determine if a warrant or something less will be required in future cases, general Fourth Amendment principles must suffice until the courts provide further guidance.

The "ultimate touchstone" of the Fourth Amendment is reasonableness, as required by the history and text of the prohibition against "unreasonable searches and seizures."[98] That is to say, once a court determines a *search* has occurred, it must then inquiry whether it was reasonable. In most instances, the Supreme Court has required the government to obtain a warrant based upon probable cause for a search to be considered reasonable.[99] A review of the cases, however, shows that this rule is not ironclad, and that the exceptions are commonplace.[100]

Some commentators argue that the automobile exception could apply to the use of a GPS tracking device.[101] The automobile exception—one of the warrantless search exceptions—evolved from the exigency requirement.[102] It was first formulated in the 1925 case of *Carroll v. United States*, in which the Court permitted the police, who had probable cause to suspect that the defendant's car was carrying bootlegged liquor, to conduct a warrantless vehicle search.[103] The Court noted that it was not practicable to obtain a warrant for evidence secreted on a "ship, motor boat, wagon or automobile" because the vehicle can be "quickly moved out of the locality or jurisdiction."[104] In later cases, the Court developed a second rationale for the automobile exception, reasoning that drivers have a diminished expectation of privacy when in their vehicles.[105] This is based on the notion that cars travel on public thoroughfares where the driver and occupants are in plain view of the public.[106] Further, cars and drivers alike are subject to extensive government regulation,[107] and vehicles must undergo periodic inspections.[108]

As noted in *Carroll*, because a vehicle can be moved quickly from the jurisdiction, requiring a warrant to attach a GPS device may not be feasible.[109] Also, tracking someone's public movements may not be as invasive as searching through a person's belongings as is currently permitted under the traditional automobile exception.[110] On the reverse side, police will generally know in advance when they intend to use a GPS device, thereby negating the presumed exigency that is linked with cars. A court could hold that warrants are generally required for GPS devices, unless a true exigency existed beyond that presumed in general automobile cases, for example, in a case of kidnapping or a fleeing suspect.

Additionally, some commentators believe that the general reasonableness standard may apply, vitiating a need for a warrant.[111] These theories suppose that the intrusion on the individual is minimal and the government interest significant. In line with this reasoning, one observer posited that a *Terry*-type standard would be sufficient—that is, that the police must have reasonable suspicion to conduct a search, but need neither probable cause nor a warrant.[112] A court would review the reasonableness after the fact, unlike warrants, where the review comes before the search.

Conclusion

Nine Justices are seemingly in agreement that, based on the facts of *Jones*, the attachment of a GPS device to the bottom of Jones's car and tracking him for a month-long period was a constitutional search. Presented with a different set of facts, the Court's unanimity may disintegrate. For instance, if the police need not attach the device, but it is preinstalled, for example, in a cell phone or a navigation system in a car, the outcome may differ. Further, even though this surveillance was considered a search, the Court gave no guidance on whether a warrant is required or what quantum of suspicion is enough to use GPS monitoring.

That said, it is within the power of Congress or state legislatures to propose their own requirements. The federal Constitution sets the minimum constitutional standard. Legislatures (state or federal) may create more protection of privacy and property. Congress has done this on several occasions, most notably in the field of communications with the wiretap statutes.[113] When technology is in flux, one may argue that the institutional capabilities of a legislature may be the better venue to develop these rules.[114] Justice Alito suggested this approach in his *Jones* concurrence: "In circumstances involving dramatic technological change, the best solution to privacy concerns may be legislative. A legislative body is well situated to gauge changing public attitudes, to draw detailed lines, and to balance privacy and public safety in a comprehensive way."[115]

There has been legislative activity in recent Congresses to update privacy laws to cover new technologies such as GPS. Senator Leahy has introduced the Electronic Communications Privacy Act Amendments Act of 2011 (S. 1011), which would prohibit the government from accessing or using a device to acquire geolocation information, unless it obtains a warrant based upon probable cause or a court order under Title I or Title IV of the Foreign Intelligence Surveillance Act (FISA) of 1978.[116] Similarly, Senator Ron Wyden and Representative Jason Chaffetz have introduced identical legislation, S. 1212 and H.R. 2168, entitled the Geolocational Privacy and Surveillance Act, or GPS bill, which would make it unlawful for law enforcement to intercept or use a person's location unless they obtained a warrant based upon probable cause or one of the limited exceptions applied.[117]

With each advance in technology, the courts and Congress are asked to balance a host of competing interests including privacy, property, technology, and the needs of law enforcement. It will take future cases and statutes to better delineate a proper balance.

NOTES

1. U.S. Const. amend. IV.

2. United States v. Jones, 132 S. Ct. 945, 948 (2012).

3. GPS is a network of 24 government satellites that constantly send out radio signals and allow a receiver on Earth to determine its position. Aaron Renenger, *Satellite Tracking and the Right to Privacy*, 53 HASTINGS L. J. 549, 550 (2002).

4. John Ganz, *It's Already Public: Why Federal Officers Should Not Need Warrants to Use GPS Vehicle Tracking Devices*, 95 CRIM. L. & CRIMINOLOGY 1325, 1330 (2005).

5. United States v. Knotts, 460 U.S. 276, 278–79 (1983) (holding that use of tracking device while suspect was on public thoroughfares was not a violation of the Fourth Amendment as he had no reasonable expectation of privacy in his public movements); United States v. Karo, 468 U.S. 705, 718 (1984) (holding that use of tracking device while in private home was a violation of the Fourth Amendment).

6. This reasonable expectation of privacy test was formulated by Justice Harlan in his *Katz* concurrence. Katz v. United States, 389 U.S. 347, 361 (1967) (Harlan, J., concurring).

7. *Jones*, 132 S. Ct. at 952.

8. *Id.* at 951 n.5.

9. *Id.* at 958 (Alito, J., concurring).

10. *Id.* at 957 (Sotomayor, J., concurring).

11. *Id.* at 948.

12. A pen register is a device that determines the outgoing telephone numbers dialed from a telephone. 18 U.S.C.§ 3127(3).

13. Since the device was attached one day late and in the wrong jurisdiction, the installation was considered warrantless.

14. *Id.*

15. *Id.* at 948–49.

16. United States v. Jones, 451 F. Supp. 2d 71, 88 (D. D.C. 2006).

17. *Jones*, 132 S. Ct. at 949.

18. United States v. Maynard, 615 F.3d 544, 555 (D.C. Cir. 2010). Because Jones's case was consolidated with other codefendants on appeal, it was entitled *United States v. Maynard* before the D.C. Circuit Court of Appeals. It was subsequently changed back to *United States v. Jones* when reviewed by the Supreme Court.

19. Katz v. United States, 389 U.S. 347, 361 (1967) (Harlan, J., concurring).

20. *See* Kyllo v. United States, 533 U.S. 27, 32 (2001) ("In assessing when a search is not a search, we have applied somewhat in reverse the principle first enunciated in *Katz v. United States*, 389 U.S. 347, 19 L. Ed. 2d 576, 88 S. Ct. 507 (1967)); California v. Ciraolo, 476 U.S. 207, 215 (1986) ("The touchstone of Fourth Amendment analysis is whether a person has a 'constitutionally protected reasonable expectation of privacy.' Katz v. United States, 389 U.S. 347, 360 (1967) (Harlan, J., concurring).")).

21. The majority consisted of Chief Justice Roberts, and Justices Thomas, Kennedy, and Sotomayor. In addition to joining the majority opinion, Justice Sotomayor also wrote a concurring opinion explored below.

22. *Jones*, 132 S. Ct. at 949.

23. U.S. CONST. amend IV.

24. *Jones*, 132 S. Ct. at 949.

25. *Id.* at 950.
    The Government contends that the Harlan standard shows that no search occurred here, since Jones had no "reasonable expectation of privacy" in the area of the Jeep accessed by Government agents (its underbody) and in the locations of the Jeep on the public roads, which were visible to all. But we need not address the Government's contentions, because Jones's Fourth Amendment rights do not rise or fall with the Katz formulation. At bottom, we

must "assur[e] preservation of that degree of privacy against government that existed when the Fourth Amendment was adopted."

Id.

[. . .]

51. United States v. Hanna, No. 11-20678-CR, 2012 WL 279435, at *3 (S.D. Fla. Jan. 3, 2012) (analyzing the issue of Fourth Amendment standing under both the trespass theory and *Katz*'s privacy test); United States v. Bradshaw, No. 1:11-CR-257, 2012 WL 774964 (N.D. Ohio Mar. 8, 2012) (noting that the *Jones* majority did not adopt the mosaic theory); State v. Zahn, No. 25584, 2012 WL 862707 (S.D. Mar. 14, 2012) (holding that both the trespass approach and the mosaic theory can apply to GPS tracking).

52. This dialogue between concurring justices and those they are trying to persuade lies at the heart of the common law system—a case-by-case discussion between judges, lawyers, and the public about the progression of the law. Richard A. Posner, *The Federal Courts: Crisis and Reform* 236 (1985).

53. Igor Kirman, *Standing Apart to Be a Part: The Precedential Value of Supreme Court Concurring Opinions*, 95 COLUM L. REV. 2083, 2096–2101 (1995) (explaining that some courts will presume precedential value in a concurring opinion while others will presume no precedential value).

54. Lewis A. Kornhauser & Lawrence G. Sager, *The One and the Many: Adjudication in Collegial Courts*, 81 CAL. L. REV. 1 (1993).

55. Kirman, *supra* note 53, 2119.

56. Scott C. Idleman, *A Prudential Theory of Judicial Candor*, 73 TEX. L. REV. 1307, 1371 (1995).

57. Mark Tushnet, *Themes in Warren Court Biographies*, 70 N.Y.U. L. REV. 748, 763 (1995).

[. . .]

86. Johnson v. United States, 333 U.S. 10, 14 (1948).

87. United States v. Miller, 425 U.S. 435, 443 (1976). "The Fourth Amendment does not prohibit the obtaining of information revealed to a third party and conveyed by him to Government authorities, even if the information is revealed on the assumption that it will be used only for a limited purpose and the confidence placed in the third party will not be betrayed."

Id.

88. *Miller*, 425 U.S. at 435.

89. Smith v. Maryland, 442 U.S. 735 (1979).

90. United States v. McIntyre, 646 F.3d 1107 (8th Cir. 2011).

91. United States v. Hynson, No. 05-576, 2007 WL 2692327, at *6 (E.D. Pa. Sept. 11, 2007).

92. *See* Orin S. Kerr, *The Case for a Third-Party Doctrine*, 107 MICH. L. REV. 561, 565 (2009).

93. *Smith*, 442 U.S. at 744 ("Because the depositor [in *Miller*] 'assumed the risk' of disclosure, the Court held that it would be unreasonable for him to expect his financial records to remain private.").

94. *Jones*, 132 S. Ct. at 957 (Sotomayor, J., concurring).

95. *Id.*

96. *See* Peter Swire, *A Reasonableness Approach to Searches After the Jones GPS Tracking Case*, 64 STAN. L. REV. ONLINE 57 (2012); Daniel J. Solove, *United States v. Jones and the Future of Privacy Law: The Potential Far-Reaching Implications of the GPS Surveillance Case*, 90 CRIM. L. REPER. 632 (2012); Tom Goldstein, Why *Jones* is still less of a pro-privacy decision than most thought, SCOTUSblog (Jan. 30, 2012, 10:53 AM), http://www.scotusblog.com/2012/01/why-*Jones*-is-still-less-of-a-pro-privacy-decision-than-most-thought/.

97. *Jones*, 132 S. Ct. at 954.

98. Brigham City v. Stuart, 547 U.S. 398, 403 (2006); Nat'l Treasury Employees Union v. Von Raab, 489 U.S. 656, 665 (1989); California v. Acevedo, 500 U.S. 565, 581 (1991) (Scalia, J., concurring in the judgment).

99. Mincey v. Arizona, 437 U.S. 385, 390 (1978) (quoting Katz v. United States, 389 U.S. 347, 357 (1967)).

100. The Court often states that "[t]he Fourth Amendment proscribes all unreasonable searches and seizures, and it is a cardinal principle that 'searches conducted outside the judicial process, without prior approval by judge or magistrate, are *per se* unreasonable under the Fourth Amendment—subject only to a few specifically established and well-delineated exceptions.'" United States v. Ross, 456 U.S. 798, 825 (1982) (quoting Katz v. United States, 389 U.S. 347, 357 (1967)). One scholar aptly commented on this rule:

> In fact, these exceptions are neither few nor well-delineated. There are over twenty exceptions to the probable cause or the warrant requirement or both. They include searches incident to arrest (exceptions to both); automobile searches (exception to warrant requirement); border searches (both); searches near the border

(warrant and sometimes both); administrative searches (probable cause exception); administrative searches of regulated businesses (warrant); stop and frisk (both); plain view, open field seizures and prison "shakedowns" (both, because they are not covered by the fourth amendment at all); exigent circumstances (warrant); search of a person in custody (both); search incident to nonarrest when there is probable cause to arrest (both); fire investigations (warrant); warrantless entry following arrest elsewhere (warrant); boat boarding for document checks (both); consent searches (both); welfare searches (both, because not a "search"); inventory searches (both); driver's license and vehicle registration checks (both); airport searches (both); searches at courthouse doors (both); the new "school search" (both); and finally the standing doctrine which, while not strictly an exception to fourth amendment requirements, has that effect by causing the courts to ignore fourth amendment violations.

Craig M. Bradley, *Two Models of the Fourth Amendments*, 83 MICH. L. REV. 1468, 1473–74 (1985) (internal citations omitted).

101. Goldstein, *supra* note 96.

102. Carol A. Chase, *Privacy Takes a Back Seat: Putting the Automobile Exception Back on Track after Several Wrong Turns*, 41 B.C. L. REV. 71, 75 (1999).

103. Carroll v. United States, 267 U.S. 132 (1925).

104. *Id.* at 153.

105. United States v. Chadwick, 433 U.S. 1, 12–13 (1977).

106. Cardwell v. Lewis, 417 U.S. 583, 590 (1974).

107. Cady v. Dombrowski, 413 U.S. 433, 441 (1973) ("All States require vehicles to be registered and operators to be licensed. States and localities have enacted extensive and detailed codes regulating the condition and manner in which motor vehicles may be operated on public streets and highways.").

108. South Dakota v. Opperman, 428 U.S. 364, 367–8 (1976).

109. *See* Orin Kerr, Jones, *the Automobile Exception, and the Warrant Requirement*, THE VOLOKH CONSPIRACY (Feb. 2, 2012 12:45 AM), http://volokh.com/2012/02/02/Jones-the-automobile-exception-and-the-warrant-requirement/.

110. *Id.*

111. *See* Swire, *supra* note 96; Goldstein, *supra* note 96.

112. Swire, *supra* note 96.

113. Kerr, *supra* note 73, at 839. For an in-depth look at the statutory regulation of communication surveillance, *See* CRS Report R41733, *Privacy: An Overview of the Electronic Communications Privacy Act*, by Charles Doyle.

114. *Id.* at 857.

> The difference favors legislatures when technology is in flux because the privacy implications of particular rules can fluctuate as technology advances. To ensure that the law maintains its intended balance, it needs mechanisms that can adapt to technological change. Legislatures are up to the task; courts generally are not. Legislatures can experiment with different rules and make frequent amendments; they can place restrictions on both public and private actors; and they can even "sunset" rules so that they apply only for a particular period of time. The courts cannot. As a result, Fourth Amendment rules will tend to lack the flexibility that a regulatory response to new technologies may require. . . . The statutory framework that governs Internet privacy demonstrates the flexibility and creative potential of legislative approaches.

Id. at 871.

115. *Jones*, 132 S. Ct. at 964 (Alito, J., concurring).

116. S. 1011, 112th Cong., 1st Sess. (2011).

117. S. 1212, H.R. 2168, 112th Cong., 1st Sess. (2011).

*Richard M. Thompson II is a legislative attorney for members and committees of Congress employed by the Congressional Research Service.

Thompson, Richard M., II. "*United States v. Jones*: GPS Monitoring, Property, and Privacy," Congressional Research Service Report for Congress, April 30, 2012.

Testimony of The Honorable Joseph I. Cassilly

WRITTEN TESTIMONY OF THE HONORABLE JOSEPH I.
CASSILLY*
STATE'S ATTORNEY FOR HARFORD COUNTY, MARYLAND
AND PAST PRESIDENT, NATIONAL DISTRICT ATTORNEYS
ASSOCIATION

Hearing on H.R. 2168, the "Geolocational Privacy and
Surveillance Act"

House Judiciary Committee, Subcommittee on Crime,
Terrorism, and Homeland Security

May 17, 2012

Chairman Sensenbrenner, Ranking Member Scott, members of
the Subcommittee, thank you for inviting me to testify today on
behalf of the National District Attorneys Association (NDAA),
the oldest and largest organization representing over 39,000
district attorneys, State's attorneys, attorneys general and
county and city prosecutors with responsibility for prosecut-
ing 95% of criminal violations in every state and territory of
the United States.

As an Army Ranger who served in Viet Nam and a State's
Attorney for over thirty-three years I have pledged my honor
and life to defending the Constitution and the rights of my fellow citizens.

The Founders of our Country, in adopting the Fourth Amendment, wanted to protect its citizens from unreasonable searches. Obtaining geolocation information from a third party has been determined not to be a search; although the U. S. Supreme Court may weigh in on that decision. Even if it is a search, obtaining a warrant is not required for a lawful search when the circumstances of getting the warrant would be unreasonable or frustrate the lawful purposes of the government; i.e., search incident to arrest, search resulting from exigent circumstances or "hot pursuit," and search of a vehicle, among other recognized exceptions to the warrant requirement.

NDAA has serious concerns with the potential impact that H.R. 2168, the Geolocational Privacy and Surveillance Act (GPS Act), would have on State or local law enforcement's ability to most effectively and efficiently protect the citizens we serve. The GPS Act, as currently written, has been drafted so broadly that the bill would require a search warrant to gather many forms of information that can currently be obtained by subpoena. The new standards set through the GPS Act would hamper law enforcement's ability to quickly obtain important information that could be used to save lives. NDAA feels that any legal reforms to the current system should be implemented to *shorten* the investigative timeline instead of lengthening it, which we feel would be an unintentional consequence of the GPS Act. NDAA believes that any bill that hinders law enforcement from doing its job most effectively would lead to serious consequences for crime victims and public safety. Because so many cases are time sensitive in nature—including child abductions, other forms of kidnapping and organized criminal and/or terrorist activities—law enforcement must be able to work these cases without unnecessary administrative delay.

NDAA believes it is imperative to distinguish between historical data compiled from cell tower hits, referred to as cell-site information, and real time GPS ping information. The overwhelming majority of the requests for geolocation data in my jurisdiction are for the historical data. These requests are often made to confirm or rebut information which does not meet the probable cause standard. For example, in a gang shooting in my jurisdiction an anonymous caller who states they fear gang retaliation if their identity is known gives the police the identity of two gang members who committed the murder. The police receive cell phone information regarding these individuals from prior arrest reports. The cell-site historical information for the time of the killing shows that those two cell phones were hitting off the same tower at the same time in the area of the murder. Even with this information, the police do not have probable cause to arrest, but to require probable cause to access historical records would have deprived the officers of this vital information. Gang crimes are domestic terrorism which rules with fear, silences witnesses and deprives whole communities of life and liberty. Denying law enforcement the ability to use this critical tool is to decide to refuse to allow America's communities to protect themselves from the scourge of gangs.

In section 2602 (d) "Exception for Consent" allows for a parent or guardian to consent to a child's device location but it is silent as to whether such consent is available for those with mental handicaps, developmental disabilities, dementia or who may be on medication. Also, what if a child is reported missing by their peers but parents or guardians cannot be located? Do the police waste precious seconds hunting for the parents or use those seconds to hunt for the child?

Evidence of the confusion this bill will cause is obvious from the fact that section 2602 (f) "Exception for Emergency Information" sets a different standard for a law enforcement officer to access geolocation information than does section 2604(a)(1)(A) "Emergency Situation Exception," including the fact that one section does not require a subsequent order while the other does. While NDAA does appreciate the "Emergency Situation Exception" contained in section 2064(a) of the GPS Act, we also feel the bill as currently written leaves too much of a grey area on what geolocational information can be legally obtained by law enforcement in such emergency situations. For example, the exception allows for interception of geolocation information when "such officer reasonably determines that an emergency situation exists that . . . involves . . . immediate danger of death or serious physical injury to any person." It is unclear, however, whether this exception would permit interception of geolocation information relating to others—such as the perpetrator of a crime—or only information relating to the person whose life or safety is threatened. Take a kidnapping case, for example; it is currently unclear whether law enforcement could use this exception to track the kidnapper's phone or only the victim's phone or other electronic devices belonging to the victim. It is also important to point out that the ability to gather GPS information lasts only so long as the battery continues to power the device. Stopping to investigate to gather information or draft a warrant or find a judge may exhaust the battery and frustrate the effort to use geolocation.

It may not be clear at first whether a missing person is in danger or just out of touch and yet frantic relatives often demand that law enforcement use every opportunity to locate that person. Given that the proposed law subjects electronic communication service providers' employees to possible criminal and civil liability if they cooperate with an officer, as well as loss of their job if the employer wishes to separate itself from an employee's decision, the employee might challenge the officer's determination that an exception to the warrant requirement exists.

If Congress chooses to elevate the standard for location evidence to probable cause, law enforcement will be forced to adapt to these changes and such changes would extend the investigative timeline and decrease the number of leads law enforcement can pursue in a given time period. Additionally, with deep cuts in federal spending to important State and local law enforcement programs over the past several years—including to COPS, Byrne-JAG, Byrne Competitive and cuts to information sharing programs like the Regional Information Sharing System (RISS)—law enforcement has been forced to do more with less; the GPS Act would seem to present yet another burdensome obstacle for State and local law enforcement to overcome in order to effectively protect and serve.

State statutes and court rules impose additional burdens on the use of warrants. For example, in Maryland, law enforcement officers are required to deliver a copy of the warrant to the person being searched at the execution of the warrant. Is the person being searched the person carrying the phone? This means that the target of the investigation would be alerted to the investigation and afforded an opportunity to intimidate witnesses, destroy evidence, turn off the wireless communication device and flee. In addition, Maryland law enforcement is required to deliver the statement of probable [cause] to the person searched at least sixty days after the warrant is executed; therefore, warrants in Maryland generally come at the conclusion of the investigation, but most law enforcement needs geolocation information at the beginning of the investigation. Additionally, on weekends, holidays and evenings law enforcement may use hours trying to locate a judge and another hour driving to their location with the warrant. These are just some examples from one of fifty states and several territories of how the Federal requirement of a warrant translated to the States will result in uncounted obstacles and frustrate or destroy law enforcement efforts.

Whatever level of investigative process is deemed appropriate by the Congress, NDAA urges the Committee to take steps to guarantee that law enforcement is able to access the required communications records—including location information—once that process is implemented. The emergency exceptions outlined in section 2602(f) of the GPS Act may provide the necessary recourse, but if there is no statutory mandate for a service provider to turn over the records, and no time frame for compliance, law enforcement may effectively be denied the information we need despite being in accordance with the legal process. The law should provide a course of action that will enable the rapid transfer of information when needed and possibly provide penalties for service providers who are intentionally slow to respond in providing critical location information.

NDAA appreciates the privacy concerns of America's citizens and strives for all of America's State and local prosecutors to minimize unnecessary intrusions into citizens' privacy. While there are countless articles expressing concern about the amount of location evidence obtained by law enforcement and private companies, not a lot has been publicized about the good that has come from the proper use of location evidence by law enforcement to solve crimes and to save lives. There are literally thousands of instances where the proper gathering and use of this important evidence has led to the rescue of abducted children, the identification and prosecution of sexual predators, and the apprehension and conviction of a terrorist looking to harm innocent Americans. We assert that this legislation is a solution in search of a problem and as the true defenders of the public's freedom and rights America's prosecutors believe that the current system of police discretion and judicial oversight is working; for if it were not the evidence would be found in cases challenging the conduct of the police in the Courts.

Chairman Sensenbrenner, Ranking Member Scott, members of the Subcommittee, I appreciate the opportunity to testify before you on this important legislation and will answer any questions which you may have.

*Joseph I. Cassilly** is a state's attorney for Harford County, Maryland, and past president of the National District Attorneys Association.

Written testimony of Joseph I. Cassilly. "Geolocational Privacy and Surveillance Act." U.S. Congress. House of Representatives. Hearing before the House Judiciary Committee, Subcommittee on Crime, Terrorism, and Homeland Security, 112th Congress, 2012

Statement of Catherine Crump

STATEMENT OF CATHERINE CRUMP,* STAFF ATTORNEY AMERICAN CIVIL LIBERTIES UNION

On The Geolocational Privacy and Surveillance Act

Before the House Judiciary Subcommittee on Crime, Terrorism, and Homeland Security

May 17, 2012

Good morning Chairman Sensenbrenner, Ranking Member Scott and Members of the Subcommittee. Thank you for the opportunity to testify on behalf of the American Civil Liberties Union, its more than half a million members, countless additional activists and supporters, and fifty-three affiliate organizations nationwide.

The ACLU supports passage of H.R. 2168, the Geolocational Privacy and Surveillance Act. Requiring law enforcement agents to secure a warrant based upon probable cause before obtaining geolocational information would allow legitimate investigations to proceed, while ensuring that innocent Americans are protected from intrusions into their privacy. Passing the GPS Act would fulfill Congress's duty to ensure that the safeguards provided by the Fourth Amendment to the Constitution are respected, and it would allow Americans to preserve the privacy they have traditionally experienced, even as technology advances.

I. Introduction

GPS and cell site technology provide law enforcement agents with powerful and inexpensive methods of tracking individuals over an extensive period of time and an unlimited expanse of space as they traverse public and private areas. In many parts of the country, the police have been tracking people for days, weeks, or months at a time, without ever having to demonstrate to a magistrate that they have a good reason to believe that tracking will turn up evidence of wrongdoing. Today, individuals' movements can be subject to remote monitoring and permanent recording without any judicial oversight. Innocent Americans can never be confident that they are free from round-the-clock surveillance by law enforcement of their activities. As Justice Sonya Sotomayor recently wrote, "The net result is that GPS monitoring—by making available at a relatively low cost such a substantial quantum of intimate information about any person whom the Government, in its unfettered discretion, chooses to track—may alter the relationship between citizen and government in a way that is inimical to democratic society."[1]

Congress should pass the GPS Act to require law enforcement agents to secure a warrant based upon probable cause before obtaining geolocational information through GPS or cell site technology. The warrant and probable cause requirements, enshrined in the Fourth Amendment, ensure that an objective magistrate weighs the need to invade privacy when enforcing the law. Requiring a warrant would fulfill Congress's obligation to ensure that the Fourth Amendment's prohibition on unreasonable searches and seizures is respected. Americans' privacy rights are threatened by warrantless access to geolocational information, and history teaches that the executive cannot be counted upon to police itself. The need for the GPS Act is real and immediate, and we urge its passage.

II. Current Technologies Allow for Detailed Tracking of Americans' Movements.

Recent technological developments make it possible to obtain geolocational information about the vast majority of Americans with great precision, in both real time and historically, regardless of whether they are tracked through their cell phones or their vehicles, or whether the police obtain GPS or cell site data.

A. TRACKING CELL PHONES

Over the past decade, cell phones have gone from a luxury good to an essential communications device. As of December 2011, there were more than 311.6 million wireless subscriber accounts in the United States—a number greater than the total U.S. population.[2] While cell phones are best known as devices used to make voice calls and send text messages, they are also capable of being used as covert tracking devices. As a result, cell phone technology has given law enforcement an unprecedented new surveillance tool. With compelled assistance from mobile phone carriers, the U.S. government now has the technical capability to covertly track any one of the nation's hundreds of millions of cell phone owners, for 24 hours a day, for as long as it likes.

Cell phones yield several types of information about their users' past and present location and movements: cell site location data, triangulation data, and Global Positioning System data. The most basic type of cell phone location information is "cell site" data or "cell site location information," which refer to the identity of the cell tower from which the phone is receiving the strongest signal and the sector of the tower facing the phone. This data is generated because whenever individuals have their cell phones on, the phones automatically scan for nearby cell towers that provide the best reception; approximately every seven seconds, the phones register their location information with the network.[3] The carriers keep track of the registration information to identify the cell tower through which calls can be made and received. The towers also monitor the strength of the telephone's signal during the progress of the call to manage the hand-off of calls from one adjacent tower to another if the caller is moving during the call.[4]

The precision of cell site location information depends, in part, on the size of the coverage area of each cell tower. This means that as the number of cell towers has increased and the coverage area for each cell tower has shrunk, cell site location information has become more precise.

The latest generation of cellular towers now may cover an area as small as a tunnel, a subway, a specific roadway, a particular floor of a building, or even an individual home or office.[5] As consumers embrace data-hungry devices such as smartphones, the carriers have installed more towers, each with smaller coverage areas. Further improvement in precision can be expected given the explosive demand for wireless technology and its new services, to the point that "[t]he gap between the locational precision in today's cellular call detail records and that of a GPS tracker is closing, especially as carriers incorporate the latest technologies into their networks."[6] As Professor Matt Blaze testified to Congress in June 2010, "[i]t is no longer valid to assume that the cell sector recorded by the network will give only an approximate indication of a user's location."[7]

In addition to cell site information, law enforcement agents can obtain location data at a high level of accuracy by requesting cell phone providers to engage in "triangulation," which entails collecting and analyzing data of the precise time and angle at which the cell phone's signal arrives at multiple cell towers. Current technology can pinpoint the location of the cell phone to an accuracy of within 50 meters or less anytime the phone is on, and the accuracy will improve with newer technology.[8]

Finally, a cell phone that has GPS receiver hardware built into it can determine its precise location by receiving signals from global positioning satellites. An increasing number of phones, particularly smartphones, contain such GPS chips, and over half of mobile subscribers are now smartphone users.[9] Current GPS technology can pinpoint location when it is outdoors, typically achieving accuracy of within 10 meters.[10] With "assisted GPS" technology, which combines GPS and triangulation, it is possible to obtain such accurate location information even when the cell phone is inside a home or a building.

Government requests for cell site location information are usually of two types: historical cell site data, which can be used to retrace previous movements, or prospective cell site data, which can be used to track the phone in real time. The availability of historical information and the length of time this information is stored depend on the policies of the cell phone company. According to an internal Department of Justice document, obtained by the ACLU through a public records act request, cell phone companies store their customers' historical location information for significant periods of time: Verizon stores the cell towers used by a mobile phone for "one rolling year"; T-Mobile keeps this information "officially 4–6 months, really a year or more"; Sprint and Nextel store this data for "18–24 months"; and AT&T/Cingular retains it "from July 2008."[11]

B. TRACKING VEHICLES

Just as geolocation data can be gathered from cell phones, so, too, can it be gathered from vehicles. There are a number of ways this can be accomplished. As in the recent Supreme Court case *United States v. Jones*, the government can physically attach a GPS device to a car. In that case, law enforcement agents installed a GPS device on a vehicle and it remained there for 28 days. During this period, the GPS device allowed agents to track the location of the car at every moment. It had an antenna that received signals from satellites; the device used these signals to determine its latitude and longitude every ten seconds, accurately pinpointing its location to within 50–100 feet. Law enforcement agents connected that data to software that plotted the car's location and movements on a map. The software also created a comprehensive record of the car's locations.

However, law enforcement agents do not necessarily need to affix a GPS device to a car in order to track its movements. The increased prevalence of integrated car navigation systems may soon make even this minimal legwork unnecessary. *See, e.g., United States v. Coleman*, No. 07-20357, 2008 WL 495323, at *1 (E.D. Mich. Feb. 20, 2008) (discussing issuance of court order requiring car navigation company to disclose location data to law enforcement).

III. Tracking People's Location Can Invade Their Privacy Because It Reveals a Great Deal About Them.

Location tracking enables law enforcement to capture details of someone's movements for months on end, unconstrained by the normal barriers of cost and officer resources. *See United States v. Pineda-Moreno*, 617 F.3d 1120, 1124 (9th Cir. 2010) (Kozinski, J, dissenting from denial of rehearing en banc) ("The modern devices used in Pineda-Moreno's case can record the car's movements without human intervention—quietly, invisibly, with uncanny precision. A small law enforcement team can deploy a dozen, a hundred, a thousand such devices and keep track of their various movements by computer, with far less effort than was previously needed to follow a single vehicle.").

In *United States v. Jones*, 132 S. Ct. 945, 954 (2012), the Supreme Court held that a Fourth Amendment search occurred when the government placed a GPS tracking device on the defendant's car and monitored his whereabouts nonstop for 28 days. *Id.* at 954. A majority of the Justices also stated that "the use of longer term GPS monitoring . . . impinges on expectations of privacy" in the location data downloaded from that tracker. *Id.* at 953–64 (Sotomayor, J., concurring); *see also id.* at 964 (Alito, J., concurring). As Justice Alito explained, "[s]ociety's expectation has been that law enforcement agents and others would not—and indeed, in the main, simply could not—secretly monitor and catalog every single movement of an individual's car, for a very long period." *Id.* at 964 (Alito, J., concurring).

Justice Sotomayor emphasized the intimate nature of the information that might be collected by the GPS surveillance, including "trips to the psychiatrist, the plastic surgeon, the abortion clinic, the AIDS treatment center, the strip club, the criminal defense attorney, the by-the-hour motel, the union meeting, the mosque, synagogue or church, the gay bar and on and on." *Id.* at 955 (quoting *People v. Weaver*, 12 N.Y.3d 433, 442 (N.Y. 2009)). While even the limited collection of geolocation information can reveal intimate and detailed facts about a person, the privacy invasion is multiplied many times over when law enforcement agents obtain geolocation information for prolonged periods of time. As the D.C. Circuit Court of Appeals has observed, "[a] person who knows all of another's travels can deduce whether he is a weekly church goer, a heavy drinker, a regular at the gym, an unfaithful husband, an outpatient receiving medical treatment, an associate of particular individuals or political groups—and not just one such fact about a person, but all such facts." *United States v. Maynard*, 615 F.3d 544, 562 (D.C. Cir. 2010), *aff'd sub nom. United States v. Jones*, 132 S. Ct. 945 (2012).

There have always been facets of American life that have been uniquely safeguarded from the intrusive interference and observation of government. Geolocational surveillance threatens to make even those aspects of life an open book to government. As Justice Sotomayor pointed out in *Jones*, "Awareness that the Government may be watching chills associational and expressive freedoms. And the Government's unrestrained power to assemble data that reveal private aspects of identity is susceptible to abuse." *Jones*, 132 S. Ct. at 956 (Sotomayor, J., concurring) (quotations omitted).

While privacy rights are often conceptualized as belonging to individuals, they are also important because they ensure a specifically calibrated balance between the power of individuals on the one hand and the state on the other. When the sphere of life in which individuals enjoy privacy shrinks, the state becomes all the more powerful:

The net result is that GPS monitoring—by making available at a relatively low cost such a substantial quantum of intimate information about any person whom the Government, in its unfettered discretion, chooses to track—may alter the relationship between citizen and government in a way that is inimical to democratic society.

Jones, 132 S. Ct. at 956 (Sotomayor, J., concurring) (quotations omitted). Chief Judge Kozinski of the U.S. Court of Appeals for the Ninth Circuit has elaborated on this critical point:

I don't think that most people in the United States would agree with the panel that someone who leaves his car parked in his driveway outside the door of his home invites people to crawl under it and attach a device that will track the vehicle's every movement and transmit that information to total strangers. There is something creepy and un-American about such clandestine and underhanded behavior. To those of us who have lived under a totalitarian regime, there is an eerie feeling of déjà vu.

United States v. Pineda-Moreno, 617 F.3d 1120, 1126 (9th Cir. 2010) (Kozinski, C.J., dissenting). *See also United States v. Cuevas-Perez*, 640 F.3d 272, 286 (7th Cir. 2011) (Wood, J., dissenting) ("The technological devices available for [monitoring a person's movements] have rapidly attained a degree of accuracy that would have been unimaginable to an earlier generation. They make the system that George Orwell depicted in his famous novel, *1984*, seem clumsy and easily avoidable by comparison.").

Furthermore, while the government routinely argues that records of a person's prior movements deserve less privacy protection than records of where a person travels in real time, this is a meaningless distinction. As one judge has noted, "[t]he picture of [a person]'s life the government seeks to obtain is no less intimate simply because it has already been painted." *In re Application of* the *U.S. for Historical Cell Site Data*, 747 F. Supp. 2d 827, 840 (S.D.Tex. 2010) (citation omitted). A contrary conclusion would eliminate privacy protections even in real-time data, because police officers would be free to use GPS devices to record vehicles' travels so long as they waited some minutes before accessing those records, thereby rendering them "historical."

IV. A Warrant and Probable Cause for Location Tracking is Vital to the Constitution and Innovation.

While the Supreme Court held in *Jones* that affixing a GPS monitor and then tracking a suspect's whereabouts for weeks constitutes a "search" within the meaning of the Fourth Amendment, it did not address whether it is the sort of search that requires a judicial warrant supported by probable cause. It will likely take years for this question to reach the Supreme Court again. Congress should not stand by as law enforcement faces confusion over the rules for obtaining location information and Americans' privacy rights are violated.

The warrant and probable cause requirements are essential components of the Fourth Amendment. The function of the warrant clause is to safeguard the rights of the innocent by preventing the state from conducting searches solely in its discretion:

> Absent some grave emergency, the Fourth Amendment has interposed a magistrate between the citizen and the police. This was done not to shield criminals nor to make the home a safe haven for illegal activities. It was done so that an objective mind might weigh the need to invade that privacy in order to enforce the law. The right of privacy was deemed too precious to entrust to the discretion of those whose job is the detection of crime

and the arrest of criminals. Power is a heady thing; and history shows that the police acting on their own cannot be trusted.

McDonald v. United States, 335 U.S. 451, 455 (1948).

The warrant and probable cause requirements are especially important here given the extraordinary intrusiveness of modern-day electronic surveillance. Without these requirements, the low cost of collecting and storing geolocational information would permit the police to continuously track any driver and cell phone user.

The warrant requirement imposes no great burden on the state. Under the GPS Act, obtaining warrants for geolocational information would be even less burdensome than obtaining them for telephone wiretaps, and the expectation of privacy implicated in placing calls on a public phone is no greater than the expectation that the state will not, absent a warrant, monitor a citizen's every movement continuously for months on end.

In addition congressional action to require a probable cause warrant for location tracking enjoys widespread support from companies and organizations from across the political spectrum including Amazon, the American Library Association, Americans for Tax Reform, AT&T, the Campaign for Liberty, Citizens Against Government Waste, the Competitive Enterprise Institute, the Center for Democracy and Technology, Consumer Action, eBay, Facebook, Freedom Works, Google, HP, IBM, the Information Technology & Innovation Foundation, Intel, the Liberty Coalition, the Newspaper Association of America, Salesforce.com, Tech America, Tech Freedom and Twitter.[12] This list demonstrates that many businesses agree that safeguarding location information is a necessity for American competitiveness and innovation.

V. There Is a Need to Act, and Congress Is the Appropriate Branch of Government to Act.

Congress cannot afford to wait any longer to enact a warrant and probable cause requirement for location tracking. Today Americans' privacy rights are being violated routinely by invasive location tracking, particularly cell phone tracking.

In August 2011, 35 ACLU affiliates submitted public records requests with state and local law enforcement agencies around the nation seeking information about their policies, procedures, and practices for tracking cell phones.[13] The ACLU received over 5,500 pages of documents from over 200 local law enforcement agencies. The responses show that while cell phone tracking is routine, few agencies consistently obtain judicial warrants. The overwhelming majority of the more than 200 law enforcement agencies that provided documents engaged in at least some cell phone tracking. Most law enforcement agencies explained that they track cell phones to investigate crimes. Some said they tracked cell phones only in emergencies, for example to locate a missing person. Only ten said they have never tracked cell phones.

Many law enforcement agencies track cell phones quite frequently. For example, based on invoices from cell phone companies, it appears that Raleigh, N.C. tracks hundreds of cell phones a year. The practice is so common that cell phone companies have manuals for police explaining what data the companies store, how much they charge police to access that data, and what officers need to do to get it.

Most law enforcement agencies do not obtain warrants to track cell phones, and the legal standards used vary widely. For example, police in Lincoln, Neb. obtain GPS location data on telephones without demonstrating probable cause. Police in Wilson County, N.C. obtain historical cell tracking data where it is "relevant and material" to an ongoing investigation, a standard lower than probable cause. Yet some police departments do protect privacy by obtaining warrants based upon probable cause when tracking cell phones. For example, police in the County of Hawaii, Wichita, and Lexington, Ky. demonstrate probable cause and obtain a warrant when tracking cell phones. If these police departments can protect both public safety and privacy by meeting the warrant and probable cause requirements, then surely other agencies can as well.

Moreover, it is not just state and local law enforcement agencies that obtain geolocation data under inconsistent standards. The U.S. Attorney's Offices appear to do so as well. The Department of Justice maintains that the government need not obtain a warrant and show probable cause to track people's location, with only one exception: real-time GPS and triangulation data. Since at least 2007, DOJ has recommended that U.S. Attorneys obtain a warrant based on probable cause prior to engaging in these forms of cell phone tracking.[14]

However, not all U.S. Attorneys Offices obtain a warrant and show probable cause even in the limited circumstances in which DOJ recommends that they do so. Litigation by the ACLU and Electronic Frontier Foundation under the Freedom of Information Act revealed that U.S. Attorney's Offices in the District of New Jersey and the Southern District of Florida have obtained even the most precise cell tracking information without obtaining a warrant and showing probable cause.[15] Because the FOIA focused on only a small number of U.S. Attorney's Offices, it may well be that many other offices also do not follow DOJ's recommendation.

The records the ACLU has obtained from local, state, and federal law enforcement agencies conclusively demonstrate that warrantless geolocation tracking is not merely a theoretical privacy risk. Americans' privacy rights are violated by warrantless cell phone tracking routinely.

Congress is in a good position to put an end to these violations. In his concurrence in *Jones*, Justice Alito wrote: "In circumstances involving dramatic technological change, the best solution to privacy concerns may be legislative."[16] Moreover, when considering how to apply the Stored Communications Act to government requests to obtain historical cell site location information, the Third Circuit has stated that, "we are stymied by the failure of Congress to make its intention clear."[17]

Congress should act not just to protect privacy but also to safeguard law enforcement investigations. Given the changes in Fourth Amendment jurisprudence, law enforcement faces a very uncertain standard for proceeding with searches, operating in emergencies and securing information from telecommunications providers.

VI. The GPS Act Would Safeguard Americans' Privacy While Allowing Law Enforcement to Do Its Job.

The ACLU supports passage of the GPS Act because it would ensure that law enforcement agents obtain a warrant for geolocation information, subject to certain reasonable exceptions.

The heart of the Act is the requirement that "[a] governmental entity may intercept geolocation information or require the disclosure by a provider of a covered service of geolocation information only pursuant to a warrant issued using the procedures described in the Federal Rules of Criminal Procedure . . . ." § 2602(h)((2).

In turn, Federal Rule of Criminal Procedure 41 provides that "a warrant may be issued for any of the following: (1) evidence of a crime; (2) contraband, fruits of crime, or other items illegally possessed; (3) property designed for use, intended for use, or used in committing a crime; or (4) a person to be arrested or a person who is unlawfully restrained."

Thus, through its incorporation of the Rule 41 standard, the GPS Act strikes a reasonable—and constitutionally necessary—balance between privacy and law enforcement interests. Under this provision, for example, when law enforcement agents have a good reason to believe that tracking the location of a cell phone will turn up evidence of a crime, or that a cell phone was used during the commission of a crime, law enforcement agents will have little difficulty persuading magistrate judges to grant them permission to engage in location tracking.

Further, the GPS Act contains a limited number of exceptions, for:

- Emergency access when "it is reasonable to believe that the life or safety of the person is threatened";

- Foreign intelligence surveillance covered by the Foreign Intelligence Surveillance Act of 1978;

- Law enforcement emergencies where there is not time to secure a warrant;

- To retrieve lost or stolen phones;

- To allow parents or guardians to monitor children; and

- When the user has consented.

The GPS Act could be strengthened through the inclusion of reporting requirements regarding law enforcement agencies' collection of geolocation information. To be sure, law enforcement agencies may have a legitimate interest in keeping the details of specific investigations secret, but when it comes to aggregate statistical information about the use of specific surveillance techniques, the public interest is best served through disclosure.

Covert surveillance techniques are by their nature secret, which has important ramifications for the ability of both Congress and the public to engage in oversight. Robust reporting requirements play a valuable role in filling what would otherwise be a void of information regarding the activities of government. For example, each year the administrative office of the courts produces aggregate reports on the use of wiretap authorities by law enforcement agencies. Without revealing any sensitive investigative details, these reports give Congress and the public meaningful insight into the frequency with which the government uses this surveillance technique and the kinds of crimes that they are used to investigate.

Congress simply cannot perform effective oversight without data. For this reason, we urge the co-sponsors of the legislation to implement reporting requirements.

Conclusion

The ACLU agrees with Justice Alito that, in this time of rapid technological change, it is especially appropriate for Congress to step in and regulate the use of surveillance technology by government. The warrant and probable cause requirements strike the appropriate balance, ensuring that legitimate investigations can go forward without eroding the privacy rights of innocent Americans. We urge the committee to support H.R. 2168 and report it favorably from the committee.

NOTES

1. *United States v. Jones*, 132 S. Ct. 945, 956 (2012) (Sotomayor, J concurring).

2. CTIA, Wireless Quick Facts, *available at* http://www.ctia.org/advocacy/research/index.cfm/aid/10323.

3. *In re the Application of the United States for an Order Directing a Provider of Elec. Commc'n Serv. to Disclose Records to the Gov't*, 534 F. Supp. 2d 585, 589–90 (W.D. Pa. 2008) (Lenihan, M.J.), *rev'd on other grounds*, 620 F.3d 304 (3d Cir. 2010).

4. See Declaration of Henry Hodor at 7 n.6, available at http://www.aclu.org/pdfs/freespeech/cellfoia_release_4805_001_20091022.pdf

5. *Hearing on Electronic Communications Privacy Act Reform and the Revolution in Location Based Technologies and Services Before the Subcomm. on the Constitution, Civil Rights, and Civil Liberties of the H. Comm. on Judiciary*, 111th Cong. (2010) (statement of Professor Matt Blaze at 5), *available at* http://judiciary.house.gov/hearings/pdf/Blaze100624.pdf; Thomas Farely & Ken Schmidt, Cellular Telephone Basics: Basic Theory and Operation (2006), http://www.privateline.com/mt_cellbasics/iv_basic_theory_and_operation/

6. Statement of Professor Matt Blaze, supra n.5, at 13–14.

7. *Id.* at 13.

8. *Id.* at 10.

9. Keith Flagstaff, *Nielson: Majority of Mobile Subscribers Now Smartphone Owners*, Time Techland (May 7, 2012), http://techland.time.com/2012/05/07/nielsen-majority-of-mobile-subscribers-now-smartphone-owners/.

10. Statement of Professor Matt Blaze, *supra* n.5, at 5.

11. U.S. Department of Justice, *Retention Periods of Major Cellular Service Providers*, available at https://www.aclu.org/cell-phone-location-tracking-request-response-cellphone-company-data-retention-chart

12. A full list can be found here: http://digitaldueprocess.org/index.cfm?objectid=DF652CE0-2552-11DFB455000C296BA163

13. ACLU, *Cell Phone Location Tracking Public Records Request*, http://www.aclu.org/protecting-civil-liberties-digital-age/cell-phone-location-tracking-public-records-request. Supporting documentation demonstrating the factual assertions throughout this section can be found at this webpage.

14. *Senate Judiciary 2011 ECPA Hearing*, at 7 (testimony of James A. Baker, Assoc. Deputy Attorney Gen., U.S. Dep't of Justice). *available at* http://1.usa.gov/IsojNy.

15. ACLU, *ACLU v. Department of Justice: ACLU Lawsuit To Uncover Records of Cell Phone Tracking*, Sept. 6, 2011, http://www.aclu.org/free-speech/aclu-v-department-justice

16. 132 S. Ct. at 964.

17. *In the Matter of the Application of the United States of America for an Order Directing a Provider of Electronic Communication Service to Disclose Records to the Government*, 620 F.3d 304, 319 (3d Cir. 2010).

*Catherine Crump** is a staff attorney with the ACLU's Speech, Privacy and Technology Project.

Statement of Catherine Crump. "On The Geolocational Privacy and Surveillance Act." U.S. Congress. House of Representatives. Hearing before the House Judiciary Committee, Subcommittee on Crime, Terrorism, and Homeland Security, 112th Congress, 2012.

Prison Without Walls

by Graeme Wood*

Incarceration in America is a failure by almost any measure. But what if the prisons could be turned inside out, with convicts released into society under constant electronic surveillance? Radical though it may seem, early experiments suggest that such a science-fiction scenario might cut crime, reduce costs, and even prove more just.

ONE SNOWY NIGHT last winter, I walked into a pizzeria in Morrisville, Pennsylvania, with my right pant leg hiked up my shin. A pager-size black box was strapped to my sockless ankle, and another, somewhat larger unit dangled in a holster on my belt. Together, the two items make up a tracking device called the BI ExacuTrack AT: the former is designed to be tamper-resistant, and the latter broadcasts the wearer's location to a monitoring company via GPS. The device is commonly associated with paroled sex offenders, who wear it so authorities can keep an eye on their movements. Thus my experiment: an online guide had specified that the restaurant I was visiting was a "family" joint. Would the moms and dads, confronted with my anklet, identify me as a possible predator and hustle their kids back out into the cold?

Well, no, not in this case. Not a soul took any notice of the gizmos I wore. The whole rig is surprisingly small and unobtrusive, and it allowed me to eat my slice in peace. Indeed, over the few days that I posed as a monitored man, the closest I came to feeling a real stigma was an encounter I had at a Holiday Inn ice machine, where a bearded trucker type gave me a wider berth than I might otherwise have expected. All in all, it didn't seem like such a terrible fate.

Unlike most of ExacuTrack's clientele, of course, I wore my device by choice and only briefly, to find out how it felt and how people reacted to it. By contrast, a real sex offender—or any of a variety of other lawbreakers, including killers, check bouncers, thieves, and drug users—might wear the unit or one like it for years, or even decades. He (and the offender is generally a "he") would wear it all day and all night, into the shower and under the sheets—perhaps with an AC adapter cord snaking out into a wall socket for charging. The device would enable the monitoring company to follow his every move, from home to work to the store, and, in consultation with a parole or probation officer, to keep him away from kindergartens, playgrounds, Jonas Brothers concerts, and other places where kids congregate. Should he decide to snip off the anklet (the band is rubber, and would succumb easily to pruning shears), a severed cable would alert the company that he had tampered with the unit, and absent a very good excuse he would likely be sent back to prison. Little wonder that the law-enforcement officer who installed my ExacuTrack noted that he was doing me a favor by unboxing a fresh unit: over their lifetimes, many of the trackers become encrusted with the filth and dead skin of previous bearers, some of whom are infected with prison plagues such as herpes or hepatitis. Officers clean the units and replace the straps between users, but I strongly preferred not to have anything rubbing against my ankle that had spent years rubbing against someone else's.

Increasingly, GPS devices such as the one I wore are looking like an appealing alternative to conventional incarceration, as it becomes ever clearer that, in the United States at least, *traditional prison* has become more or less synonymous with *failed prison*. By almost any metric, our practice of locking large numbers of people behind bars has proved at best ineffective and at worst a national disgrace. According to a recent Pew report, 2.3 million Americans are currently incarcerated—enough people to fill the city of Houston. Since 1983, the number of inmates has more than tripled and the total cost of corrections has jumped sixfold, from $10.4 billion to $68.7 billion. In California, the cost per inmate has kept pace with the cost of an Ivy League education, at just shy of $50,000 a year.

This might make some sense if crime rates had also tripled. But they haven't: rather, even as crime has fallen, the sentences served by criminals have grown, thanks in large part to mandatory minimums and draconian three-strikes rules—politically popular measures that have shown little deterrent effect but have left the prison system overflowing with inmates. The vogue for incarceration might also make sense if the prisons repaid society's investment by releasing reformed inmates who behaved better than before they were locked up. But that isn't the case either: half of those released are back in prison within three years. Indeed, research by the economists Jesse Shapiro of the University of Chicago and M. Keith Chen of Yale indicates that the stated purpose of incarceration, which is to place prisoners under harsh conditions on the assumption that they will be "scared straight," is actively counterproductive. Such conditions—and U.S. prisons are astonishingly harsh, with as many as 20 percent of male inmates facing sexual assault—typically harden criminals, making them *more* violent and predatory. Essentially, when we lock someone up today, we are agreeing to pay a large (and growing) sum of money merely to put off dealing with him until he is released in a few years, often as a greater menace to society than when he went in.

Devices such as the ExacuTrack, along with other advances in both the ways we monitor criminals and the ways we punish them for their transgressions, suggest a revolutionary possibility: that we might turn the conventional prison system inside out for a substantial number of inmates, doing away with the current, expensive array of guards and cells and fences, in favor of a regimen of close, constant surveillance on the outside and swift, certain punishment for any deviations from an established, legally unobjectionable routine. The potential upside is enormous. Not only might such a system save billions of dollars annually, it could theoretically produce far better outcomes, training convicts to become law-abiders rather than more-ruthless lawbreakers. The ultimate result could be lower crime rates, at a reduced cost, and with considerably less inhumanity in the bargain.

Moreover, such a change would in fact be less radical than it might at first appear. An underappreciated fact of our penitentiary system is that of all Americans "serving time" at any given moment, only a third are actually behind bars. The rest—some 5 million of them—are circulating among the free on conditional supervised release either as parolees, who are freed from prison before their sentences conclude, or as probationers, who walk free in lieu of jail time. These prisoners-on-the-outside have in fact outnumbered the incarcerated for decades. And recent innovations, both technological and procedural, could enable such programs to advance to a stage where they put the traditional model of incarceration to shame.

In a number of experimental cases, they already have. Devices such as the one I wore on my leg already allow tens of thousands of convicts to walk the streets relatively freely, impeded only by the knowledge that if they loiter by a school-yard, say, or near the house of the ex-girlfriend they threatened, or on a street corner known for its crack trade, the law will come to find them. Compared with incarceration, the cost of such sur-veillance is minuscule—mere dollars per day—and monitoring has few of the hardening effects of time behind bars. Nor do all the innovations being developed depend on technology. Simi-lar efforts to control criminals in the wild are under way in pilot programs that demand adherence to onerous parole guide-lines, such as frequent, random drug testing, and that provide for immediate punishment if the parolees fail. The result is the same: convicts who might once have been in prison now walk among us unrecognized—like pod people, or Canadians.

There are, of course, many thousands of dangerous felons who can't be trusted on the loose. But if we extended this form of enhanced, supervised release even to just the nonviolent offenders currently behind bars, we would empty half our prison beds in one swoop. Inevitably, some of those released would take the pruning-shears route. And some would offend again. But then, so too do those convicts released at the end of their brutal, hardening sentences under our current system. And even accepting a certain failure rate, by nearly any measure such "prisons without bars" would represent a giant step forward for justice, criminal rehabilitation, and society.

IN THE 18TH CENTURY, the English philosopher and social theorist Jeremy Bentham designed the Panopticon, a hypotheti-cal prison. Inside the Panopticon (the name is derived from the Greek word for "all-seeing"), the prisoners are arranged in a ring of cells surrounding their guard, who is concealed in a tower in the center. The idea is that the guard controls the prisoners through his presumed observation: they constantly imagine his eyes on them, even when he's looking elsewhere. Bentham promoted the concept of the Panopticon for much the same reasons that spur criminal-justice innovation today—a ballooning prison population and the need for a cheap solution with light manpower demands. Whereas the guard in Bentham's day had only two eyes, however, today's watcher can be virtually all-seeing, thanks to GPS monitoring technology. The modern prisoner, in other words, need not wonder whether he is being observed; he can be sure that he is, and at all times.

The hub of the American penal system's largest open-air Panopticon is in the Indianapolis suburb of Anderson, population 57,496, at the call center of a company called BI Incorporated. The firm manufactures and services the ankle device I test-drove, as well as a suite of other law-enforcement gadgets designed to track offenders. Though BI has a handful of rivals in the monitoring business, it is the most prominent and best-known, with 55,000 offenders wearing BI anklets at any given moment. (The company monitors another 10,000 using lower-tech means: for instance, by having them call from particular landlines at designated times.)

I drove to Anderson from Indianapolis, past clapboard houses and cornfields, to visit BI's offices, located on a few discreet and highly secure floors above the local branch of KeyBank. I was buzzed up to meet Jennifer White, the BI vice president in charge of monitoring. From her office window, we looked out not on the backs of the 30,000 offenders this branch monitors, but on the sedate midwestern bedroom community that is, by her description, "a little bit less happening than Muncie," 20 miles away. Even the sleepy streets of Anderson have their secrets, though. White told me that below us were about 120 criminals with BI anklets—roughly one for every 500 residents in the town.

White, an Indiana native, has been at BI since 1988. Over a turkey salad from Bob Evans, she explained that the company's first "clients" (as the monitored are always called) were not human beings but Holsteins. In 1978, BI began selling systems that allowed dairy farmers to dispense feed to their cows automatically. The company fitted a radio-frequency tag on each cow's ear so that when the cow approached the feed dispenser, a sensor in the latter caused it to drop a ration of fodder. If the same cow returned, the sensor recognized the unique signal of the tag and prevented the cow from getting a second helping until after enough time had passed for her to digest the first. (The worlds of bovine and criminal management have in fact been oddly intertwined for many years. Just as modern abattoirs have studied the colors that can distract and agitate cows during their final moments—thus ruining their meat with adrenaline—prisons have painted their walls in soothing shades to minimize anxiety and aggression in their inmates.)

In the 1980s, BI expanded into "tethering people." As an early mover in the outpatient prison industry, BI grew fast, and the Anderson office contains a one-room museum of the bulky devices from its early days, some the size of a ham-radio set. The company now counts tracking people as its core business, and as a sideline it facilitates their reentry into society, through treatment programs and counseling. BI monitors criminals in all 50 states, "everyone from people who owe child support to ax murderers," White told me. Most use the lowest-tech tracking equipment, a radio-frequency-based technology that monitors house arrest. The system works simply: you keep a radio beacon in your home and a transmitter around your ankle. If you wander too far from your beacon, an alert goes out to the BI call center in Anderson, which then notifies your probation officer that you have left your designated zone—as Martha Stewart allegedly did during her BI-monitored house arrest in 2005, earning a three-week extension of her five-month sentence.

The truly revolutionary BI devices, though, are the new generation of GPS trackers, which monitor criminals' real-time locations down to a few meters, enabling BI to control their movements almost as if they were marionettes. If you were a paroled drunk driver, for instance, your parole officer could mandate that you stay home every day from dusk until dawn, be at your workplace from nine to five, and go to and from work following a specific route—and BI would monitor your movements to ensure compliance. If your parole terms included not entering a bar or liquor shop, the device could be programmed to start an alert process if you lingered near such a location for more than 60 seconds. That alert could take the form of an immediate notice to the monitors—"He's at Drinkie's again"—or even a spoken warning emanating from the device itself, instructing you to leave the area or face the consequences. Another BI system, recently deployed with promising results, features an electrostatic pad that presses against the offender's upper arm at all times, chemically "tasting" sweat for signs of alcohol. (In May, starlet Lindsay Lohan was ordered to wear a similar device, manufactured by a BI competitor, after violating her probation stemming from DUI charges.)

To see the BI systems at work is to realize that Jeremy Bentham was thinking small. The call center consists of just a few rows of desks, with a dozen or so men and women wearing headsets and speaking in Spanish and English to their "customers" (the law-enforcement agents, as distinguished from the tracked "clients"). Each sits in front of a computer monitor, and at the click of a mouse can summon up a screen detailing the movements of a client as far away as Guam, ensuring not only that he avoids "exclusion zones"—schoolyards or bars or former associates' homes, depending on the circumstances—but also that he makes his way to designated "*in*clusion zones" at appointed times.

As a fail-safe against any technological glitch, whether accidental or malicious, BI is immensely proud of its backup systems, which boast an ultrasecure data room and extreme redundancy: if, say, a toxic-gas cloud were to wipe out the town of Anderson, the last act of the staff there would be to flip the switches diverting all call traffic to BI's corporate office in Boulder, Colorado, where a team capable of taking over instantly in case of disaster is always on duty.

I asked Jamie Roberts, a call-center employee who had previously been a BI customer as a corrections officer in Terre Haute, Indiana, to show me a parolee on the move, and in seconds he pulled up the profile of a criminal in Newport News, Virginia. The young man's parole officer had used a Microsoft Bing online map to build a large irregular polygon around his high school—an inclusion zone that would guarantee an alert if he failed to show up for class on time, every day. Roberts showed me one offender after another: names and maps, lives scheduled down to the minute. There was a gambler whose anklet was set to notify Roberts if the client approached the waterfront, because he might try his luck on the gaming boats; an addict who couldn't return to the street corners where he used to score crack; and an alcohol abuser who had to squeeze himself into an inclusion zone around a church basement for an Alcoholics Anonymous meeting from 9 to 10 p.m., three times a week.

A strict parole officer could plausibly sketch out a complete weekly routine for his parolee, with specific times when he would have to leave home and specific stations he would have to tag throughout the week. He might allow, or even require, the parolee to go to the grocery store on a Sunday afternoon, and go for a jog along an authorized route every morning. Roberts pulled up another Bing map for me, and set in motion a faster-than-real-time playback of one client's day. As his dot carefully skirted the exclusion zones around a school and a park, staying away from kids because of the absolute certainty that BI would report him if he did not, his life on the outside looked fully set out in advance, as if he moved not on his own feet but on rails laid by his parole officer. For BI clients, technology has made detection of any deviation a near certainty—and with detection a swift response, one that often leads straight back to the Big House.

CRIMINALS TYPICALLY DIFFER from the broader population in a number of ways, including poor impulse control, addictive personality, and orientation toward short-term gratification rather than long-run consequences. More than a fifth of all incarcerated criminals are in for drug offenses, and a large portion of the others abuse legal and illegal substances. If one were to design a criminal-justice system from scratch with these characteristics in mind, it would be difficult to come up with something less effective than what we have today.

Take the world of supervised release, for example. With some exceptions (BI clients prominent among them), parolees and probationers know that if they violate the terms of their release, they are unlikely to be caught—and even less likely to be punished. So, impulsive as many of them are, they will transgress, perhaps modestly at first, but over time with growing recklessness, until many have resumed the criminal habits—drug use, theft, or worse—that got them arrested in the first place.

This prevailing condition is something Mark A. R. Kleiman, a professor of public policy at the University of California at Los Angeles and a leading advocate of non-prison alternatives, calls "randomized severity": some transgressors will be punished for violations, sometimes quite harshly, but others will not be punished at all, whether because their delinquencies go undetected or because judges, police, and parole officers decline to pursue the severe penalties that could apply. In his 2009 book, *When Brute Force Fails*, Kleiman argues that such capricious enforcement undermines efforts to reduce crime, and moreover that tough penalties—such as the long sentences that have contributed to clogged prisons don't do much to help, despite their high cost. The alternative, Kleiman suggests, is a paradigm called "swift and certain" justice, first proposed by Cesare Beccaria in the 18th century: immediate, automatic penalties—though not necessarily severe ones—doled out by credible, identifiable figures.

One way to achieve this result is through monitoring devices like those supplied by BI. But a pioneering judge in Hawaii has demonstrated that it can also be accomplished without the technological assist. In the early 2000s, Steven Alm, a circuit judge in Honolulu, grew increasingly frustrated with what he viewed as a farcical probation system. The majority of the cases he saw were drug-related offenses, including property crimes such as burglaries and thefts from tourists' rental cars. Many of the defendants in his court received probation, but once they were back on the street, they might as well never have been convicted. Drug tests, for instance, were scheduled a full month in advance, even though the test could detect meth use only within the previous three days. Despite this, probationers still tested positive about half of the time, indicating that they couldn't stay clean for even that short interval.

One reason for the backsliding, presumably, was that violators knew that in practice they had little to fear. Probation officers had limited time and resources, and to ask for a convict's probation to be revoked would require a great deal of work. Moreover, officers weren't always eager to send someone to prison for five years just for getting high. Since the probationers viewed the enforcers of their probation as lenient, overworked, and somewhat unpredictable, they correctly assumed there was a good chance they could get away with toking up at will.

Then, in 2004, Judge Alm decided to test the "swift and certain" paradigm. "It's something we always talk about in the sociology classes," he told me. "It just never happens in the criminal-justice system." Alm, a former U.S. attorney who was born in Hawaii, instituted what academics such as Kleiman describe as one of the most innovative and successful alternatives to incarceration in recent years. The basic tenet will be familiar to anyone who has ever trained a puppy: punishment must be consistent and immediate, in order to maintain a clear linkage between transgression and consequences. Alm began by assembling 34 probationers chosen because their profiles suggested they were especially incorrigible. He told them: "Everybody in this courtroom wants you to succeed on probation. But for you not to be in prison means you are making a deal with me to follow the rules. If you don't want to follow the rules, tell me now, and I will send you to prison."

The rules were simple: each probationer had to call in to the courthouse every weekday to find out whether he was required to come in for an observed urine test. These tests occurred frequently, and if a probationer ever failed a test or failed to report for a test or a meeting with his probation officer, he was locked away for two days and hauled before the judge for immediate continued sentencing. The justice system under Alm was a consistent and unforgiving machine, dispensing instant punishment for every transgression. The effect was to make life on the outside a little more like life on the inside, with strict, regular monitoring of everyone in the system. If you used illegal drugs, you would be caught.

Alm worked with Kevin Takata, a supervisor in the prosecutor's office, to come up with a form that reduced the paperwork time for demanding a probation modification from hours or days to minutes. And rather than require a complete overhaul of the terms of a violator's probation, the judge simply handed down jail time. In practice, the sentences were not especially long—days or weeks, in most cases—but, as Kleiman argues, it was not the duration of punishment but the certainty that was crucial.

The results of Alm's program, called Hawaii's Opportunity Probation with Enforcement, or HOPE, astonished everyone. The probationers shaped up quickly, and over time they showed remarkably little inclination to go astray. The urine tests came back dirty a tenth as often as before. "We discovered that most of these guys can stop using on their own," Alm explained, given the discipline imposed by HOPE. For most probationers, the strict observation was as good as, or better than, any drug-treatment program. It generally took no more than one stint in jail before an offender realized that the consequences of a relapse were real; second violations were unusual. And according to a study co-authored by Kleiman, recidivism—that is, arrests for the commission of new crimes, rather than just violations of probation—dropped by half.

Alm was inherently skeptical that prison is the appropriate remedy for many types of offenses. "You don't want to send a 20-year-old who's driving a stolen car and has a little dope on him when he's caught to prison," he said. "He's not going to come out better. I belong to the school of judge-thought that says we should be sending to prison the people we are afraid of, or who won't stop stealing."

Probation officers started volunteering their problem cases to Alm's court, and now all of his cases—more than 1,300—are HOPE probationers. Still more remarkable, the demands of the program—constant testing, appearances before the judge—have not overwhelmed the court system. Violators come in to see the judge, and attorneys complain about having to show up for hearings over even the smallest violations of probation. But overall, the court's volume of work per offender has declined, as has the cost to the state. "You can get someone out working, versus having the state lock them up at a cost of $35,000 per year," explained Myles Breiner, the president of Hawaii's association of criminal defense lawyers. "Who wants to spend more money on the Corrections Corporation of America?"

Outside Hawaii, prison analysts are cautiously optimistic. "Certainly it should be tried in other jurisdictions," said Gerald Gaes, a social scientist and former director of research at the Bureau of Prisons in Washington, D.C., though he was quick to caution that certain aspects of Hawaii may make the state unique in the U.S. criminal-justice system, and therefore its experience may not be generalizable to the country at large. To date, no other state has attempted a program as streamlined as HOPE, or as capable of meting out swift and certain punishment. But Alm is evangelizing aggressively. This year, he met with Attorney General Eric Holder and testified before a House subcommittee on crime about the possibility of expanding HOPE nationwide. "Down the road, I'm convinced: probation, pre-trial, parole," he said. "We try to use best practices. Well, this truly is the best practice."

ALM'S PROGRAM CERTAINLY seems effective—much like BI's technological solution to a similar set of problems. But as I stood in the security line at the courthouse where HOPE probationers report to urinate each morning, I couldn't help but wonder how much the constant monitoring takes over their lives, and whether this carefully demarcated kind of freedom is more wearying than it appears. Some of the probationers had come in from an hour away to take their test, and they all had to monitor, on pain of incarceration, whether there was ever a whiff of spliff in the air at their friends' places.

Back on the mainland, I asked law-enforcement officers and BI personnel, who have installed hundreds of monitoring anklets, how their clients first reacted when they felt the cinch of the band around their ankle and knew that, from that moment, they would be under constant surveillance. In most cases, Jennifer White told me, "they are just relieved to be at home and with their families and working." Some were even grateful, because the device gave them an excuse to avoid criminal friends: after all, no one wants to commit a crime with an accomplice who's being monitored. But not all were so upbeat. Some cursed. Others wept.

If the future of prisons is to be turned inside out, with criminals in the wild and their guards in a suburban midwestern office, how will the experience of being a convict change? The psychology of incarceration is well known not only to research-ers, but to readers of Dostoyevsky and viewers of *Oz*. But to have your every step monitored as you make your way through life, ostensibly free—well, that is, so to speak, a brave new world.

In Anthony Burgess's novel *A Clockwork Orange*, a dystopian British prison-state famously brainwashes a sociopathic youth into feeling physically ill at the very thought of inflicting pain. But he ultimately crumbles at the violence around him, and the state is forced to un-brainwash him. BI is of course installing its devices on the ankle, not in the mind. But the real purpose of any form of Panopticon justice—that is, the certainty of discov-ery and punishment—is to force the criminal to monitor himself. The Panopticon effectively outsources the role of prison guard to the prisoners themselves. And to be constantly on watch may wear at the psyche in ways difficult to predict. In a boast that could also serve as a warning, Bentham himself described his Panopticon as offering "a new mode of obtaining power of mind over mind, in a quantity hitherto without example."

In February, I visited Trenton, New Jersey, to observe a BI client in his native environment and to find out how life is for a man in a prison without bars. The New Jersey State Parole Board monitors about 250 sex offenders via GPS, and has had great success, in terms of cost and results, as a BI customer. The board's public-information officer, Neal Buccino, offered to intro-duce me to a local child-molester, who allowed me to attend his regular parole meeting on the condition that I not use his real name. I will call him Mick.

Mick was 57, with a bad back, rotten teeth, and hepatitis. He'd worn a BI tracker for two years. When he walked in from the icy streets of Trenton, my eyes darted to the electronic components hanging off his leg and clothing, and I sympathized with him immediately. Mick had tried to kill himself a few months earlier in a bout of depression, possibly brought on by poverty and estrangement from his son and daughter, both of whom he had been convicted of molesting. He was tall and lanky, with glasses and a moustache, and, in the way of some depressives, was disarmingly funny. If I'd met Mick in the hallway of my apartment building, I would have thought he was there to fix the heater.

His parole officer, an intelligent young guy named John Goldin, meets Mick weekly to confirm where he has been, and why. He started by checking off the signs that Mick had kept away from kids and continued living his desperate and carefully observed life. "Any contact with police?" Goldin asked. "Drugs? Alcohol? Minors?"

Mick gave four quick, weary *No*s.

Did Mick still plan to go fishing to supplement the $480 he had left over from his monthly disability payment after he paid child support? Were bedbugs still feasting on him and the other residents of his rooming house? Why had he gone to Broad Street on Wednesday?

Mick answered the questions with the resignation of someone who had become used to explaining every minute of his life to a man barely half his age. Yes, he was going to start fishing again. The bedbugs were gone for now. He'd gone to Broad Street to visit the TD Bank and count the loose change he'd found on the street.

As for the anklet itself, he told me his diabetes made him worry about where the band rubbed his skin. "I can't afford no infections," he said. In the summer, when the weather was hot and he didn't wear long pants to conceal his tracker, he said the stares were constant: "I get tired of people asking me every day, 'That a phone?' I mean, shut the fuck up."

Mick said he had trouble visiting his mother in her retirement home, because she worried about explaining why her son always wore a device on his leg. "She gets upset, and I can't say that I blame her," he said dejectedly. "It feels like it has grown into my skin sometimes." It seemed also to have grown into his brain.

WHATEVER ITS MERITS, the idea of increasing the number of free-range felons such as Mick is unlikely to make for good politics. Willie Horton still haunts the dreams of every aspiring politician. Even Steven Alm says it was largely his reputation as a former prosecutor and "hanging judge" that enabled him to institute HOPE, since no one could plausibly accuse him of being soft on crime. "I'm convinced this is one of those Nixon-in-China things," he explained. "If I hadn't been a career prosecutor, there's no way the law-enforcement people would have gotten on board."

Nevertheless, there are moves under way to experiment with HOPE-like programs outside Hawaii. In addition to the conversations Alm has held with Attorney General Holder, legislation introduced by Representatives Adam B. Schiff (a California Democrat) and Ted Poe (a Texas Republican) would establish a competitive grant program to provide seed money for HOPE-style probation systems. Small programs are in place in Nevada and Oregon, and Alaska launched its own effort this summer. And the market for monitoring devices seems destined to expand, as the technology involved becomes more widespread and hardware costs continue to fall. Already, I have an application on my iPhone that broadcasts my exact location to selected friends at all times. If I were ever convicted of a crime and forced to submit to GPS tracking, I would, in theory, need only to add my probation officer to my Google Friends list and keep my phone handy. (When I showed the app to BI's Jennifer White, she had trouble fathoming that anyone would use such a thing without a court order. "Do you keep that on all the time?" she asked suspiciously.) And with prison costs rising, and the pernicious effects of incarceration becoming clearer all the time, the problem of selling prisons without walls will presumably grow easier over time.

There are also, of course, worries about the creeping power of government, and the routinization of surveillance. Right now, BI monitors mostly offenders who have done something seriously wrong, and although its anklets enable parole and probation officers to lay down very specific location itineraries, in practice most just mark off home and work spaces. But there is no reason, as the technology gets cheaper and the monitoring ever more fine-grained, why electronic monitoring could not be used to impose an ever wider range of requirements on an ever wider range of "criminals." A serious felon might have every second of his day tracked, whereas a lighter offender like myself—recently caught lead-footed by a traffic camera—might be required to carry a tracker that issues an alert any time I move faster than 65 miles per hour. (If such an intervention sounds far-fetched, recall that many jurisdictions in the United States already require convicted drunk drivers to pass an ignition-mounted Breathalyzer test before they can start their cars.)

The technology is already largely in place for such forms of Big Brother surveillance. In theory, they'd require little more than a creative judge to impose them, and someone behind a monitor in an office somewhere to enforce them. And that's before you even begin spinning out the science-fiction scenarios, which themselves might not be so very far off. Right now the electrostatic patches made by BI and others monitor the sweat of parolees only for alcohol. But why stop there? Despite some practical hurdles, they could perhaps be upgraded to taste other substances, such as amphetamines or other drugs. And if patches can ensure that certain foreign substances remain out of the bloodstream, why not ensure that others are added to it—pharmaceuticals, say, to inhibit libido or muzzle aggression or keep psychosis at bay. They could even, again in theory, police the natural substances in our sweat, our hormones and neurotransmitters, the juices that determine our moods and desires. No machine currently exists that could sniff out criminal intent, or schizophrenia, or sexual arousal, from the armpits of a parolee or probationer, but the forward march of technology suggests that such a device is far from impossible, and that perhaps someday routine monitoring by authorities could be used to map convicts not just geographically but emotionally as well. If, for instance, the parole officer for a convicted rapist saw that his charge was in a state of highly elevated aggression, fear, and arousal, he might ask the police to pay an immediate visit to deter a possible crime—or, perhaps, interrupt a consensual encounter.

Future generations of devices could also be programmed to interact more directly with a client's immediate surroundings. They might, for instance, react to the radio-frequency chips embedded in commercial products for the next generation of retail checkout scanners, and sound a warning if a parolee approached cigarettes like those he once shoplifted, or the liquor he liked to abuse. Or anklets could be set up to react with one another, preventing ex-cons from getting together without sounding an alert. Monitors could even be sold to store owners or other private citizens to let them know when particular categories of criminals set foot on their property.

These are the kinds of possibilities that give privacy advocates nightmares. Erik Luna, a law professor at Washington and Lee University, is a critic of mandatory sentencing and other measures that have packed U.S. jails, but he urges caution when viewing electronic monitoring as an alternative. "There should be a general concern about the extent of the power of the state to follow and track individuals and gather information about their lives," Luna says. "What is the minimum ambit of privacy, to maintain the level of human dignity that a liberal form of government should provide?"

At the same time, if the people being monitored are those who would otherwise be in prison, then the infringement on their privacy is substantially less intrusive than that entailed in being required to sit in a cell all day. BI's White made exactly this point when I raised the question with her. "They are doing their time in lieu of incarceration," she said, with some exasperation. When I asked whether the privacy concerns of inmates should be considered at all, her answer, in essence, was no: "A person's rights, when they are incarcerated, or a ward of the state, are different from yours and mine."

And what of our rights, those of us outside the realm of the criminal-justice system? If the past several years in the shadow of a war against terrorism have taught us anything, it is that, once available, surveillance technologies rarely go unused, or un-abused. Could yesterday's warrantless wiretapping become tomorrow's clandestine cell-phone tracking? The technology already exists: even a cell phone that lacks a GPS can be traced to within a few city blocks. Once the legal and technical infrastructures were in place to allow the monitoring of criminals, it would be a relatively simple step to extend that monitoring to any person the government considered, for whatever reason, to be "of interest."

For now, of course, none of these scenarios is close to taking place. Even HOPE, a narrow, low-tech program, is limited to Hawaii, and the number of convicts wearing BI's anklets still make up a tiny fraction of those serving time, even outside prison walls. When close monitoring of probationers and parolees emerges as an ever more obvious alternative to expensive incarcerations, we would be wise to remain vigilant against Orwellian abuses. But potential drawbacks and pitfalls notwithstanding, it seems likely that the invasive surveillance model, combining tracking technology and the Kleiman/Alm paradigm of "swift and certain" justice, could offer an alternative to much of the waste—in human as well as economic terms—of our current, dysfunctional system.

In a way, the goal of Panopticon justice is as old as morality itself. It aims to install a tiny voice in each offender's head, a warning that someone is watching and that wrongdoing will be punished. Most of us call that tiny voice a conscience. But for some that voice is overwhelmed by other, louder voices expressing need or impulse or desire, voices less bound by reason or consequence. If a device strapped to an ankle can help restore the balance, can amplify the voice of conscience relative to the others, is that such a bad thing? For optimists of human nature, it is a melancholy realization that the highest function of humanity can be, to some extent, outsourced to a plastic box. But the American criminal-justice system has become in many ways a graveyard of optimism. And surely it is better to outsource the fragile voice of conscience to a plastic box than to do what our brick-and-bar prisons so often do, which is to extinguish that voice altogether.

***Graeme Wood** is a contributing editor at *The Atlantic* in Washington, D.C.

Wood, Graeme. "Prison Without Walls," *The Atlantic*, September 2010. http://www.theatlantic.com/magazine/archive/2010/09/prison-without-walls/8195/.

Copyright 2010, The Atlantic Media Co. as published in The Atlantic Online. Distributed by Tribune Media Services.

Used by permission.

On Locational Privacy, and How to Avoid Losing it Forever

by Andrew J. Blumberg and Peter Eckersley*

Over the next decade, systems which create and store digital records of people's movements through public space will be woven inextricably into the fabric of everyday life. We are already starting to see such systems now, and there will be many more in the near future.

Here are some examples you might already have used or read about:

- Monthly transit swipe-cards

- Electronic tolling devices (FastTrak, EZpass, congestion pricing)

- Cellphones

- Services telling you when your friends are nearby

- Searches on your PDA for services and businesses near your current location

- Free Wi-Fi with ads for businesses near the network access point you're using

- Electronic swipe cards for doors

- Parking meters you can call to add money to, and which send you a text message when your time is running out

These systems are marvelously innovative, and they promise benefits ranging from increased convenience to transformative new kinds of social interaction.

Unfortunately, these systems pose a dramatic threat to locational privacy.

What Is "Locational Privacy"?

Locational privacy (also known as "location privacy") is the ability of an individual to move in public space with the expectation that under normal circumstances their location will not be systematically and secretly recorded for later use. The systems discussed above have the potential to strip away locational privacy from individuals, making it possible for others to ask (and answer) the following sorts of questions by consulting the location databases:

- Did you go to an anti-war rally on Tuesday?

- A small meeting to plan the rally the week before?

- At the house of one "Bob Jackson"?

- Did you walk into an abortion clinic?

- Did you see an AIDS counselor?

- Have you been checking into a motel at lunchtimes?

- Why was your secretary with you?

- Did you skip lunch to pitch a new invention to a VC? Which one?

- Were you the person who anonymously tipped off safety regulators about the rusty machines?

- Did you and your VP for sales meet with ACME Ltd on Monday?

- Which church do you attend? Which mosque? Which gay bars?

- Who is my ex-girlfriend going to dinner with?

Of course, when you leave your home you sacrifice some privacy. Someone might see you enter the clinic on Market Street, or notice that you and your secretary left the Hilton Gardens Inn together. Furthermore, in the world of ten years ago, all of this information could be obtained by people who didn't like you or didn't trust you.

But obtaining this information used to be expensive. Your enemies could hire a guy in a trenchcoat to follow you around, but they had to pay him. Moreover, it was hard to keep the surveillance secret—you had a good chance of noticing your tail ducking into an alley.

In the world of today and tomorrow, this information is quietly collected by ubiquitous devices and applications, and available for analysis to many parties who can query, buy or subpoena it. Or pay a hacker to steal a copy of *everyone's* location history.

It is this transformation to a regime in which information about your location is collected *pervasively, silently*, and *cheaply* that we're worried about.

Threats and Opportunity

Some threats to locational privacy are overt: it's evident how cameras backed by face-recognition software could be misused to track people and record their movements. In this document, we're primarily concerned with threats to locational privacy that arise as a hidden side-effect of *clearly useful* location based services.

We can't stop the cascade of new location-based digital services. Nor would we want to—the benefits they offer are impressive. What urgently needs to change is that these systems need to be built with privacy as part of their original design. We can't afford to have pervasive surveillance technology built into our electronic civic infrastructure by accident. We have the opportunity now to ensure that these dangers are averted.

Our contention is that the easiest and best solution to the locational privacy problem is to build systems which *don't collect the data in the first place*. This sounds like an impossible requirement (how do we tell you when your friends are nearby without knowing where you and your friends are?) but in fact as we discuss below it is a reasonable objective that can be achieved with modern cryptographic techniques.

Modern cryptography actually allows civic data processing systems to be designed with a whole spectrum of privacy policies: ranging from complete anonymity to limited anonymity to support law enforcement. But we need to ensure that systems aren't being built right at the zero-privacy, everything-is-recorded end of that spectrum, simply because that's the path of easiest implementation.

Location-based Services That Don't Know Where You Are

Surprisingly, modern cryptography offers some really clever ways to deploy road tolls and transit tickets and location searches and all the other mobile services we want, without creating a record of where you are. This isn't at all intuitive, but it's really important that policymakers and engineers working with location systems know about it. This section lists just a few examples of the kinds of systems that are possible.

AUTOMATED TOLLING AND STOPLIGHT ENFORCEMENT

In many metropolitan areas, drivers are encouraged to use small electronic transponders (FastTrak, EZpass) to pay tolls at bridges and tunnels. As momentum builds behind nuanced usage tolling and congestion pricing schemes, we expect to see an explosion of such devices and tolling methods.

For simple point tolls (e.g. bridge tolls), protocols that cryptographers call *electronic cash* are an excellent solution. In its cryptographic sense, electronic cash refers to means by which an individual can pay for something using a special digital signature which is anonymous but which guarantees the recipient that he can redeem it for money; it acts just like cash! See this paper[1] for the details of a modern implementation. Thus, a driver "Vera" would buy a wad of electronic cash every few months and "charge up" her transponder. As Vera drives over bridges and through tunnels, the tolling transponder would anonymously pay her tolls.

For more complicated tolling systems (in which the price depends on the specific path taken), a somewhat more involved implementation can be used (discussed in detail in this technical paper[2]).

Straightforward but privacy-insensitive implementations of congestion-pricing systems simply track drivers and use the tracking information to generate tolls. For instance, you might have all of the cars using a little radio gadget to report their location all the time. As Vera drives throughout the congestion pricing area (e.g. down a street in central London[3]), the gadget says "Hi, this is Vera's car." That creates a record of everywhere Vera went. Equivalently, one might put cameras everywhere which record Vera's license plate as she drives and keeps track of everywhere she goes to subsequently compute his tolls. Both of these solutions violate Vera's locational privacy.

The less obvious but much better way to run such tolls is to have Vera's gadget commit to a secret list of "dynamic license plates"—a long list of random-looking cryptographic numbers. This commitment takes the form of a digital signature given to the tolling authority. As Vera drives through the tolling region, her gadget cycles through these numbers rapidly, sending the current number to the monitoring devices she passes. None of those numbers actually identifies Vera, and since they keep changing there's no way to string them together to track her.

But, at the end of the month, Vera has to pay her road toll by plugging the gadget in her car into her computer. The computers execute a fancy cryptographic process called a "secure multiparty communication." At the end, her computer *proves* that she owes $17.00 in road tolls this month, *without* revealing how she accumulated that total. The commitment exchanged at the beginning ensures that Vera can't cheat: she can't prove a lower total if she actually drove across a bridge with the gadget active.

This kind of approach can be used to solve various automated traffic enforcement needs, as well. For instance, every time Vera passes a traffic light a monitoring device can collect the current "dynamic license plate." Although again, the collected data can't be used to track Vera around, if Vera runs a red light the system can detect this and issue Vera a ticket.

LOCATION-BASED SEARCH

A location-based search on a mobile device is another important example. Phones are starting to be able to locate themselves based on the signal strength[4] or visibility[5] of nearby wireless networks or on GPS data. Naturally, companies are also racing to provide search tools which use this data to offer people different search results depending on where they are at any given moment. The naive way to do mobile location search is for the device to say "This is Frank's Nokia here. I see the following five WiFi networks with the following five signal strengths." The service replies "okay, that means you're at the corner of 5th and Main in Springfield." Then your device replies, "What burger joints are nearby? Are any of Frank's friends hanging out nearby?" That kind of search creates a record of everywhere you go and what you're searching for while you're there.

A better way to do location-based services and search is something like this: "Hi, this is a mobile device here. Here is a cryptographic proof that I have an account on your service and I'm not a spammer. I see the following five wireless networks." The service replies "okay, that means you're at the corner of 5th and Main in Springfield. Here is a big list of encrypted information about things that are nearby." If any of that encrypted information is a note from one of Frank's friends, saying "hey,

I'm here," then his Nokia will be able to read it. If he likes, he can also say "hey, here's an encrypted note to post for other people who are nearby." If any of them are his friends, they'll be able to read it. (An excellent and detailed discussion of a related approach via secure multi-party computation is presented in this paper[6].)

TRANSIT PASSES AND ACCESS CARDS

Another broad area of application is for passcards and devices allowing access to protected areas; for instance, passcards which allow access to bike lockers near train stations, or cards which function as a monthly bus pass. A simple implementation might involve an RFID card reporting that Bob has checked his bike into or out of the storage facility (and deducts his account accordingly), or equivalently that Bob has stepped onto the bus (and checks to make sure Bob has paid for his pass). This sort of scheme might put Bob at risk.

A better approach would involve the use of recent work[7] on *anonymous credentials*. These give Bob a special set of digital signatures with which he can prove that he is entitled to enter the bike locker (i.e. prove you're a paying customer) or get on the bus. But the protocols are such that these interactions can't be linked to him specifically and moreover repeated accesses can't be correlated with one another. That is, the bike locker knows that *someone authorized to enter* has come by, but it can't tell who it was, and it can't tell when this individual last came by. Combined with *electronic cash*, there are a wide-range of card-access solutions which preserve locational privacy.

Privacy Concerns and Anonymized Databases

We should note that even the existence of location databases stripped of identifying tags can leak information. For instance, if I know that Vera is the only person who lives on Dead End Lane, the datum that someone used a location-based service on Dead End Lane can be reasonably linked to Vera. This problem is widely acknowledged (and studied) in the context of epidemiological data as well: it turns out to be relatively easy to deduce the identity of individual disease victims from "anonymized" geographic information about the location of cases. Generally speaking, one solution to this problem is to restrict the use of location-based services to high density areas. There are more complicated cryptographic solutions that are also possible. See this paper[8] for a discussion (and proposed solution) to this problem in the context of collection of aggregate traffic statistics, and this paper[9] for discussion of "differential privacy," a formalization of ideal privacy guarantees in the face of the existence of databases.

For More Information

Safely and correctly implementing such modern cryptographic protocols can be a substantial engineering challenge. And implementing them efficiently takes work. But it can be done—this is exactly the kind of cryptographic software that protects the security of our financial network (e.g. ATMs), makes it safe for us to buy things online, and encodes our phone calls. Big software contractors (e.g. IBM and Siemens) maintain large staffs of cryptographers.

We've linked to some of the sources that would be useful for engineers who want to understand how these protocols work.

But, if you're a policymaker or an engineer and you have questions about how these methods work, don't hesitate to contact us: we can point you at literature and connect you with experts to answer your questions.

Why Should Private Sector Firms Prioritize Locational Privacy?

We believe that governments have a civic responsibility to their citizens to ensure that the infrastructure they deploy protects locational privacy. But there are also financial reasons for the private sector to go to some length to design privacy into the locational systems they build.

Avoid Legal Compliance Costs

If a corporation retains logs that track individuals' locations, they may be subject to legal requests for that information. Such requests may come in different forms (including informal questions, subpoenas or warrants) and from different parties (law enforcement or civil litigants). There are complex legal questions as to whether compliance with a particular request is legally required, optional, or even legally prohibited and a liability risk.

This legal complexity may even involve international law. For instance, US corporations which also have operations in the European Union might be subject to European data protection laws when EU citizens visit the United States and use the US company's services.

Corporations with large locational datasets face a risk that lawyers and law enforcement will realize the data exists and begin using legal processes to obtain it. The best way to avoid this costly compliance risk is to avoid having identifiable location data in the first place.

OBTAIN A COMPETITIVE EDGE

The public is slowly becoming aware of the potential downsides of having their location tracked on a continuous basis. The ability to demonstrate reliable privacy protections will increasingly offer firms a competitive edge if they can persuade individual customers—or government clients—that their product offers more robust and trustworthy privacy protections.

Isn't There an Easier/Different Alternative?

Using cryptography and careful design to protect location privacy from the outset requires engineering effort. So it's important to ask whether there are other adequate ways to preserve privacy in these systems. Unfortunately, we believe the alternatives are unreliable or harder to implement and enforce.

DATA RETENTION AND ERASURE

One kind of protection you might hope for is that your location records will be deleted before your adversary gets to them. If the company that's offering you a fancy location search on your cell phone doesn't need to remember your history a week later, perhaps they can be persuaded to forget it quickly. Perhaps they promise that they will.

Unfortunately, there isn't much basis for optimism on the data retention front. Search companies have incentives to keep extensive records of their users' queries, so that they can learn how to improve their results (and sell more effective advertisements). Storage space is cheap and getting cheaper. Tolling agencies have incentives to keep extensive records of toll usage, to settle complaints and provide aggregate statistics and accounting data.

Even if the collecting outfit does promise to delete the data after a set interval, there's no guarantee that they're actually going to do that properly. Firstly, secure deletion tools are necessary to make sure that deleted data is really gone; many sys admins will fail to use them correctly. Secondly, all it takes is the flip of a switch to suddenly change policies from deletion to retention. To make matters worse, there's no guarantee that a government won't suddenly pass a law requiring such companies and government agencies to keep all of their records for years, just in case the records are needed for "national security" purposes. This last concern isn't just idle paranoia: this has already happened in Europe, and the Bush administration has toyed with the same idea.

And as for government agencies, experience so far with data retention has not been reassuring. An interesting example is provided by automated tolling data (records from FastTrak and EZpass). Different states have made different promises about how long they keep the data, and there have been varying degrees of effectiveness in carrying out these promises. Data has often remained available for subpoena after a number of years. Legal penalties for the violation of these promises are currently minimal.

Limiting data retention is an important protection for privacy, but it's no substitute for the best protection: not recording that information in the first place.

Opting Out

Sometimes people respond to these sorts of worries with the claim that the free market will solve this problem. "People who are worried about privacy shouldn't use these services," they say. "If people really care, a company offering privacy as an explicit feature will arise."

We don't believe this is an acceptable viewpoint—there is too much coercion in play. Often, there's no adequate replacement for the service in question, and it is or will soon be a dramatic hardship to avoid its use. Suppose that parts of the United States began to adopt mandatory "pay as you drive" insurance, or congestion pricing, that was based on location tracking. In most parts of the United States, it's not really reasonable to suggest that people who are worried about privacy shouldn't drive (or shouldn't drive to their religious institution of choice). And in the case of location-based services, it's clear that the deck is stacked. against people choosing to take inconvenient measures to protect themselves: it's too hard to know what is being recorded by whom, too hard to know what options there are to avoid being recorded, and too hard to keep researching these questions as you interact with new pieces of technology. In this environment, people simply haven't adjusted to the potential for the loss of the *reasonable expectation* of privacy in public places, and our standard intuitions haven't kept up with advances in technology.

Cell Phones and Credit Cards Already Create a Trail

It's true that most cell phones provide some amount of tracking information to the carriers as long as they're on, and that credit card records provide a pervasive trail of activity. This is no reason to surrender further locational privacy, but rather a reason to fight for better practices or laws for cell phone technology and credit card data. The problems we're having now with identity theft[10] make it clear how problematic the handling of sensitive personal data is.

Law-abiding Citizens Don't Need Privacy

Another common response to worries about locational privacy is to say that law-abiding citizens don't need privacy. "I don't commit adultery, I don't break the law," people say (and tacitly, "I'm not in the closet, and I don't belong to any non-majority religious or political groups").

One answer to this concern is a reminder that there are more subtle reasons for needing privacy. It's not just the government, or law enforcement, or political enemies you might want to be protected from.

- Your employer doesn't need to know things about whether, when, and where you went to church.

- Your co-workers don't need to know how late you work or where you shop.

- Your sister's ex-boyfriend doesn't need know how often she spends the night at her new boyfriend's apartment.

- Your corporate competitors don't need to know who your salespeople are talking to.

Preserving locational privacy is about maintaining dignity and confidence as you move through the world. Locational privacy is also about knowing when other people know things about you, and being able to tell when they are making decisions based on those facts.

Suppose that an insurance company manages to obtain a record of Alice's movements over the past year, and decides that there is some aspect of that record which is grounds for raising her premiums or denying her coverage. The problem with that decision is not just that it is unfair, but that Alice may have no ability to dispute it. If the insurance company's reasoning is misinformed, will Alice have a practical way of knowing that and disputing it?

The `I've got nothing to hide' argument against privacy is criticized at greater length in this article.[11]

Conclusion

In the long run, the decision about when we retain our location privacy (and the limited circumstances under which we will surrender it) should be set by democratic action and lawmaking. Now is a key moment for organizations that are building and deploying location data infrastructure to show leadership and select designs that are responsible and do not surrender the locational privacy of users simply for expediency.

LINKS

1. http://www.cs.brown.edu/%7Eanna/papers/chl05-full.pdf
2. http://math.stanford.edu/%7Eblumberg/traffic/vpriv.pdf
3. http://transportforlondon.gov.uk/

4. http://gigaom.com/2007/11/28/google_my_location/

5. http://www.herecast.com/

6. http://www.cypherpunks.ca/%7Eiang/pubs/locpriv.pdf

7. http://en.wikipedia.org/wiki/Digital_credential

8. http://www.traffic.berkeley.edu/conference%20publications/virtual_trip_lines.pdf

9. http://research.microsoft.com/en-us/projects/databaseprivacy/dworks.pdf

10. http://www.ftc.gov/opa/2003/09/idtheft.shtm

11. http://papers.ssrn.com/sol3/Delivery.cfm/SSRN_ID1098449_code249137.pdf?abstractid=998565andmirid=5

*__Andrew J. Blumberg__ is an assistant professor of mathematics, University of Texas at Austin.

__Peter Eckersley__ is Technology Projects Director for the Electronic Frontier Foundation.

Blumberg, Andrew J., and Peter Eckersley. "On Locational Privacy and How to Avoid Losing it Forever," The Electronic Freedom Foundation, August 2009. https://www.eff.org/wp/locational-privacy.

The publisher has made an online version of this work available under a Creative Commons Attribution License.

PART 6:

Online Privacy

The Internet has fundamentally changed the way we use and share information. Social networks help us stay in touch with friends and families around the world; we turn to search engines with sensitive questions, and we browse websites for interesting content. Historically, this type of information-seeking activity was a private endeavor. Prior to the Internet, we could read letters and newspaper articles and flip through the latest celebrity gossip magazine without outside scrutiny. Today, however, we leave a digital footprint each time we use the Internet, whether on our home computers, laptops, tablet computers, or Smartphones. Small files known as cookies are installed on our computers, linking one online session to another. While cookies can be helpful for finding frequently visited pages, they can also be used to track a user's activities across websites, revealing very detailed information about individual preferences and behavior. Few federal laws regulate the tracking and collection of personal data online; it is generally up to companies to self-regulate these practices.

Marketing and advertising companies argue that extensive data collection is beneficial to the consumer. Such information helps these businesses better identify consumer needs—for which they can provide more useful targeted advertisements. Third-party marketing and advertising helps pay for the free online content and services we have all come to both rely on and take for granted—free search engines, mapping systems, and games. These companies oppose government regulation of online data collection, arguing that such regulation may result in less Internet innovation and fewer free services. And, in their view, regulation will never be able to keep up with the rapid pace of technological development.

Privacy advocates, however, believe that online tracking erodes our right to privacy. Surveys report that consumers find these practices intrusive. Advocates argue that most companies do not inform customers well enough about how and why they are being tracked. Nor do they provide users with adequate mechanisms to choose how their data are used. Companies that do provide such features often use confusing language that the average person has difficulty understanding. And, with so much information collected in business and other databases, privacy advocates fear that governments can too easily access the data—a private database is only one court order away from the government's hands. Comprehensive laws to govern online tracking practices would, therefore, provide consumers with control over their data and would prevent unwarranted government access.

How can we strike a balance between preserving personal privacy so we can be ourselves online, while fostering innovation on the Internet? Should laws be passed to address these issues? If so, what should they say?

In this section, journalist Julia Angwin presents a panel discussion covering the opinions of a diverse group of privacy experts on how much people should care about privacy and whether there should be more laws governing privacy. Next, Alexis Madrigal explores the complex world of online tracking and the tools, or lack thereof, that help us control who is tracking us. In the Economist.com online privacy debate, Marc Rotenberg claims that current self-regulatory efforts are inadequate and that new privacy laws are necessary to regulate unscrupulous private-sector online data collection. Nicholas Carr argues that users do not understand the trade-offs made for the online services that tracking affords, and, as a result, tracking is eroding our right to privacy. Finally, Jim Harper responds to Carr by maintaining that users must sacrifice some privacy to enjoy the free online services they have come to rely on.

As you read the materials in this section, think about the following questions:

1. Should we care about our online privacy and, if so, for what reasons?

2. Should the government regulate online tracking and, if so, to what extent? Will government regulation hamper innovation on the Internet?

3. Do we live in an era where we cannot reasonably expect to have privacy on the Internet? Do we need to sacrifice online privacy for free services? If so, what are the implications for privacy in other areas of our lives?

How Much Should People Worry About the Loss of Online Privacy?

by Julia Angwin*

Privacy in the digital age means a lot of things to a lot of people. Some people fret about the privacy controls on social networks, some worry about the companies that track their online behavior, and others are concerned about government surveillance. We asked a diverse group of panelists how much our readers should worry about the vast array of privacy threats.

Our panelists are, in alphabetical order:

Stewart Baker, a partner in Washington, D.C., at the law firm of Steptoe & Johnson. His book "Skating on Stilts" describes his battles with privacy advocates during his tenure at the U.S. Department of Homeland Security.

Danah Boyd, a senior researcher at Microsoft Corp., conducted one of the most comprehensive ethnographic studies of how teenagers shape—and are shaped by—their interactions with social networks.

Jeff Jarvis, associate professor at the CUNY Graduate School of Journalism, whose recent book, "Public Parts," argues that living in public opens up unprecedented personal and professional opportunities for collaboration.

Christopher Soghoian, a fellow at the Open Society Institute, created the first browser software—called TACO—that blocked online tracking.

What follows are edited excerpts of the conversation.

The Value of Sharing

WSJ: How much should people care about privacy?

MR. JARVIS: Privacy is important. It deserves protection. And it is receiving protection from no end of self-appointed watchdogs, legislators, regulators, consultants, companies, and chief privacy officers—an entire regulatory/industrial complex. Privacy is in good hands.

It's publicness I worry about: our corresponding right and newfound ability to use this Gutenberg press we all now own—the Internet—to speak, assemble, act, connect and collaborate in a more open society. If we over-regulate privacy, managing only to the worst case, we could lose sight of the benefits of publicness, the value of sharing.

Our new sharing industry—led by Facebook, Twitter, Google +, YouTube, Foursquare, blogs and new services launched every day—is premised on an innate human desire to connect. These aren't privacy services. They are social services.

But the private/public discussion to date has focused almost exclusively on privacy and worry. New technologies that cause disruption have often led to collective concern about privacy. It is well to worry about what could go wrong so we may guard against it, to assure that companies and especially government do not surveil us to our detriment. But I ask us to also recognize and guard the publicness our new tools empower.

DR. BOYD: Positioning privacy and publicness in opposition is a false dichotomy. People want privacy, and they want to be able to participate in public. This is why I think it's important to emphasize that privacy is not about controlling information, but about having the ability to control a social situation. People want to share and they gain a lot from sharing. But that's different than saying that people want to be exposed by others.

Protecting privacy is about making certain that people have the ability to make informed decisions about how they engage in public. I do not think we've done enough here.

That said, I am opposed to approaches that protect people by disempowering them. I want to see approaches that force powerful entities to be transparent about their data practices. And I want to see approaches that put restrictions on how data can be used to harm people.

For example, people should have the ability to share their medical experiences without being afraid of losing their health insurance. The answer is not to silence consumers from sharing their experiences, but rather to limit what insurers can do with information that they can access.

MR. BAKER: How much should people care about privacy?

That's like asking how much they should care about the weather. Some, for sure. If we don't pay any attention, we're liable to end up deeply uncomfortable from time to time.

But let's not kid ourselves. Privacy is like the weather in another way, too. For all the complaining, no one is going to do much about it. Because they can't. The price of storing and analyzing data is dropping exponentially, and keeping that data hidden is a hopeless task.

So, in the end, we will adjust to these changes. Privacy is the most adaptable of rights.

Sometimes our sense of what is private shrinks. The man who invented the right to privacy, Louis Brandeis, was appalled that ordinary newsmen could snap his picture and print it in the paper without so much as a by-your-leave. And most of us can sympathize, if we remember the shock of seeing ourselves in a photo, looking quite different than we imagined. But no one today thinks that photography is a privacy violation. We've adjusted to the new technology.

And sometimes our sense of privacy grows. Most of us would be deeply uncomfortable at the idea of having strangers sleeping in our homes, listening to our family conversations and gossiping about us over the back fence. But Brandeis never gave the privacy risk posed by his servants a second thought.

The Cost of Free Content

MR. SOGHOIAN: Mr. Jarvis is engaging in some sleight of hand. The online services that the public benefits from largely involve intentional sharing and communication by consumers. No privacy advocate is calling for Twitter or Foursquare to be regulated—as there really aren't any major privacy issues associated with these services.

Although consumers knowingly share information via Facebook, the privacy issues associated with that company are not related to the way consumers use it, but rather the other things the company does. These include the tricks the company has pulled to expose users' private data to third-party app developers, the changing privacy defaults for profile data, as well as Facebook's covert surveillance of your browsing activities on non-Facebook websites, as long as a "Like" button is present (even if you don't click on it).

The dirty secret of the Web is that the "free" content and services that consumers enjoy come with a hidden price: their own private data. Many of the major online advertising companies are not interested in the data that we knowingly and willingly share. Instead, these parasitic firms covertly track our web-browsing activities, search behavior and geolocation information. Once collected, this mountain of data is analyzed to build digital dossiers on millions of consumers, in some cases identifying us by name, gender, age as well as the medical conditions and political issues we have researched online.

Although we now regularly trade our most private information for access to social-networking sites and free content, the terms of this exchange were never clearly communicated to consumers.

WSJ: Why is that a problem?

MR. SOGHOIAN: Many of the dangers posed by digital dossiers do not occur regularly, but are incredibly destructive to people's lives when they do. An unlucky few will be stalked, fired, surveilled, arrested, deported or even tortured, all as a result of the data kept about them by companies and governments. Much more common are the harms of identity theft or public embarrassment. Even when companies follow best practices—and few do—it is impossible to be completely secure.

The personal data collected by these firms is like toxic waste—eventually, there will be an accident that will be impossible to clean up, leaving those whose data has spewed all over the Internet to bear the full costs of the breach.

WSJ: Do we need more laws to protect privacy, and if so what kinds of laws?

MR. JARVIS: Privacy legislation and regulation are awash with unintended consequences.

Germany's head of consumer protection, Ilse Aigner, surely believes she is guarding citizens' privacy when she urges them to exercise their so-called right to have photos of buildings taken from public streets pixelated in Google Street View.

But she sets a precedent that could affect the free-speech rights of journalists and citizens. She diminishes the public square at the public's cost.

The Do Not Track legislation making its way through Congress threatens ad tracking and cookies. Taken too far, Do Not Track could devalue online media, resulting in less content, more pay walls and a less-informed populace. The road to ignorance may be paved with good intentions.

The U.S. Children's Online Privacy Protection Act says sites may not use information specific to a child under 13 without written (that is, faxed, scanned, or videoconferenced) parental consent. The result: Children learn to lie about their age. And young people are likely the worst-served sector of society online. That is a tragedy of lost opportunity.

DR. BOYD: I completely agree with Jeff on this point. In our efforts to protect youth, we often exclude them from public life. Nowhere is this more visible than with respect to the Children's Online Privacy Protection Act (COPPA). This well-intended law was meant to empower parents. Yet, in practice, it has prompted companies to ban any child under the age of 13 from joining general-purpose communication services and participating on social-media platforms. In other words, COPPA has inadvertently locked children out of being legitimate users of Facebook, Gmail, Skype, and similar services. Interestingly, many parents help their children circumvent age restrictions. Is this a win? I don't think so.

MR. BAKER: It's tempting, in that first uncomfortable moment when new technology starts to shrink our old sense of privacy, to ask for new laws to protect us from change. But these laws won't really stop change. And in the long run, they can do a lot of damage.

Maybe it made sense to tell the FBI in Hoover's day that its agents couldn't compile clippings files on Americans who weren't suspected of acting improperly. But by the time of 9/11, when any coed could assemble clips files on her blind dates—in seconds, for free, with the help of Google—did it really make sense for FBI agents to be the only people in the country barred from printing out name searches?

So, sure, we should care about privacy. But we should also care about dumb privacy laws whose cost we won't appreciate until it's too late.

MR. SOGHOIAN: The history books are flush with examples of governments violating the privacy of their citizens. Once those in power have the ability to covertly monitor the communications of others, these capabilities prove irresistible—allowing them to monitor dissidents, political opponents, and even their own colleagues.

There is one grain of truth in Mr. Baker's claims. It is true that it would be easier for the government to catch criminals and even terrorists if we had no privacy laws. It would be much easier for the government to detect and even prevent crimes if all of our calls and emails were intercepted, if our homes could be searched or our locations tracked for any reason, or if the police could stop us on the street, looking through our pockets and bags whenever they like. Our laws, including the Fourth Amendment to our Constitution, that protect us from such violations to our privacy are probably a nuisance to law-enforcement and intelligence agencies. Instead of wasting their time obtaining "evidence" or "probable cause" of crimes, I'm sure it would save the government a lot of time if the police or spies could simply search every Americans' email and phone calls for hints of criminal behavior.

Our founding fathers experienced life without privacy protections under the British, when writs of assistance permitted searches of homes at the whim of customs agents. Life without privacy laws was hell under the British, and it would be even worse now, given the powerful surveillance technologies that governments around the world now possess.

***Julia Angwin** is an award-winning technology journalist at the *Wall Street Journal*.

Angwin, Julia. "How Much Should People Worry About the Loss of Online Privacy?" *Wall Street Journal*. November 14, 2011.

Reprinted by permission of the *Wall Street Journal*. Copyright © 2011 Dow Jones & Company, Inc. All Rights Reserved Worldwide. License number 2923660742529.

I'm Being Followed: How Google—and 104 Other Companies—Are Tracking Me on the Web

by Alexis Madrigal*

Who are these companies and what do they want from me? A voyage into the invisible business that funds the web.

This morning, if you opened your browser and went to NYTimes.com, an amazing thing happened in the milliseconds between your click and when the news about North Korea and James Murdoch appeared on your screen. Data from this single visit was sent to 10 different companies, including Microsoft and Google subsidiaries, a gaggle of traffic-logging sites, and other, smaller ad firms. Nearly instantaneously, these companies can log your visit, place ads tailored for your eyes specifically, and add to the ever-growing online file about you.

There's nothing necessarily sinister about this subterranean data exchange: this is, after all, the advertising ecosystem that supports free online content. All the data lets advertisers tune their ads, and the rest of the information logging lets them measure how well things are actually working. And I do not mean to pick on *The New York Times*. While visiting the Huffington Post or *The Atlantic* or Business Insider, the same process happens to a greater or lesser degree. Every move you make on the Internet is worth some tiny amount to someone, and a panoply of companies want to make sure that no step along your Internet journey goes unmonetized.

Even if you're generally familiar with the idea of data collection for targeted advertising, the number and variety of these data collectors will probably astonish you. Allow me to introduce the list of companies that tracked my movements on the Internet in one recent 36-hour period of standard web surfing: Acerno. Adara Media. Adblade. Adbrite. ADC Onion. Adchemy. ADiFY. AdMeld. Adtech. Aggregate Knowledge. AlmondNet. Aperture. AppNexus. Atlas. Audience Science.

And that's just the As. My complete list includes 105 companies, and there are dozens more than that in existence. You, too, could compile your own list using Mozilla's tool, Collusion, which records the companies that are capturing data about you, or more precisely, your digital self.

While the big names—Google, Microsoft, Facebook, Yahoo, etc.—show up in this catalog, the bulk of it is composed of smaller data and advertising businesses that form a shadow web of companies that want to help show you advertising that you're more likely to click on and products that you're more likely to purchase.

To be clear, these companies gather data without attaching it to your name; they use that data to show you ads you're statistically more likely to click. That's the game, and there is substantial money in it.

As users, we move through our Internet experiences unaware of the churning subterranean machines powering our web pages with their cookies and pixels trackers, their tracking code and databases. We shop for wedding caterers and suddenly see ring ads appear on random web pages we're visiting. We sometimes think the ads following us around the Internet are "creepy." We sometimes feel watched. Does it matter? We don't really know what to think.

The issues the industry raises did not exist when Ronald Reagan was president and were only in nascent form when the Twin Towers fell. These are phenomena of our time and while there are many antecedent forms of advertising, never before in the history of human existence has so much data been gathered about so many people for the sole purpose of selling them ads.

"The best minds of my generation are thinking about how to make people click ads," my old friend and early Facebook employee Jeff Hammerbacher once said. "That sucks," he added. But increasingly I think these issues—how we move "freely" online, or more properly, how we pay one way or another—are actually the leading edge of a much bigger discussion about the relationship between our digital and physical selves. I don't mean theoretically or psychologically. I mean that the norms established to improve how often people click ads may end up determining *who you are* when viewed by a bank or a romantic partner or a retailer who sells shoes.

Already, the web sites you visit reshape themselves before you like a carnivorous school of fish, and this is only the beginning. Right now, a huge chunk of what you've ever looked at on the Internet is sitting in databases all across the world. The line separating all that it might say about you, good or bad, is as thin as the letters of your name. If and when that wall breaks down, the numbers may overwhelm the name. The unconsciously created profile may mean more than the examined self I've sought to build.

Most privacy debates have been couched in technical. We read about how Google bypassed Safari's privacy settings, whatever those were. Or we read the details about how Facebook tracks you with those friendly Like buttons. Behind the details, however, are a tangle of philosophical issues that are at the heart of the struggle between privacy advocates and online advertising companies: What is anonymity? What is identity? How similar are humans and machines? This essay is an attempt to think through those questions.

The bad news is that people haven't taken control of the data that's being collected and traded about them. The good news is that—in a quite literal sense—simply thinking differently about this advertising business can change the way that it works. After all, if you take these companies at their word, they exist to serve users as much as to serve their clients.

***

Before we get too deep, let's talk about the reality of the online display advertising industry. (That means, essentially, all the ads not associated with a web search.) There are a dizzying array of companies and services who can all make a buck by helping advertisers target you a teensy, weensy bit better than the next guy. These are companies that must prove themselves quite narrowly in measurable revenue and profit; the competition is fierce, the prize is large, and the strategies are ever-changing. . . .

. . . There are three basic categories [in display advertising]: Essentially, there are people who help the buyers (on the left), people who help the sellers (on the right), and a whole lot of people who assist either side with more data or faster service or better measurement. Let's zoom in on three of them—just from the As—to give you an idea of the kinds of outfits we're talking about.

Let's look at three companies from our list of As. Adnetik is a standard targeting company that uses real-time bidding. They can offer targeted ads based on how users act (behavioral), who they are (demographic), where they live (geographic), and who they seem like online (lookalike), as well as something they call "social proximity." They also give advertisers the ability to choose the types of sites on which their ads will run based on "parameters like publisher brand equity, contextual relevance to the advertiser, brand safety, level of ad clutter and content quality."

It's worth noting how different this practice is from traditional advertising. The social contract between advertisers and publications used to be that publications gathered particular types of people into something called an audience, then advertisers purchased ads in that publication to reach that audience. There was an art to it, and some publications had cachet while others didn't. Online advertising upends all that: Now you can buy the audience without the publication. You want an Atlantic reader? Great! Some ad network can sell you someone who has been to The Atlantic but is now reading about hand lotion at KnowYourHandLotions.com. And they'll sell you that set of eyeballs for a fifth of the price. You can bid in real-time on a set of those eyeballs across millions of sites without ever talking to an advertising salesperson. (Of course, such a tradeoff has costs, which we'll see soon.)

Adnetik also offers a service called "retargeting" that another A-company, AdRoll, specializes in. Here's how it works. Let's say you're an online shoe merchant. Someone comes to your store but doesn't purchase anything. While they're there, you drop a cookie on them. Thereafter you can target ads to them, knowing that they're at least mildly interested. Even better, you can drop cookies on everyone who comes to look at shoes and then watch to see who comes back to buy. Those people become your training data, and soon you're only "retargeting" those people with a data profile that indicates that they're likely to purchase something from you eventually. It's slick, especially if people don't notice that the pairs of shoes they found the willpower not to purchase just happen to be showing up on their favorite gardening sites.

There are many powerful things you can do once you've got data on a user, so the big worries for online advertisers shift to the inventory itself. Purchasing a page in a magazine is a process through which advertisers have significant control; but these types of online ads could conceivably run anywhere. After all, many ad networks need all the inventory they can get, so they sign up all kinds of content providers. And that's where our third company comes into play.

AdExpose, now a comScore company, watches where and how ads are run to determine if their purchasers got their money's worth. "Up to 80% of interactive ads are sold and resold through third parties," they put it on their website. "This daisy-chaining brings down the value of online ads and advertisers don't always know where their ads have run." To solve that problem, AdExpose claims to provide independent verification of an ad's placement.

All three companies want to know as much about me and what's on my screen as they possibly can, although they have different reasons for their interest. None of them seem like evil companies, nor are they singular companies. Like much of this industry, they seem to believe in what they're doing. They deliver more relevant advertising to consumers and that makes more money for companies. They are simply tools to improve the grip strength of the invisible hand.

***

And yet, the revelation that 105 different outfits were collecting and presumably selling data about me on the Internet gives me pause. It's not just Google or Facebook or Yahoo. There are literally dozens and dozens of these companies and the average user has no idea what they do or how they work. We just know that for some reason, at one point or another, an organization dropped a cookie on us and have created a file on some server, steadily accumulating clicks and habits that will eventually be mined and marketed.

The online advertising industry argues that technology is changing so rapidly that regulation is not the answer to my queasiness about all that data going off to who-knows-where. The problem, however, is that the industry's version of self-regulation is not one that most people would expect or agree with, as I found out myself.

After running Collusion for a few days, I wanted to see if there was an easy method to stop data collection. Naively, I went to the self-regulatory site run by the Network Advertising Initiative and completed their "Opt Out" form. I did so for the dozens of companies listed and I would say that it was a simple and nominally effective process. That said, I wasn't sure if data would stop being collected on me or not. The site itself does not say that data collection will stop, but it's also not clear that data collection will continue. In fact, the overview of NAI's principles freely mixes talk about how the organization's code "limits the types of data that member companies can use" with information about the opt-out process.

After opting out, I went back to Collusion to see if companies were still tracking me. I found that many, many companies appeared to be logging data for me. According to Mozilla, the current version of Collusion does not allow me to see precisely what companies are still tracking, but Stanford researchers using Collusion found that at least some companies continue to collect data. All that I had "opted out" of was receiving targeted ads, not data collection. There is no way, through the companies' own self-regulatory apparatus, to stop being tracked online. None.

After those Stanford researchers posted their results to a university blog, they received a sharp response from the NAI's then-chief, Chuck Curran.

In essence, Curran argued that users do not have the right to *not* be tracked. "We've long recognized that consumers should be provided a choice about whether data about their likely interests can be used to make their ads more relevant," he wrote. "But the NAI code also recognizes that companies sometimes need to continue to collect data for operational reasons that are separate from ad targeting based on a user's online behavior."

Companies "need to continue to collect data," but that contrasts directly with users' desire "not to be tracked." The only right that online advertisers are willing to give users is the ability not to have ads served to them based on their web histories. Curran himself admits this: "There is a vital distinction between limiting the use of online data for ad targeting, and banning data collection outright."

But based on the scant survey and anecdotal data that we have available, when users opt out preventing data collection is *precisely* what they are after.

In preliminary results from a survey conducted last year, Aleecia McDonald, a fellow at Stanford Center for Internet and Society, found that users expected a lot more from the current set of tools than those tools deliver. The largest percentage of her survey group (34 percent) who looked at the NAI's opt-out page thought that it was "a website that lets you tell companies not to collect data about you." For browser-based "Do Not Track" tools, a full 61 percent of respondents expected that if they clicked such a button, no data would be collected about them.

Do Not Track tools have become a major point of contention. The idea is that if you enable one in your browser, when you arrive at The New York Times, you send a herald out ahead of you that says, "Do not collect data about me." Members of the NAI have agreed, in principle, to follow the DNT provisions, but now the debate has shifted to the details.

There is a fascinating scrum over what "Do Not Track" tools should do and what orders websites will have to respect from users. The Digital Advertising Alliance (of which the NAI is a part), the Federal Trade Commission, W3C, the Internet Advertising Bureau (also part of the DAA), and privacy researchers at academic institutions are all involved. In November, the DAA put out a new set of principles that contain some good ideas like the prohibition of "collection, use or transfer of Internet surfing data across Websites for determination of a consumer's eligibility for employment, credit standing, healthcare treatment and insurance."

This week, the White House seemed to side with privacy advocates who want to limit collection, not just uses. Its Consumer Privacy Bill of Rights pushes companies to allow users to "exercise control over what personal data companies collect from them and how they use it." The DAA heralded its own participation in the White House process, though even it noted this is the beginning of a long journey.

There has been a clear and real philosophical difference between the advertisers and regulators representing web users. On the one hand, as Stanford privacy researcher Jonathan Mayer put it, "Many stakeholders on online privacy, including U.S. and EU regulators, have repeatedly emphasized that effective consumer control necessitates restrictions on the *collection* of information, not just prohibitions on specific *uses* of information." But advertisers want to keep collecting as much data as they can as long as they promise to not to use it to target advertising. That's why the NAI opt-out program works like it does.

Let's not linger too long on the technical implementation here: there may be some topics around which compromises can be found. Some definition of "Do Not Track" that suits industry and privacy people may be crafted. Various issues related to differences between first- and third-party cookies may be resolved. But the battle over data collection and ad targeting goes much deeper than the tactical, technical issues that dominate the discussion.

Let's assume good faith on behalf of advertising companies and confront the core issue head on: Should users be able to stop data collection, even if companies aren't doing anything "bad" with it? Should that be a right as the White House contends, and more importantly, why?

***

Companies' ability to track people online has significantly outpaced the cultural norms and expectations of privacy. This is not because online companies are worse than their offline counterparts, but rather because what they can do is *so, so different.* We don't have a language for talking about how these companies function or how our society should deal with them.

The word you hear over and over and over is that targeted ads can be "creepy." It even crops up in the academic literature, despite its vague meaning in this context. My intuition is that we use the word "creepy" precisely because it is an indeterminate word. It connotes that tingling-back-of-the-neck feeling, but not necessarily more than that. The creepy feeling is a sign to pay attention to a possibly harmful phenomenon. But we can't sort our feelings into categories—dangerous or harmless—because we don't actually know what's going to happen with all the data that's being collected.

Not only are there more than 100 companies that are collecting data on us, making it practically impossible to sort good from bad, but there are key unresolved issues about how we relate to our digital selves and the machines through which they are expressed.

At the heart of the problem is that we increasingly live two lives: a physical one in which your name, social security number, passport number, and driver's license are your main identity markers, and one digital, in which you have dozens of identity markers, which are known to you and me as cookies. These markers allow data gatherers to keep tabs on you without your name. Those cookie numbers, which are known only to the entities that assigned them to you, are persistent markers of who you are, but they remain unattached to your physical identity through your name. There is a (thin) wall between the self that buys health insurance and the self that searches for health-related information online.

For real-time advertising bidding, in which audiences are being served ads that were purchased milliseconds *after* users arrive at a webpage, ad services "match cookies," so that both sides know who a user is. While that information may not be stored by both companies, i.e. it's not added to a user's persistent file, it means that the walls between online data selves are falling away quickly. Everyone can know who you are, even if they call you by a different number.

Furthermore, many companies are just out there collecting data to sell to other companies. Anyone can combine multiple databases together into a fully fleshed out digital portrait. As a Wall Street Journal investigation put it, data companies are "transforming the Internet into a place where people are becoming anonymous in name only." Joe Turow, who recently published a book on online privacy, had even stronger words.

> If a company can follow your behavior in the digital environment—an environment that potentially includes your mobile phone and television set—its claim that you are "anonymous" is meaningless. That is particularly true when firms intermittently add off-line information such as shopping patterns and the value of your house to their online data and then simply strip the name and address to make it "anonymous." It matters little if your name is John Smith, Yesh Mispar, or 3211466. The persistence of information about you will lead firms to act based on what they know, share, and care about you, whether you know it is happening or not.

Militating against this collapse of privacy is a protection embedded in the very nature of the online advertising system. No person could ever actually look over the world's web tracks. It would be too expensive and even if you had all the human laborers in the world, they couldn't do the math fast enough to constantly recalculate web surfers' value to advertisers. So, machines are the ones that do all of the work.

When new technologies come up against our expectations of privacy, I think it's helpful to make a real-world analogy. But we just do not have an adequate understanding of anonymity in a world where machines can parse all of our behavior without human oversight. Most obviously, with the machine, you have more privacy than if a person were watching your clickstreams, picking up collateral knowledge. A human could easily apply analytical reasoning skills to figure out who you were. And any human could use this data for unauthorized purposes. With our data-driven advertising world, we are relying on machines' current dumbness and inability to "know too much."

This is a double-edged sword. The current levels of machine intelligence insulate us from privacy catastrophe, so we let data be collected about us. But we know that this data is not going away and yet machine intelligence is growing rapidly. The results of this process are ineluctable. Left to their own devices, ad tracking firms will eventually be able to connect your various data selves. And then they will break down the name wall, if they are allowed to.

***

Your visit to this story probably generated data for 13 companies through our website. The great downside to this beautiful, free web that we have is that you have to sell your digital self in order to access it. If you'd like to stop data collection, take a look at Do Not Track Plus. It goes beyond Collusion and browser based controls in blocking data collection outright.

But I am ultimately unclear what I think about using these tools. Rhetorically, they imply that there will be technological solutions to these data collection problems. Undoubtedly, tech elites will use them. The problem is the vast majority of Internet users will never know what's churning beneath their browsers. And the advertising lobby is explicitly opposed to setting browser defaults for higher levels of "Do Not Track" privacy. There will be nothing to protect them from unwittingly giving away vast amounts of data about who they are.

On the other hand, these are the tools that allow websites to eke out a tiny bit more money than they otherwise would. I am all too aware of how difficult it is for media businesses to survive in this new environment. Sure, we could all throw up paywalls and try to make a lot more money from a lot fewer readers. But that would destroy what makes the web the unique resource in human history that it is. I want to keep the Internet healthy, which really does mean keeping money flowing from advertising.

I wish there were more obvious villains in this story. The saving grace may end up being that as companies go to more obtrusive and higher production value ads, targeting may become ineffective. Avi Goldfarb of Rotman School of Management and Catherine Tucker of MIT's Sloan School found last year that the big, obtrusive ads that marketers love do not work better with targeting, but worse. "Ads that match both website content are obtrusive [and] do worse at increasing purchase intent than ads that do only one or the other," they wrote in a 2011 Marketing Science journal paper. "This failure appears to be related to privacy concerns: the negative effect of combining targeting with obtrusiveness is strongest for people who refuse to give their income and for categories where privacy matters most."

Perhaps there are natural limits to what data targeting can do for advertisers and when we look back in 10 years at why data collection practices changed, it will not be because of regulation or self-regulation or a user uprising. No, it will be because the best ads could not be targeted. It will be because the whole idea did not work and the best minds of the next generation will turn their attention to something else.

*Alexis Madrigal** is a senior editor at the *Atlantic*. He's the author *of Powering the Dream: The History and Promise of Green Technology*.

Madrigal, Alexis. "I'm Being Followed: How Google—and 104 Other Companies—Are Tracking Me on the Web." *The Atlantic*, February 2012. http://www.theatlantic.com/technology/archive/2012/02/im-being-followed-how-google-151-and-104-other-companies-151-are-tracking-me-on-the-web/253758/.

Copyright 2012. The Atlantic Media Co. as published in The Atlantic Online. Distributed by Tribune Media Services.

Used by permission.

Economist Debates: Online Privacy

by The Economist*

MOTION: THIS HOUSE BELIEVES THAT GOVERNMENT MUST DO FAR MORE TO PROTECT ONLINE PRIVACY

Opening Statements

DEFENDING THE MOTION
Marc Rotenberg, President and executive director, Electronic Privacy Information Center

Today there is no meaningful check on private-sector data collection. Companies post "privacy policies" on websites and then do as they wish with the personal information they collect.

AGAINST THE MOTION
Jim Harper, Director of information policy studies, Cato Institute

The internet is not for couch potatoes. It is an interactive medium. While internet users enjoy its offerings, they should be obligated to participate in watching out for themselves.

The Moderator's Opening Remarks

Aug 25th 2010, Martin Giles

When Facebook announced recently that it would allow users of its mobile service to alert all their friends on the social network to their whereabouts, it immediately triggered another bout of hand-wringing about the implications for people's privacy. Social networks, location-based services on mobile phones and a host of other innovations have greatly increased our ability to share large amounts of information online. But at the same time, they have increased the risk that companies, governments and criminals may exploit the same information without our knowledge.

To some, worries about "Privacy2.0" seem greatly overblown. People are indeed making more information public than ever before on the internet, they say. But that is because societal norms are changing and it has become more acceptable to share details of one's daily life online. The rise of reality TV shows such as "Big Brother" is another example of this trend. Moreover, there is plenty of evidence to suggest that folk use the detailed privacy controls provided by firms such as Facebook to limit access to their information. Several studies have shown that teenagers, who are often criticised for plastering intimate details of their lives online, use these controls as much as adults.

But is self-regulation enough? Not according to some critics of internet firms who argue that economic self-interest inevitably encourages them to make more information public by default. Companies such as Google and Facebook, they say, are engaged in a form of digital data-collection arms race, with each trying to gather and exploit as much information as possible about individuals' likes, habits and tastes. The international fuss over Google's Street View service, which inadvertently collected data from private Wi-Fi systems as part of an ambitious project to photograph streets around the world, has highlighted the threat to privacy that this arms race poses.

Hence growing calls for more robust government action to protect individuals' online privacy. But are new laws and regulations really needed? Or is the solution to step up industry-led and public efforts to educate people about the implications of "over-sharing" on the web?

These questions lie at the heart of our latest online debate. To address them we welcome Marc Rotenberg, president and executive director of the Electronic Privacy Information Center in Washington, DC, and Jim Harper, director of information policy studies at the Cato Institute.

Mr Rotenberg, who is proposing the motion, claims that the privacy policies offered by many web services are often smokescreens behind which companies do what they like with the data they gather. And he warns that as business practices become more opaque, consumers will find it ever more difficult to exercise control over their personal information. So new privacy laws and regulations specifically tailored for the online world are urgently needed.

Mr Harper, who is opposing the motion, points out that some erosion in personal privacy is the price that people accept they must pay in return for enjoying the huge benefits that web-based services provide. And he argues that individuals have very different comfort levels when it comes to revealing personal information, so a state-mandated, one-size-fits-all online privacy regime would be worse than the status quo.

These thoughtful and provocative opening statements lay the groundwork for a stimulating debate. But it will be contributions from our readers that help to bring it alive. Don't hesitate to make them public!

The Proposer's Opening Remarks

Aug 25th 2010, Marc Rotenberg

Today there is no meaningful check on private-sector data collection. Companies post "privacy policies" on websites and then do as they wish with the personal information they collect. Not surprisingly, identity theft, security breaches and growing unease about online privacy are all on the rise. New service offerings are met with both enthusiasm about technology and worries about personal privacy.

The pressures will only mount as competition among internet firms for advertising dollars heats up. Business practices will become more opaque and consumers will find it more difficult to exercise meaningful control over their personal information. The launch of Facebook Places this past week, with its complicated and confusing opt-out requirements for user location data, is exhibit A in our case

We will concede that many privacy threats emerge from government. In fact, EPIC has led the charge against such government-inspired surveillance schemes as the NSA's clipper chip, the FBI's digital wiretap plan and John Poindexter's Total Information Awareness project. We are currently trying to get the Department of Homeland Security to shut down the intrusive and ineffective airport body-scanner programme. Our opposition to government surveillance is well established.

So, why do we favour the proposition? Because government can also play a substantial role in safeguarding privacy when it is directed by law to do so. Those who opposed the Patriot Act recognised that one of the solutions was to give judges, that is to say "the government," greater authority to review warrant applications so that prosecutors could not simply gather digital data unchecked. Congressional oversight, another form of government intervention, also plays a critical role in safeguarding privacy rights.

In similar fashion, we need the government agencies charged with consumer protection, privacy protection and antitrust review to play a more active role on behalf of internet users. Companies that collect personal information for one purpose and then turn around and use it for a completely unrelated purpose should not get a free pass from regulators. And the consolidation of large internet firms, particularly in the online advertising world, should set off alarm bells for competition authorities. Not only does the massive profiling of users by incumbents place users in a digital fishbowl, it also makes it more difficult for new entrants to compete. Competition, innovation and privacy protection could easily become allies as the internet economy evolves.

We also need independent privacy agencies to speak up when the private sector or the government cross into Big Brother territory. Requiring RFID tags in products and identity documents, gathering up DNA samples for law enforcement use and consumer products, and tracking the location of internet users without their knowledge or consent all pose new challenges that cannot be ignored.

Some who draw a bright line between data collection by the private sector and data collection by the government do not understand that the private sector has become the primary means for government to collect data on citizens. Government agencies are often the top clients of those companies in the data broker business. And what governments cannot buy they can often obtain through legal authority and data retention mandates. So, the reluctance to impose meaningful limits on private sector data collection has made it far easier for governments to build elaborate databases.

Of course, it can be said that those who are concerned about privacy can always choose not to use the internet. But that is a remarkably short-sighted and unproductive view, a bit like saying that anyone who does not like air pollution should simply stop breathing.

To be sure, there are real challenges in crafting effective and meaningful privacy rules for the internet. Policies should be technology neutral, stable, forward-looking and non-discriminatory. Some policies will fail. Others will work beyond expectation. Innovation with public policy, as with technology, should be welcome.

In the long run it will become obvious that government—that is, the legal institutions established to safeguard the rights of citizens—will need to do more to protect online privacy. The question now is only how long it will take.

In the meantime, Facebook users who "check in" will be left to wonder to whom, other than their friends, the social networking firm has decided to reveal their location.

The Opposition's Opening Remarks
Aug 25th 2010, Jim Harper

The internet is not for couch potatoes. It is an interactive medium. While internet users enjoy its offerings, they should be obligated to participate in watching out for themselves. Government efforts to provide online privacy will almost certainly make a hash of things.

Internet-connected devices and computers both retrieve information and send out information. This interactivity is why the internet's usefulness and entertainment stand head and shoulders—and chest and waist—above static media like TV, movies and (many) books.

The blessings of interactivity come at a cost. There is someone (well, something—a server) on the other end of every mouse-click, and sometimes every keystroke. The cost of interactivity is privacy. But many internet users do not know the full price they are paying. Unaware of how internet connections, browsers, websites, plug-ins and various other technical tools work, lots of people do not know what information they share when they go online, how much of it, or how revealing it is. Obviously, this deprives them of the opportunity to do anything about it.

There are concerns and complaints beyond control, of course. Potential unfair uses of information posted or released online are a "privacy" concern. People worry about the security of their financial accounts and reputations against identity fraud, or even about risks of theft or violence produced by information put online. Other "privacy" concerns include intrusive protocols and practices—spam, pop-ups and the like—that interfere with peaceful enjoyment of the net.

It is understandable for people, feeling bowled over, to wish government would take these challenges from their hands. The promises of regulation are lavish, though the results are not so great. Witness the American government's Minerals Management Service, which did not prevent a recent massive oil spill in the Gulf of Mexico. The American Securities and Exchange Commission did not discover Bernie Madoff's multibillion-dollar scam despite being told of it repeatedly. Should consumers abdicate responsibility for privacy to such institutions?

For some privacy problems, law and government are already appropriately on the case. Law is rightly recognising privacy policies as enforceable contractual promises. Fraud is already a crime, irrespective of medium or subject matter. The problem with online law enforcement is not the need for new law or for government to "do more." Government should get better at carrying out its existing responsibilities.

In the meantime, controlling identity fraud requires people to watch out for themselves by monitoring their financial statements and credit reports. The financial-services and credit-reporting industries must similarly keep watch on their end. Waiting for government help will not do.

Government help will not do for protecting privacy in its stronger "control" sense either. Privacy is a value that varies from person to person and from context to context. Perfectly nice, normal people can be highly protective of information about themselves or indifferent to what happens with data about their web surfing. Any government regulation would cut through this diversity.

Government "experts" should not dictate social rules. Rather, interactions among members of the internet community should determine the internet's social and business norms.

There is a response to this argument: industry defaults, set against privacy, are as uniform as government rules would be. But they are not. Apple's Safari browser blocks third-party cookies, denying ad networks their most common source of consumer demographic information. If stronger cookie controls are warranted, coders can write plug-ins—as they have for Mozilla's Firefox.

The limiting factor on the success of such efforts so far has been consumer awareness and interest. All major browsers allow users to control online tracking, for example. (In Internet Explorer and Firefox, go to the "Tools" pull-down menu, select "Options", click on the "Privacy" tab and then customise cookie settings.) Yet few web surfers take these rudimentary steps.

The social engineer takes consumer indifference as a signal that people should be forced to prioritise privacy, but this would undercut consumer welfare as indicated by the best evidence available: consumer behaviour. People appear generally to prefer the interactivity and convenience of today's web, and the free content made more abundant by ad network tracking.

Appeals like this—to revealed consumer interest—typically fall on deaf ears because people involved in privacy debates care more about privacy than the average person. Each of us believes ourselves to be typical, and we take our own opinions as the best evidence of consumer interest. Indeed, if you have read this far, you care more about privacy than most, and you probably favour government regulation to serve your slightly peculiar interests. Rare will be the reader willing to suspend personal opinion on privacy in favour of evidence.

The privacy challenges of the online environment are real and difficult. But asking the government to fix them is the couch potato's solution. And it is an unsatisfactory one. Government regulation will make consumers worse off than they could be. The better alternative is to get people educated and involved in their own privacy protection.

The Economist is a weekly news and international affairs publication based in the United Kingdom.

Economist Debates. "Online Privacy: Opening Statements." August 25, 2010. http://www.economist.com/debate/days/view/564/print.

Copyright © The Economist Newspaper Limited, London (August 25, 2010).

Used by permission.

Tracking Is an Assault on Liberty, With Real Dangers

by Nicholas Carr*

In a 1963 Supreme Court opinion, Chief Justice Earl Warren observed that "the fantastic advances in the field of electronic communication constitute a great danger to the privacy of the individual." The advances have only accelerated since then, along with the dangers. Today, as companies strive to personalize the services and advertisements they provide over the Internet, the surreptitious collection of personal information is rampant. The very idea of privacy is under threat.

Most of us view personalization and privacy as desirable things, and we understand that enjoying more of one means giving up some of the other. To have goods, services and promotions tailored to our personal circumstances and desires, we need to divulge information about ourselves to corporations, governments or other outsiders.

This tradeoff has always been part of our lives as consumers and citizens. But now, thanks to the Net, we're losing our ability to understand and control those tradeoffs—to choose, consciously and with awareness of the consequences, what information about ourselves we disclose and what we don't. Incredibly detailed data about our lives are being harvested from online databases without our awareness, much less our approval.

Even though the Internet is a very social place, we tend to access it in seclusion. We often assume that we're anonymous as we go about our business online. As a result, we treat the Net not just as a shopping mall and a library but as a personal diary and, sometimes, a confessional. Through the sites we visit and the searches we make, we disclose details not only about our jobs, hobbies, families, politics and health, but also about our secrets, fantasies, even our peccadilloes.

But our sense of anonymity is largely an illusion. Pretty much everything we do online, down to individual keystrokes and clicks, is recorded, stored in cookies and corporate databases, and connected to our identities, either explicitly through our user names, credit-card numbers and the IP addresses assigned to our computers, or implicitly through our searching, surfing and purchasing histories.

A few years ago, the computer consultant Tom Owad published the results of an experiment that provided a chilling lesson in just how easy it is to extract sensitive personal data from the Net. Mr. Owad wrote a simple piece of software that allowed him to download public wish lists that Amazon.com customers post to catalog products that they plan to purchase or would like to receive as gifts. These lists usually include the name of the list's owner and his or her city and state.

Using a couple of standard-issue PCs, Mr. Owad was able to download over 250,000 wish lists over the course of a day. He then searched the data for controversial or politically sensitive books and authors, from Kurt Vonnegut's "Slaughterhouse-Five" to the Koran. He then used Yahoo People Search to identify addresses and phone numbers for many of the list owners.

Mr. Owad ended up with maps of the United States showing the locations of people interested in particular books and ideas, including George Orwell's "1984." He could just as easily have published a map showing the residences of people interested in books about treating depression or adopting a child. "It used to be," Mr. Owad concluded, "you had to get a warrant to monitor a person or a group of people. Today, it is increasingly easy to monitor ideas. And then track them back to people."

What Mr. Owad did by hand can increasingly be performed automatically, with data-mining software that draws from many sites and databases. One of the essential characteristics of the Net is the interconnection of diverse stores of information. The "openness" of databases is what gives the system much of its power and usefulness. But it also makes it easy to discover hidden relationships among far-flung bits of data.

In 2006, a team of scholars from the University of Minnesota described how easy it is for data-mining software to create detailed personal profiles of individuals—even when they post information anonymously. The software is based on a simple principle: People tend to leave lots of little pieces of information about themselves and their opinions in many different places on the Web. By identifying correspondences among the data, sophisticated algorithms can identify individuals with extraordinary precision. And it's not a big leap from there to discovering the people's names. The researchers noted that most Americans can be identified by name and address using only their ZIP Code, birthday and gender—three pieces of information that people often divulge when they register at a website.

The more deeply the Net is woven into our work lives and leisure activities, the more exposed we become. Over the last few years, as social-networking services have grown in popularity, people have come to entrust ever more intimate details about their lives to sites like Facebook and Twitter. The incorporation of GPS transmitters into cellphones and the rise of location-tracking services like Foursquare provide powerful tools for assembling moment-by-moment records of people's movements. As reading shifts from printed pages onto networked devices like the Kindle and the Nook, it becomes possible for companies to more closely monitor people's reading habits—even when they're not surfing the Web.

"You have zero privacy," Scott McNealy remarked back in 1999, when he was chief executive of Sun Microsystems. "Get over it." Other Silicon Valley CEOs have expressed similar sentiments in just the last few months. While Internet companies may be complacent about the erosion of personal privacy—they, after all, profit from the trend—the rest of us should be wary. There are real dangers.

First and most obvious is the possibility that our personal data will fall into the wrong hands. Powerful data-mining tools are available not only to legitimate corporations and researchers, but also to crooks, con men and creeps. As more data about us is collected and shared online, the threats from unsanctioned interceptions of the data grow. Criminal syndicates can use purloined information about our identities to commit financial fraud, and stalkers can use locational data to track our whereabouts.

The first line of defense is, of course, common sense. We need to take personal responsibility for the information we share whenever we log on. But no amount of caution will protect us from the dispersal of information collected without our knowledge. If we're not aware of what data about us are available online, and how they're being used and exchanged, it can be difficult to guard against abuses.

A second danger is the possibility that personal information may be used to influence our behavior and even our thoughts in ways that are invisible to us. Personalization's evil twin is manipulation. As mathematicians and marketers refine data-mining algorithms, they gain more precise ways to predict people's behavior as well as how they'll react when they're presented with online ads and other digital stimuli. Just this past week, Google CEO Eric Schmidt acknowledged that by tracking a person's messages and movements, an algorithm can accurately predict where that person will go next.

As marketing pitches and product offerings become more tightly tied to our past patterns of behavior, they become more powerful as triggers of future behavior. Already, advertisers are able to infer extremely personal details about people by monitoring their Web-browsing habits. They can then use that knowledge to create ad campaigns customized to particular individuals. A man who visits a site about obesity, for instance, may soon see a lot of promotional messages related to weight-loss treatments. A woman who does research about anxiety may be bombarded with pharmaceutical ads. The line between personalization and manipulation is a fuzzy one, but one thing is certain: We can never know if the line has been crossed if we're unaware of what companies know about us.

Safeguarding privacy online isn't particularly hard. It requires that software makers and site operators assume that people want to keep their information private. Privacy settings should be on by default and easy to modify. And when companies track our behavior or use personal details to tailor messages, they should provide an easy way for us to see what they're doing.

The greatest danger posed by the continuing erosion of personal privacy is that it may lead us as a society to devalue the concept of privacy, to see it as outdated and unimportant. We may begin to see privacy merely as a barrier to efficient shopping and socializing. That would be a tragedy. As the computer security expert Bruce Schneier has observed, privacy is not just a screen we hide behind when we do something naughty or embarrassing; privacy is "intrinsic to the concept of liberty." When we feel that we're always being watched, we begin to lose our sense of self-reliance and free will and, along with it, our individuality. "We become children," writes Mr. Schneier, "fettered under watchful eyes."

Privacy is not only essential to life and liberty; it's essential to the pursuit of happiness, in the broadest and deepest sense. We human beings are not just social creatures; we're also private creatures. What we don't share is as important as what we do share. The way that we choose to define the boundary between our public self and our private self will vary greatly from person to person, which is exactly why it's so important to be ever vigilant in defending everyone's right to set that boundary as he or she sees fit.

*__Nicholas Carr__ writes about technology, culture, and economics. His most recent book, _The Shallows: What the Internet Is Doing to Our Brains_, was a 2011 Pulitzer Prize nominee and a _New York Times_ best-seller.

Carr, Nicholas. "Tracking Is an Assault on Liberty, With Real Dangers." _Wall Street Journal_. August 6, 2010.

Reprinted by permission of the _Wall Street Journal_, Copyright © 2010 Dow Jones & Company, Inc. All Rights Reserved Worldwide. License number 2923660872424.

It's Modern Trade: Web Users Get as Much as They Give

by Jim Harper*

If you surf the web, congratulations! You are part of the information economy. Data gleaned from your communications and transactions grease the gears of modern commerce. Not everyone is celebrating, of course. Many people are concerned and dismayed—even shocked—when they learn that "their" data are fuel for the World Wide Web.

Who is gathering the information? What are they doing with it? How might this harm me? How do I stop it?

These are all good questions. But rather than indulging the natural reaction to say "stop," people should get smart and learn how to control personal information. There are plenty of options and tools people can use to protect privacy—and a certain obligation to use them. Data about you are not "yours" if you don't do anything to control them. Meanwhile, learning about the information economy can make clear its many benefits.

It's natural to be concerned about online privacy. The Internet is an interactive medium, not a static one like television. Every visit to a website sends information out before it pulls information in. And the information Web surfers send out can be revealing.

Most websites track users, particularly through the use of cookies, little text files placed on Web surfers' computers. Sites use cookies to customize a visitor's experience. And advertising networks use cookies to gather information about users.

A network that has ads on a lot of sites will recognize a browser (and by inference the person using it) when it goes to different websites, enabling the ad network to get a sense of that person's interests. Been on a site dealing with SUVs? You just might see an SUV ad as you continue to surf.

Most websites and ad networks do not "sell" information about their users. In targeted online advertising, the business model is to sell space to advertisers—giving them access to people ("eyeballs") based on their demographics and interests. If an ad network sold personal and contact info, it would undercut its advertising business and its own profitability.

Some people don't like this tracking, for a variety of reasons. For some, it feels like a violation to be treated as a mere object of commerce. Some worry that data about their interests will be used to discriminate wrongly against them, or to exclude them from information and opportunities they should enjoy. Excess customization of the Web experience may stratify society, some believe. If you are poor or from a minority group, for example, the news, entertainment and commentary you see on the Web might differ from others', preventing your participation in the "national" conversation and culture that traditional media may produce. And tied to real identities, Web surfing data could fall into the hands of government and be used wrongly. These are all legitimate concerns that people with different worldviews prioritize to differing degrees.

"Surreptitious" use of cookies is one of the weaker complaints. Cookies have been integral to Web browsing since the beginning, and their privacy consequences have been a subject of public discussion for over a decade. Cookies are a surreptitious threat to privacy the way smoking is a surreptitious threat to health. If you don't know about it, you haven't been paying attention.

But before going into your browser settings and canceling cookies, Web users should ask another question about information-sharing in the online world. What am I getting in return?

The reason why a company like Google can spend millions and millions of dollars on free services like its search engine, Gmail, mapping tools, Google Groups and more is because of online advertising that trades in personal information.

And it's not just Google. Facebook, Yahoo, MSN and thousands of blogs, news sites, and comment boards use advertising to support what they do. And personalized advertising is more valuable than advertising aimed at just anyone. Marketers will pay more to reach you if you are likely to use their products or services. (Perhaps online tracking makes everyone special!)

If Web users supply less information to the Web, the Web will supply less information to them. Free content won't go away if consumers decline to allow personalization, but there will be less of it. Bloggers and operators of small websites will have a little less reason to produce the stuff that makes our Internet an endlessly fascinating place to visit. As an operator of a small government-transparency web site, WashingtonWatch.com, I add new features for my visitors when there is enough money to do it. More money spent on advertising means more tools for American citizens to use across the Web.

Ten years ago—during an earlier round of cookie concern—the Federal Trade Commission asked Congress for power to regulate the Internet for privacy's sake. If the FTC had gotten authority to impose regulations requiring "notice, choice, access, and security" from websites—all good practices, in varying measure—it is doubtful that Google would have had the same success it has had over the past decade. It might be a decent, struggling search engine today. But, unable to generate the kind of income it does, the quality of search it produces might be lower, and it may not have had the assets to produce and support all its fascinating and useful products. The rise of Google and all the access it provides was not fated from the beginning. It depended on a particular set of circumstances in which it had access to consumer information and the freedom to use it in ways that some find privacy-dubious.

Some legislators, privacy advocates and technologists want very badly to protect consumers, but much "consumer protection" actually invites consumers to abandon personal responsibility. The *caveat emptor* rule requires people to stay on their toes, learn about the products they use, and hold businesses' feet to the fire. People rise or fall to meet expectations, and consumer advocates who assume incompetence on the part of the public may have a hand in producing it, making consumers worse off.

If a central authority such as Congress or the FTC were to decide for consumers how to deal with cookies, it would generalize wrongly about many, if not most, individuals' interests, giving them the wrong mix of privacy and interactivity. If the FTC ruled that third-party cookies required consumers to opt in, for example, most would not, and the wealth of "free" content and services most people take for granted would quietly fade from view. And it would leave consumers unprotected from threats beyond their jurisdiction (as in Web tracking by sites outside the United States). Education is the hard way, and it is the only way, to get consumers' privacy interests balanced with their other interests.

But perhaps this is a government vs. corporate passion play, with government as the privacy defender. The [Wall Street]Journal reported last week that engineers working on a new version of Microsoft's Internet Explorer browser thought they might set certain defaults to protect privacy better, but they were over-ruled when the business segments at Microsoft learned of the plan.

Privacy "sabotage," the Electronic Frontier Foundation called it. And a Wired news story says Microsoft "crippled" online privacy protections.

But if the engineers' plan had won the day, an equal, opposite reaction would have resulted when Microsoft "sabotaged" Web interactivity and the advertising business model, "crippling" consumer access to free content.

The new version of Microsoft's browser maintained the status quo in cookie functionality, as does Google's Chrome browser and Firefox, a product of the nonprofit Mozilla Foundation. The "business attacks privacy" story doesn't wash.

This is not to say that businesses don't want personal information—they do, so they can provide maximal service to their customers. But they are struggling to figure out how to serve all dimensions of consumer interest, including the internally inconsistent consumer demand for privacy along with free content, custom Web experiences, convenience and so on.

Only one thing is certain here: Nobody knows how this is supposed to come out. Cookies and other tracking technologies will create legitimate concerns that weigh against the benefits they provide. Browser defaults may converge on something more privacy-protective. (Apple's Safari browser rejects third-party cookies unless users tell it to do otherwise.) Browser plug-ins will augment consumers' power to control cookies and other tracking technologies. Consumers will get better accustomed to the information economy, and they will choose more articulately how they fit into it. What matters is that the conversation should continue.

***Jim Harper** is Director of Information Policy Studies at the CATO Institute.

Harper, Jim. "It's a Modern Trade: Web Users Get as Much as They Give." *Wall Street Journal*, August 6, 2010.

Reprinted by permission of the *Wall Street Journal*, Copyright © 2010 Dow Jones & Company, Inc. All Rights Reserved Worldwide. License number 2923660982507.